Camel Karma

Twenty Years Among India's Camel Nomads

Ilse Köhler-Rollefson

SPEAKING TIGER

SPEAKING TIGER BOOKS LLP
125A, Ground Floor, Shahpur Jat, near Asiad Village,
New Delhi 110049

First published in India in Tranquebar Press by Westland Ltd 2014
This edition published by Speaking Tiger Books 2023

ISBN: 978-93-5447-646-4
eISBN: 978-93-5447-648-8

10 9 8 7 6 5 4 3 2 1

Line drawings by Shariq Parvez

Typeset by Ram Das Lal
Printed at Chaman Enterprises, New Delhi

To those we lost on this long journey,
but whose memory we cherish.

To the Raika leaders, Bagdiramji and Bhopalaramji, my 'guru' Adoji Raika, and our dear friend, Namitha Dipak

CONTENTS

"Shiva was meditating. Waiting for him to be finished and trying to pass the time, his consort Parvati started shaping animals out of clay. She created one particularly strange animal with five legs. Then she asked Shiva to blow some life into it. He refused, saying that such a misshaped animal would be beset by a host of problems. But Parvati persisted in begging him. Finally, Shiva gave in. He folded the fifth leg over the animals back and then said '*uth*' – get up! The camel got up and walked away. After some time it started making a lot of trouble and creating a big nuisance. Parvati once again came to Shiva and asked for his help. She requested him to make a man that could look after the camel. Shiva then rolled of a little bit of skin and dust from his arm and out of this he made the first Raika."

Raika Myth of Origin, Census of Rajmarwar (1896)

FOREWORD

The camel is an inextricable part of our Marwari heritage and Rajasthani identity. When Pabuji Rathore brought the first she-camels to Marwar some seven hundred years ago, these animals revolutionised transportation, communication and warfare in the harsh and waterless environment of the Thar Desert. In order to breed and manage them, the unique camel culture of the Rebari or Raika developed. For centuries, this Hindu caste took care of the breeding camel herds of my ancestors and other royal families. They did not only develop an amazing body of traditional knowledge around all aspects of camel husbandry, but also felt responsible for the welfare of this animal.

The humane and ethical relationship between the Raika and the camel is one of its kind in the world. It cast a spell over Ilse Köhler-Rollefson when she first came to Rajasthan in 1990 to study camels and their keepers and motivated her to come back again and again and eventually make Rajasthan her permanent home. By now, she has spent almost a quarter of a century living among and listening to the Raika, turning from a researcher into an advocate for the Raika and other traditional livestock keepers. During this period, she was able to witness first-hand how camels lost their meaning as transport animals, how the herds declined and how a unique human-animal relationship began to unravel. In 2005, she, Hanwant Singh Rathore and a Raika team undertook an arduous 800 km long yatra on camelback to draw attention to the situation. In this book, she chronicles this journey as well as many other adventures in a manner that also provides deep insight into rural Rajasthani culture.

Ilse's book comes at the right time, just when the Rajasthan government has decided to declare the camel as state animal and to accord it special heritage protection. It provides important pointers on how Rajasthan's camel population can be saved for the future and remain part of our Rajasthani identity even in the twenty-first century – for real and not only on glossy photographs: by making full use of its potential for a range of eco-friendly products from its milk, hair and dung, by respecting and protecting it as part of the Thar Desert eco-system, and as a patient and reliable companion animal.

I do hope that this book will help the camel to be revived in a new avatar so that it can be cherished by countless future generations as well.

H. H. MAHARAJAH SHRI GAJ SINGHJI II OF JODHPUR
2014

PREFACE TO THE SECOND EDITION

The first edition of *Camel Karma* came out barely 10 years ago, relating the story of how I experienced the Raika and Rajasthan's camel culture between 1991 and 2014. In the meantime, almost all has changed in the Raika-camel universe and the world surrounding it. Externally, fields have become fenced, roads are being built, towns and cities are sprawling, and mining operations are growing like cancer; all these developments are displacing precious grazing land. Internally, only a very small percentage of Raika are active herders and many of its youth are not even aware of the community's unique heritage.

But that does not mean that *Camel Karma* is of interest only as a historical record of a now vanquished culture. Far from it. The "Raika way" of breeding and managing camels, as well as other livestock, is now more relevant and pertinent than ever. Considering the ecological challenges that humanity and the planet face, well into the third decade of the twenty-first century, this body of knowledge and practice is of immeasurable value providing us much needed guidance on how humans, animals and the environment can exist in harmony with each other and to mutual benefit.

In much of the world, farm animals, especially cows, have become enemy number one. They are held to be bad for the climate because of emitting greenhouse gases, and bad for biodiversity by taking away too much land from nature. Their products are said by some to be causing heart problems or even cancer. And besides, it is cruel to raise farm animals, because they are kept under inhumane conditions in factories. Therefore, it is best to stop keeping livestock altogether, has become a common tenor.

All these accusations may be true to some degree, but only when farm animals are kept in confined settings, amassed in large numbers, and fed with soybeans or other concentrate feed, which is the conventional way that is promoted as modern and scientific and seems to be taking over the world.

The Raika, as well as other nomads, offer a compassionate alternative by keeping farm animals as part of nature, allowing them to move and do so in herds. Farm animals can thus extend their potential as humanity's greatest asset. They can help produce food in the places where crops cannot be grown, depending only on solar energy without need for fossil fuels, and also help conserve biodiversity, besides supplying natural fertiliser for organic agriculture. And they can do this while having the benefit of human care in addition to living together in families or the natural social units they would form if they were in the wild.

There is fantastic news that the Indian government is now beginning to recognise the value and importance of such systems and has recently established a Pastoral Cell in the Ministry of Animal Husbandry and Dairying whose task is to motivate young people to take up herding and establish supportive policies.

Other good news is that 2024 has been declared the International Year of Camelids by the United Nations General Assembly, with the stated goal of *raising awareness of the* ***contribution of camelids*** *to* ***livelihoods, food security and nutrition*** *and* ***encouraging all stakeholders****, including national governments, to work towards* ***recognising and valuing the economic, social and cultural importance of camelids*** *in the lives of communities, especially those that are highly* ***vulnerable*** *to extreme poverty. It is also intended to highlight the need for* ***enhanced responsible investment*** *for the development of the sub-sector.*

With their ability to convert thorny, fibrous, scarce, and salty native vegetation into highly nutritious and healthy food, and this under high ambient temperatures, camels are indeed crucial for achieving a good number of the Sustainable Development Goals declared by the United Nations. Globally, camel milk production and consumption is increasing. When *Camel Karma* was written, camel milk was just on the cusp of being recognised for its health-enhancing properties. Over the time span of less than a quarter of a century, camel milk in India has made an amazing journey from being deemed "not fit for human consumption" and being the morsel for the "poorest of the poor" to a status as a superfood that helps with autism and cancer, immune system weakness, skin problems and other ailments. Camel dairies have sprung up even in places where camels were never at home, for instance in Europe and North America. In the rich Arabian countries mega-camel dairies have been set up where thousands of camels are fed with imported feed and milked with machines. Camel cheese is now a delicacy on offer in Rajasthan's top hotels. Globally, there is huge investment in developing a camel dairy industry.

In a scenario where companies and countries are competing for shares in the globalising market, the unique selling point of Rajasthan's camel milk is the Raika heritage of producing milk humanely and with compassion. The biodiverse diet of the state's camels is composed of ayurvedic plants that add another unique quality.

This is why it is appropriate and fitting that *Camel Karma* goes into a second edition – to let the world know about the unique Raika heritage and to serve as a baseline to look back on ten or twenty years from now. My guess is both camels and much of the Raika culture will be here to stay and reclaim their past glory.

PROLOGUE

THE KISS

> *"Many Englishmen have written about camels. When I open a book and see the familiar disparagement, the well-worn humour, I realize that the author's knowledge of them is slight, that he has never lived among the Bedu, who know the camel's worth: 'Ata Allah', or 'God's gift', they call her and it is her patience that wins the Arab's heart. I have never seen a Bedu strike or ill-treat a camel. Always the camels' needs come first. It is not only that the Bedu's existence depends upon the welfare of his animals, but that he has a real affection for them. Often I have watched my companions fondling and kissing them while they murmured endearments."*
>
> – Wilfred Thesiger, *Arabian Sands, p 83*

February 1991

We make eye contact. Although I am about six feet tall, she towers over me. She bends her long neck in a smooth, elegant movement, bringing her face within a foot of mine. I freeze. I don't want to give her a reason to get startled. At the same time, tales of camels ripping off their caretakers' heads go through my mind. I have heard several such stories – tales of a camel's revenge, of their eternal memory which makes them viciously attack – and kill – people that have mistreated them decades before.

But maybe they are just tales to impress me, the foreigner and intruder in this inside world of old camel hands. And, anyway, I like camels and have never done the slightest harm to any of them.

So I try to relax and breathe normally. The camel I stand beside must have sensed this and, after the brief, cautious halt, her nostrils gradually inch closer. I feel her whiskers and harelips on my right cheek, feel her inhaling my scent and then gently move over my nose to the other cheek. It feels like being tipped by a fairy with a wand, it's so subtle and innocent.

Then the magic moment is over. Her curiosity satisfied, she swings her head up and again is out of reach, seemingly pondering what or whom to investigate next or whether to go and nibble on one of the thorny acacia trees that dot the field.

Bedazzled, I traipse back to the *bhakal* – the camel-hair rug – that marks the temporary residence of a group of Raika herders whom I have just been introduced to and who are huddled around a small fire made from sticks and kindled with camel dung. They are wearing turbans in a rainbow of colours – red, orange, yellow, white and olive green – and have wrapped rough blankets over their white gowns. Their grizzled faces haven't seen a shave for a few days and they pass around a clay pipe from which each one inhales a few deep puffs.

They hand me a metal bowl of tea made from freshly squeezed camel milk with a handful of tea leaves and a generous amount of sugar.

The place where they have spread out the bhakal is perfectly chosen to oversee their herd of maybe 150 camels awakening and stirring after a night among the shimmering mustard stalks. Their massive bodies are in various stages of waking up and getting ready for the day. Many of them are sitting upright and ruminating away contentedly; others are still snoozing flat out on their sides, their long legs with knobby knees and elastic, saucer-shaped feet lazily stretched out. A few are already standing, albeit on three legs, as one forelimb has been tied to prevent them from wandering away during the night. A couple of steps away, a serene-faced female is nursing a newborn that is balancing precariously on its long stilt-like legs while forcefully nudging against its mother's udder. There is also a camel kindergarten: a small troop of frisky baby camels darting around, seemingly involved in a cameline version of playing tag. The cast is completed by a huge male camel, the *pater familias*, whose front legs are hobbled but who nevertheless prances around in short jumps, arching back his head and neck and making dark grumbly noises, showing off his position as boss and head of the extended family.

The first rays of the sun are now pouring over the ridge of the Aravalli range in the east, coating the cast of camels with blinding silver halos. For a few precious moments, I am overwhelmed by a quiver of deep fulfilment. For, finally, after a series of false starts, I have arrived among camels and their keepers.

The last four months had been frustrating. I had come to Rajasthan to undertake a research project about Indian camel husbandry, but all my attempts to track down a nomadic camel herd had been elusive. My quest had begun at a government camel-research farm in the north of Rajasthan, which had its own camels, but they had been individually stabled and fed scientifically ordained feed rations and somehow were not the real thing. I had also visited several villages where I met camel breeders, but the camel herds themselves had never been around, reportedly roaming around on their own in the desert or "in migration".

The fact that I am here now is thanks to the efforts of Dr Dewaram, a young veterinarian from the Raika camel-breeding community. He has been my companion and indefatigable translator over the last few days and has taken me to a number of Raika villages at the edge of the Aravalli Hills that dissect Rajasthan into the Thar Desert in the west and a more fertile eastern part. My dependence on him is total as, without him, I am unable to communicate with the camel herders, except through smiles and grimaces. I am lucky and grateful that he has taken me under his wing, eager to teach me all about his community and its proud history of taking care of the maharajahs' camel herds.

Now, Dr Dewaram supervises the pouring of tea into a number of small metal bowls and makes sure that the first portion is served to me. "Is it okay?" he asks with a worried expression on his face. He is always concerned about my wellbeing. The grey-brownish concoction is unlike any other tea I have tasted – sweet, but with a hint of bitterness – and is delicious and invigorating. Once I have finished, one of the Raika takes the bowl, scrubs it with sand, gives it a short polish with a fold from his dhoti, and then pours the next dose.

Dr Dewaram, who acts a bit like my personal event-manager, had earlier urged me to meet the kissing camel. Now he has more exciting treats in store. "Come here and look! Take some photos of traditional treatment!" he says, pointing to two Raikas standing next to a reclining camel. One of them grips the animal's head and turns its neck sideways, while the other one dabs on a slight wound on the shoulderblade a white fluid that he pours out of a small bottle. "Camels often get scratched by acacia trees, and if the wounds aren't disinfected, they can cause very bad blisters," Dr Dewaram explains.

While I try to document the procedure photographically, another Raika with a pale-yellow turban joins us. He is Adoji, one of the owners of the camel herd, a feisty man in his fifties, with regular well-cut features and an aquiline nose that gives him the air of a Persian nobleman. From his demeanour it is obvious that he is the leader of this group of camel breeders. He starts talking to me and motions us over to the bhakal to take a seat. I give Dr Dewaram a questioning look asking him to interpret what Adoji has been saying. "Madam, Adoji is enquiring if the camels in your country are any different from ours."

"Actually, we don't really have any camels in our country – only cattle and pigs, and some sheep," I reply lamely, sensing that this answer sounds unsatisfactory.

"Then why are you so interested in camels?" Adoji probes, while stuffing the brass bowls from which we have sipped our tea into a big burlap sack.

"Well...I don't know. I just like them and think they are great. They're also really useful," I say, looking for a convincing answer when there is none. One can't always explain matters of the heart.

Adoji gazes at me intensely as if he is trying to figure out what makes me tick, a bit like a scientist who has found a new type of insect and is wondering whether it is good for anything, or should be classified as a pest. He has stowed away most of the necessities of his nomadic life into the burlap sack. His gently barking voice becomes gradually more insistent and Dr Dewaram translates obediently. "He says that they have had a lot of breeding problems in this herd. At least ten of his twenty pregnant camels miscarried. This is causing great economic loss."

Adoji is trying to get his message across to me, his tone becoming more and more fervent.

"Because we have no grazing and because miscarriages have become so frequent, we people from Anji-ki-dhani have become very poor. We used to have many more camels. When I was small, at least 10,000 camels belonged to our village. Now there are only about 1,000! And if nothing happens, then within ten years, there will be no camels left."

Dr Dewaram adds, on his own account, "It is true what

Adoji says. Camel numbers are steadily dwindling. And these miscarriages *are* a huge problem."

Adoji's eyes now focus on my camera. "Taking photos will not help us. And we need help. We need medicines for our camels and we need grazing grounds for them." He pauses and looks straight into my eyes. "For the medicines, why don't you arrange a camp?"

"What is a 'camp'? I don't understand..."

"He means a treatment camp for sick camels – where they are given injections and vaccinations and so on," explains Dr Dewaram. "Sometimes the Animal Husbandry Department or some wealthy *seths* organise such camps. Adoji requests you to sponsor one," he elaborates.

"But I am a researcher! How can I help? I don't know anything about miscarriages in camels and what is causing them! I have forgotten all my veterinary skills! And how could I do anything about grazing problems?" I cry out in frustration, simultaneously realising that this is a decidedly un-Indian way to react.

Tactfully, Dr Dewaram refrains from translating my outburst, but its meaning is clear anyway. Adoji gives me a hurt and curt look that seems to say, "What good are you to us, you white person from far away? Sure, it's easy to say that you 'really' like camels, but what does it matter, if you don't do anything for them. You're useless to us!"

While we have been talking, the other Raika have readied the herd for going to pasture. The camels' ropes are untied and the group's sparse luggage has been secured on to two burden camels. Like well-behaved pupils, the camels have assembled in one corner of the field and are waiting to be let out. Two of the herdsmen remove a huge, thorny branch that serves as a gate to the embankment. Adoji is suddenly in a hurry. He straightens his turban and hastily excuses himself to join the other herders. In a cacophony of otherworldly noises, the camels, one by one, step through the opening and head out into the acacia-studded plain. The herders fan out behind them to make sure that no animal strays in another direction. By the time we reach our car, the herd has disappeared, and its only trace is the dust-haze in the air.

It could have been a mirage. But Dr Dewaram is still there with me in flesh and blood, living testimony to the exchange with Adoji that resonates deeply and viscerally through my whole body and has turned my cheeks red with embarrassment.

MAP OF RAJASTHAN

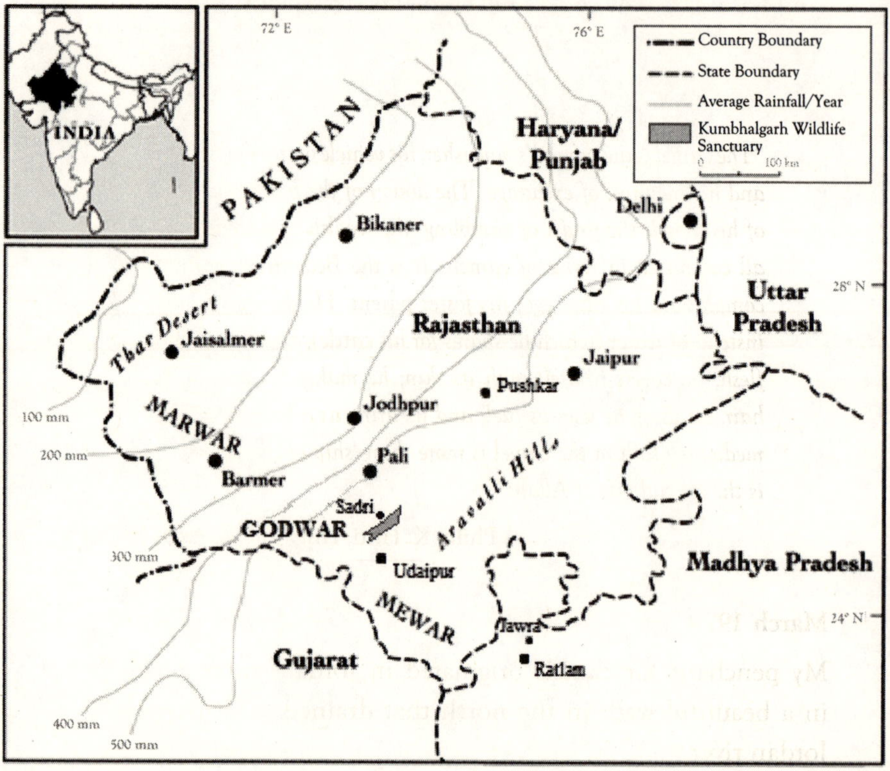

Chapter 1

CAMELS

"The camel is the nomad's nourisher, his vehicle of transportation and his medium of exchange. The dowry of the bride, the price of his blood, the profit of gambling, the wealth of a sheikh are all computed in terms of camels. It is the Bedouin's constant companion, his alter ego, his foster parent. He drinks its milk instead of water (which he spares for his cattle); he feasts on his flesh; he covers himself with its skin; he makes his tent of its hair. Its dung he uses as fuel, and its urine as a hair tonic and medicine. To him the camel is more than 'ship of the desert'; it is the special gift of Allah."

– Philip K. Hitti, *History of the Arabs* (1970)

March 1979

My penchant for camels originated in Jordan, more precisely in a beautiful wadi in the north that drained into the nearby Jordan river.

I was working on an archaeological dig as a "faunal analyst". My assignment was to identify and analyse the animal bone scraps that always turn up at such excavations in large numbers and that can provide information about the diet and economies of past periods. In real life, I was a veterinarian, but I had wanted a break from artificially inseminating cows and castrating male piglets – the tasks that made up the daily routine in rural practice. My anatomical knowledge had helped to get me this new job which I was enjoying tremendously, even though it only provided room and board and involved long hours. The setting and the whole flavour of the operation more than made up for it. Our dighouse overlooked the Jordan Valley and we had the exciting task of unearthing a settlement that was about 7,000 years old. The team was a congenial mix of an ambitious director, a cast of eccentric specialists and fresh-faced college students, supplemented by dozens of workmen from the village who were doing the actual digging with shovels and picks, while little boys carried away the dirt in rubber baskets. It could not have been more Agatha Christiesque.

Our site was placed alongside a lush and flower-dotted wadi that was the main water source for the nearby hamlet. Every morning I observed how the villagers funnelled their daily water supply into jerry cans tied to the backs of their donkeys. One morning I was sauntering down the *tell* to the excavation squares when a movement on the steep escarpment on the other side of the wadi caught my eye. A long string of camels zigzagged its way down into the wadi to drink at the rivulet. I stopped in my tracks to better focus on them. There were about a hundred animals that, with perfect discipline, trailed along in a single file. Most of them were mothers with frisky and fluffy baby camels following on their heels. Only the bull camel was behaving rather pompously, strutting around in circles and emitting gurgling noises from a fleshy pink balloon that protruded from the corner of his mouth. A single man wearing a long brown cloak and a red-chequered kuffieh accompanied the herd. When the camels reached the waterhole, something amazing happened: instead of all crowding around and pushing each other out of the way, they stepped forward in orderly rows of fives. The others waited obediently until the batch before them had finished and the Bedouin herder let them know by voice and gesture that it was the turn for the next five.

This display of obedience...the wonder how such a huge herd of big strong animals could be controlled by just one person...the cuddliness of the baby camels...the way the herd blended into the environment...the scent of oriental mystique that hovered over the whole scene, it somehow touched a raw nerve deep inside that I had not known to be there. Some inner force propelled me down the tell to meet the Bedouin who accompanied this magnificent herd. Groping for the dozen words that composed my Arab vocabulary, I tried to get across how fascinated I was by his animals. My emotional outburst did not perturb the man in the red-and-white kuffieh in the least. With flourishing hospitality, he invited me for tea in his goat-hair tent that was pitched at the bottom of our tell. I immediately made friends with his wife, Umm Juma'a, and his band of ragged-looking but gorgeous kids. They were a congenial family. Their material belongings amounted to a tent, a few foam mattresses, some cooking equipment and that's it – except for the camels which were probably their main asset. Nevertheless, they seemed happy as they joked around, and plied me with endless glasses of mint tea.

From then on, whenever there was a quiet moment in the hectic dig routine, I would sneak away and join the camel herd on its daily perambulation around our site. It was springtime and the meadows were bursting with blooming dandelions. Watching the female camels dive their noses deep into the lush forage, fastidiously selecting their favourite greens, filling their stomachs and padding their humps, filled me with deep satisfaction and peace. I could have spent hours observing the baby camels frolicking around on their stilt-like legs, playing tag, cautiously exploring their surroundings, and occasionally darting back to their placid mothers for protection. It was a scene oozing abundance and a perfect example of a harmonious, mutually beneficial relationship between animals and humans. There was no obvious sign of human domination, except maybe for the udder bags some of the nursing camels were equipped with to ensure that not all the milk was guzzled up by the camel babies but left over to feed the human family too. It was in stark contrast to the calf-raising practices I had seen in my veterinary practice back in Germany where newborn calves were separated from their mothers immediately after birth, put into a crate and raised on milk powder.

I did not like to dwell on my experiences as a vet in large-animal practice. I had chosen veterinary medicine because I loved animals, especially horses, but that had turned out to be entirely the wrong reason. With farm animals, decisions on how and whether to treat an animal were always made based on economic considerations – the value of the animal versus the cost of the treatment and the likelihood of its success. I did not enjoy visiting and advising farmers with intensive animal-production systems – rows of sows confined in metal cages or lines of oxen chained up for fattening. It had gradually dawned on me that, as a veterinarian, my role was not to help animals, but to support their owners in making maximum profits. My sojourn with cattle and pigs had been followed by a brief spell in a racehorse practice in Kentucky. This had brought about my final disillusionment. The horses were only valued for the money they earned. Spirited and gorgeous two-year-old youngsters were raced without mercy, so that frequently their bones and tendons gave up before the end of their first season, and only the knacker was left for them.

The relationship between the Bedouin and his herd of breeding camels seemed of a different nature. The animals were not subjected to any pressure, or forced to do anything that was against their nature. Abu Juma'a was a caretaker in the true sense, making sure that his herd spent a maximum amount of time feeding from the seasonally lush pasture. He would sing a lot and this was maybe not only a way of expressing his joy, but also a means of communicating with the camels. I could not understand a single word, let alone the meaning of his songs, but I imagined that they also were about camels.

Unfortunately, within two weeks, the friendship with the Bedouin family came to an abrupt end when they packed up their tent and left. I never found out for what purpose they kept such a big herd and what economic benefits they had from it. Camels remained absent from the scenery around the dig for the remainder of my stay and I did not see many during my travels through Jordan after the excavation. It was almost as if it had all been a fantasy.

After returning home, I started reading everything on camels that I could get my hands on. I leafed through the fascinating volumes written by early travellers to Arabia, who described how the camel could fulfil virtually all the needs of the Bedouin, ranging from the material to the social. Small wonder then that their tradition valued the camel as a special gift of Allah, and the Arabic word for camel – *jamal* – is synonymous with beautiful. I learnt that the Bedouins are not the only culture that has a close emotional bond with this animal. For the Tuareg in North Africa, the camel symbolises love. The Afar of Ethiopia are even said to prefer the death of a son to that of a camel, because without the latter there is no survival – while one can always have another son. Among the Rendille and Gabra tribes in Kenya, ritual life revolves around the camel. The people with the closest relationship to the camel are said to be the Somali whose copious poetry and oral literature centres on the camel, culminating in a verse covering the art of camel husbandry from A to Z.

The relationship of these traditional camel people was in strange contrast to the attitude of European commentators on the camel who generally heaped shame and ridicule on the species. *Brehm's Animal Life*, a German standard work on natural history, reported, even in a comprehensively revised edition:

> It can not be denied that the dromedary has truly surprising abilities to annoy human beings in a continuous and incredible manner. Stupidity and nastiness are standard attributes. But if cowardice, stubbornness, resistance against reason, spitefulness, and apathy towards its caretaker are joined by a hundred other vices, then the person who has to do with such an animal, eventually has no choice but to go crazy...

After enumerating how male camels routinely dismember their masters of their limbs, even the newborn camels are described as "misshapen creatures from the first day of their lives".

Thankfully, many of the famous explorers of the Arabian Desert, such as Anne and Wilfried Blunt and Wilfred Thesiger, eventually came to share the affection of desert people for the camel and their travelogues immortalise the virtues of this species. They describe it as an animal sent from heaven for all people compelled by fate or choice to live in the hot and dry stretches of the world. In fact, without the camel, the Bedouin could not live in the desert and these areas would not be inhabitable. Because they thrive on a diet of thorny, fibrous and often salty plants, camels convert the otherwise useless vegetation of the desert into highly nutritious food and other forms of energy. From very scant and scattered resources, camels are able to produce large quantities of milk all year round, and this forms the principal, or only, food, for months. Meat, wool and dung are thrown in as by-products.

The handful of ecologists that had studied the camel was raving about it. It was a machine perfectly designed to make use of the desert, equipped with a variety of water-saving mechanisms. To start with, it did not have a constant body temperature but functioned more like a reptile or cold-blooded animal by adapting its body heat to the environs. A camel's body temperature reaches its maximum during the hottest part of the day, and drops to a minimum in the early morning cool. This is a clever way of saving water: it minimises the need to perspire and thereby prevents the loss of water. Famously, camels have oval-shaped red blood cells that can swell to 240 per cent of their original size without any damage.

There was no difficulty in justifying the positive vibrations about camels that I had felt in my gut with any number of rational arguments. Eventually, I found a way of combining my two new-found interests – camels and archaeology – by choosing to write my doctoral thesis on camel domestication. "Domestication" means the process by which previously wild animals are integrated into human society and during which they turn from wolf into dog, from wild boar into pig, and from aurochs into cattle. During this process, animals undergo subtle changes: their brain-size shrinks, their colour patterns become more varied, and they develop qualities of use to humans, such as wool, the capacity to yield milk, docility, and many other traits. But it is not only the animals that change. The people and societies that obtain control over the species also develop and evolve in response to the new opportunities that are created. The historical significance of camel domestication was that it made long-distance transportation in inhospitable territories possible. Commerce along the Silk Road, the incense trade between southern Arabia and the Mediterranean, travel through the Sahara – would never have been possible without this beast of burden. It also allowed desert warfare and thus contributed substantially to the rise of Arab society and culture.

But camel domestication had not only impacted the course of history, it also had profound effects on the people who specialised in camel breeding. There are certain parallels between the different camel pastoralist societies in their respective parts of the world. They are usually nomadic. And according to one anthropological study, because camels reproduce very slowly, the associated human societies have also developed mechanisms for controlling population growth, because otherwise there would be an imbalance between people and camels.

The early stages of camel domestication were not well understood, because of a paucity of archaeological remains that could testify about the process. So I set about systematically reviewing the known archaeological finds – the bones, figurines, rock drawings, painted pot shards and other indications – that provided evidence about the presence and the use of the camel during the various prehistoric and historical periods. My conclusion was that the one-humped camel or dromedary had been domesticated in the third millennium BC in south-eastern Arabia, whereas the two-humped or Bactrian camel had begun to be made use of at around the same time, but in Iran and Turkmenistan.

After I finished the PhD, camel research turned out to be a dead-end as a career option. Although I was lucky enough to receive a fellowship for research on the camel-keeping Bedouins in Jordan, the government refused to issue me a research permit for my project. It regarded camels as an anachronism that were not really needed any more, adding that these days there were practically no Bedouin left who lived in tents and kept camels. Although this was patently not true, I had to resign myself to the situation and went back to archaeozoological research. I fell in love with an American archaeologist, Gary Rollefson, we got married and our twins, Jon and Aisha, were born in Amman. Camels were not on the cards as we moved to San Diego in California where Gary became a professor of anthropology and I taught students archaeozoology.

After a long interval, the congenial support of a friend at the University of Khartoum's Veterinary College enabled me to undertake a brief stint of camel field research in Sudan's eastern desert. In Sudan, camels were still high on the agenda and my mentor, Professor Bakri Musa, had established the most comprehensive and reputable camel-research programme worldwide. He dreamed of installing a field-research centre, but was not sure where to locate it, because the camels were kept in nomadic systems. My plan to collect more information about migration patterns of camel pastoralists, therefore, fitted in well with his agenda. Together with him and his assistant, Dr Muhammed Fadl, I drove hundreds of miles through the trackless deserts of the Eastern province, interviewed Rashaida Bedouins and collected information about herd structures, forage plants, migration routes, breeding practices and traditional treatment of camel diseases. The Rashaida Bedouins had come to Sudan from Saudi Arabia a hundred years earlier or so and kept various types of camels for different purposes. Their own, reddish-coloured breed was small, sturdy, and a good milker. They also bred camels for meat and sent them via the Forty Day Road to the slaughterhouses of Cairo. Besides, they had a special fondness for racing camels – a breed called *Anafi*. These animals whose pedigrees they memorised over seven generations fetched high prices among rich people from the Gulf countries who sometimes flew in their private planes for camel-shopping expeditions. My stay in the Eastern Province was a brief, but most productive and pleasant research experience, and I was all set to continue. But politics interfered: there was a coup, foreigners were not issued visas and my friend left the country.

Chapter 2

BIKANER

> *"The Rebaris, also called Raikas in Marwar, form nearly 3.5 per cent of the population, and are properly breeders of camels; they assert that their ancestor was brought into existence by Mahadeo in order to take care of the first camel which had just been created by Parbati for her amusement..."*
>
> – *Rajputana Gazetteer, 1908*

November 1990

That's how I now found myself in India – the country with the third-largest camel population in the world, numbering well over a million heads, at the time. I had applied for a fellowship to study the socio-economics of camel husbandry and camel-management systems. The subject was hardly researched. Judging from the scarce information at hand, camel husbandry in India was quite well integrated with crop cultivation and practised not just by nomads, but also by farmers. I had used this point in my proposal to argue that the Indian camel situation was not only easier to study but could potentially provide useful lessons for African countries. My application was successful and I had been assigned to conduct my research under the auspices of the country's premier research institution on the subject – the

National Research Centre on Camel (NRCC) in Bikaner. Luckily, Gary had received a Fulbright fellowship at the same time to do research at Deccan College in Pune. So our family set up house in Pune where Jon and Aisha were enrolled in a local school and the plan was for me to commute from there to Rajasthan.

In preparation for my fieldwork, I diligently searched all available sources for information about Indian camel keepers, looking for the subcontinent's equivalent to the Arabian and African camel cultures that I had read so much about – the Bedouin, the Tuareg, the Somali and the Rendille. They had to exist. With a camel population that statistically ranked third worldwide – after Somalia and Sudan – it was a logical conclusion that there also must be traditional camel breeders and specialised keepers, especially considering that, in India, professions are hereditary and passed on from one generation to the next through the caste system. But the Indian camel literature was strangely silent on this topic. Neither the glossy annual reports of the camel research institute that I was to be affiliated with, nor the enormous volume of recent scientific publications on the camel that have emanated from India, were of any help. The latter covered quaint facets of camel physiology, obscure anatomical details and miniscule aspects of its biochemistry, but none of these reams of scientific papers made it possible to visualise the more practical aspects of camel-keeping or its cultural foundation. How were camels actually bred and what were they used for? What did they mean to the local people? Social and economic aspects remained completely obscure in the abundant literature.

The only reference hinting at the existence of traditional camel keepers was the intriguing passage in one of the gazetteers from the time of the Raj, referring to "properly breeders of camel" that were known as Rebari or Raika. This was the sum total of what I could put my hand on and I could not really make sense of the reference to Mahadeo and Parbati – as I had not studied Indian culture, it seemed quaint and of no practical importance.

The National Research Centre on Camel, located at the outskirts of Bikaner, was an impressive set-up, but Bikaner seemed remote and backward. It had taken me a couple of months to get plane and train reservations to go there from Pune via Mumbai and Jodhpur. When I finally alighted from the train on a very chilly November morning, the only conveyance available to take me from the railway station to my hotel had been a horse-drawn tonga. But the research centre was a temple of science and technology. It was equipped with extensive labs, decked out with the most advanced equipment and technical gadgets for conducting blood analysis, checking biochemical parameters, and hormone levels, and measuring trace elements. At the more practical level, there was also a farm with about 500 camels, representing a cross-section of India's various recognised breeds – Bikaneri with typically long-haired tufted ears, speedy and long-legged Jaisalmeri, sluggish-looking animals from Kachchh in Gujarat with good milk yields, and an Arab camel sent as a gift by a visiting potentate from the Emirates. All of them were in top "hump", obviously maintained on a rich and nutritious diet. They served as guinea pigs for various new management techniques. Artificial insemination had already been perfected and embryo transfer was envisioned.

The director, Dr Khanna, gave me a hearty welcome. In his air-conditioned office, he served me a succession of tea, coffee, sweets and salty snacks and then gave me the grand tour of his centre. It concluded in one of the labs. "So what subject would you like to do research on?" Dr Khanna asked, eyeing the assemblage of gleaming high-tech devices.

"Actually, I am interested in meeting some camel breeders, especially the Raika."

"No problem! Some of them are employed here in our centre. You can talk to them, but I think tomorrow I will arrange for you to go to a Raika village and interview a camel breeder – that will be interesting for you!"

The next morning, a jeep and one of the veterinary doctors from the centre as translator whisked me away to Gadhwala, a village situated a few kilometres from Bikaner. The environs of Bikaner consisted of an ocean of sand that was gently undulating for the most part, but we also skirted some massive dunes that were sending their tentacles across the track. The jeep tackled these like a trawler braving the waves. Although dotted here and there with trees and livestock, the sand was of almost blinding whiteness, and interspersed with pristine hamlets of painted mud-brick houses. Most of the colour in this rural symphony in white and ochre was added by echelons of women, elegantly balancing water pots on their heads or going about other type of work.

My escort exuded an air of distant superiority and remained silent, maybe feeling it below his dignity to engage in small talk. Finally, the jeep pulled up next to a mud wall that surrounded a traditional compound. It belonged to a Raika whose relative worked at the NRCC, my guide explained. As we entered through the gateway, a man who was dozing on a *charpai* hastily got up, put on his turban, tucked up his dhoti, swirled his enormous white moustache back into shape, while greeting us with a series of "Ram Ram". He was introduced as Kanaram, the owner of a big camel herd.

Two more charpais were lined up in the middle of the well-swept courtyard. Although we had come unannounced, there was not a speck of sand, no clutter, no broken utensils, nor even a trace of any object not made from local material. The courtyard was ringed by a number of square mud-brick buildings that were lovingly embellished in white with decorative patterns and outlines of animals. Everything was museum perfect. Tea was served in small steel bowls, the purpose of my visit explained.

Face to face with a Raika, at last. But how do you communicate, if you have no inkling of the local language, no idea about the prevailing etiquette and not yet managed to understand the resident body language? I was grabbling for some pleasantries, but could not manage more than a friendly smile. To Kanaram, an alien from Mars could not have been any stranger than I was.

But the doctor prodded me on: "Now you ask your questions! I will translate!"

"So where are your camels?" I started meekly.

"My camels? Over there..." Kanaram answered and waved vaguely to the west. "They are running around somewhere and grazing."

The doctor clarified. "He is saying that his camels are ranging free about 20 km from here. Actually, this is the usual pattern for most of the year. The camels are gathered only in the rainy season when the crops are grown."

"You let them run totally free? How can you stop them from running away?"

"The camels come back for drinking at a well near here, every day or every few days. This area is very safe for camels – there are no thieves or big animals, so we do not have anything to worry about. They are also branded with the sign of our village, Gadhwala. Everybody knows this brand and if the camels go far, then people will return them or let us know."

My translator supplied some additional information. "Actually, if an animal gets lost, the Raikas can also trace them from their footprints. They are famous for that. The people who do this are called *pagri*. *Pag* means footprint." Shaking his head in awe, he added as an aside, "I have heard that they can distinguish the footprint of each of their camels. They can even tell whether they have become pregnant!"

This seemed a rather tall claim that I first needed to digest. So I pressed on. "How many camels do you own?"

"We are three brothers and together we have about 300 camels."

"Three hundred camels – that's a lot. But what do you do with them? What good is it to have 300 camels running around?"

"Well, eighty per cent of the camels are female. They give birth and then we sell the young male camels at the Pushkar Fair, you must have heard of it?"

"Yes, I have! But you don't use the camels for anything else? You don't milk them?"

"No, we don't. How can we, if they are roaming around? We have a buffalo and a cow for providing milk that we sell to the dairy."

"And what about the meat – is that ever made use of?"

At this stage, the doctor interjected. "That is not a good question. Here, people are Hindus and we don't eat camel meat. The Raika also feel very strongly about this and the very idea is shocking to them. So don't ask this."

Apologetically, I changed the subject. If camels were not used for milk and meat, what other meaning did they have for the Raika?

"Do you give camels as dowry or bride wealth, when a couple gets married?"

This question was welcome.

"Oh yes, when I got married, my in-laws sent one male and twenty-one female camels. But this was some time ago and now people don't do this so much any more. At that time, there were still about 2,000 camels in our village! And I remember how my grandfather told me that we Raikas from Gadhwala once looked after the camel herds of the Maharajah of Bikaner. But now times have changed. I don't think any of my sons is even going to bother about camels."

Unfortunately, before I could ask more, the doctor started showing signs of impatience. Pointing to his watch, he indicated that he had to get back to the centre so as not to miss out on one of his experiments.

The jeep dropped me in Bikaner where I had put up in the Dhola-Maru Tourist Bungalow which, incidentally, sported an illuminated signboard that depicted the silhouette of two people riding on a camel. When I picked up my key at the reception, I enquired from the manager about the meaning of "Dhola-Maru".

"Madam, Dhola and Maru are a very famous couple from Rajasthan. Dhola was a prince from Narvar and Maru a princess from Pungal. They fell in love although Dhola was already engaged to somebody else since childhood. So they ran away with the help of a talking camel," he explained.

"And then what happened? Did the story have a happy ending?" I enquired further.

He smiled. "Yes, Madam. After many adventures they finally got married." He paused for a while and then added an afterthought, "Actually, we have many love stories in which there is a camel. In Rajasthan, camel means love."

In my room, I pored over my notes and mused over the day's results. For Kanaram and the doctor, my questions must have seemed pretty strange – the equivalent of asking a European or North American farmer such pertinent questions as: "Why do you keep hogs?" "What do you do with them?" "Are they pets?"

But my curiosity was piqued. This was the first time that I had heard about camel pastoralists who abstained from eating camel meat. In Egypt, camel meat, being cheap, is favoured by the poor and thousands of camels from Sudan are driven up there on the Forty Day Road. In Kenya, the Gabbra and Rendille twice a year have huge ceremonies called "*sorio*" at which castrated and fattened camels are consumed en masse. In Jordan, camel meat is said to be the main ingredient of shwarma, a popular local snack. Scientists report that camel meat is very much like beef in fibre and taste, and the Australian Heart Association even recommends camel meat because of its low cholesterol content.

Assisted by veterinary students as interpreters, I visited more Raika settlements over the next few days. One of them was the village of Nokh, and here the Raika made the interesting statement that their forefathers had taken care of the camels of the Maharajah of Jaisalmer. But actually, there weren't too many villages with Raika *dhanis* around. So we started looking up members of other castes who also kept camels. Predominant among them were Muslims who had a special fondness for camel milk and praised its strengthening qualities. Milking their camels three times a day, they achieved a daily yield of up to 8–10 litres, much more than an Indian cow would give. The Muslims also organised camel races and some of them trained camels to do special tricks, such as bowing and dancing.

Gradually, a picture of the local pattern of camel utilisation emerged. Eating camel meat or selling camels for slaughter was absolutely unimaginable. Milk was used occasionally when the household did not have a cow or goat. It was not sold and not processed. The camel's hair was spun by hand and then woven into rugs and blankets and also used for making ropes and threading charpais. Camel dung was mixed with sand and other ingredients to make the beautiful mud walls and mud plaster of village dwellings. The bones were collected to be crushed into fertiliser and the skin was made into various types of containers, although this handling of the products of the dead animals was the domain of specialised castes. Male camels were used for work – mostly for drawing carts, but also for lifting water, and for ploughing, and as riding animals for the Border Security Force. The Raika themselves did not seem to use camels for such purposes, their role was that of specialised breeders who kept herds of female camels in order to sell the young male animals to other castes who used them for work.

The enormous role of camels for transportation was evident in and around Bikaner. Both two-wheeled and four-wheeled camel-drawn carts were a ubiquitous sight in the bustling bazaars and strings of them could be seen on the roads converging on Bikaner. Almost everything seemed to be transported by camel cart: wood, gas cylinders, bricks, fodder, cloth balls, wool, and people.

Yet, it was puzzling why the food potential of camels – after all, the main reason for keeping camels elsewhere – was not made more use of. It was practically ignored. There were no parallels to the rejection of camel meat in the rest of the world. I weighed various options why this could be so. Maybe it was because the Raika were Hindus and had transferred the concept of the holy cow to the animal closest to them? Or because they were vegetarians and did not eat meat anyway? Was there a historical explanation or an ecological reason? Furthermore, what were the economics of the breeding system? Did the Raika earn a good income from their herds? What was the average herd size, how many camels would they sell each year, and for what profit?

In search of an answer to this question, I tried my luck in the NRCC library. Although this was well equipped with camel literature, most of it was very technical and eclectic, consisting of offprints of scientific publications on such tantalising topics as copulation time, penectomy, nerves in the hind limbs and characteristics of camel meat or "venous drainage of the head of the camel with special reference to the nasal cavity". Again, there were no references to the Raika, nor did anybody ever dwell on utilisation patterns. Frustrated by this attention to detail without giving any information about the bigger picture, I consulted a series of modern reprints of *Rajputana Gazetteers* which were stacked in a corner. Compiled during the colonial period, they contained comprehensive and well-organised data on every aspect of the area. In the volume on the kingdom of Marwar where I had earlier found the only reference to the Raika, there was an interesting note attesting to the military significance of the camel. Between 1889 and 1893, the Maharajah of Bikaner, Ganga Singh, had established a 500-men-strong camel corps, the "Ganga Risala", to defend the Empire. Ganga Singh, an extremely illustrious personality, had been the representative of India in the British war cabinet and a co-sponsor of the first parliamentary reforms in British India. His Ganga Risala had gone on to see distinguished service and serve British interests in many foreign countries, including China, Egypt, Somaliland, and Afghanistan. However, there was no mention of the Raika in this context.

By now, curious about the royal and military connections of the camel, I extended my data-collection efforts to the archives of Lalgarh Palace, the erstwhile residence of Maharajah Ganga Singh, which had now been converted into a luxury hotel. I went through piles of unsorted files of brittle paper that disintegrated at the slightest touch and which I was therefore reluctant to handle. A note, "dealing with the salient features of H. H. the Maharajah's Administration of the Bikaner State, 1898–1930–31," provided new insights:

> There has been in vogue from time immemorial a system in this state to maintain State Camel Tolas, as in the olden days for want of other mode of conveyance the State found it necessary to keep camels in large numbers for its requirements. In the time of the Regency Council a set of

> rules was framed to regulate the maintenance of the State Camel Tolas with Raikas who were allowed for grazing purposes to keep in each Tola 50 State camels together with an equal number belonging to them and were permitted to graze them in crown wastelands, but the Raika abused their privileges and with a view to saving the public from harassment, H.H. the Maharajah was pleased to abolish this old system. The State camels were all disposed of so that now there are no State Camel Tolas.

This note basically confirmed what the old man in Gadhwala and the Raika from Nokh had told me: the Raika had a heritage of taking care of royal breeding camels. From some other historical records it could be deduced that the first Raikas had come to Bikaner together with Rao Bika who had founded the city in the fifteenth century. These first Raikas had settled in Gadhwala and subsequently some of them had moved out and settled elsewhere, in places where their services as camel herders were required.

In the evenings, I wandered through the town. Ganga Singh, who must have been an extraordinary personality, had also left his mark on Bikaner's architecture. He had engaged in very progressive and rather grandiose city planning. There were well-laid-out avenues, circles, a city park and even a zoo, and this area was even now almost devoid of traffic. Slightly off-centre was the majestic Junagadh Fort, a composite fortification protected by a mighty door studded with gigantic iron spikes to repel attacking elephants. Inside was a conglomerate of elaborately and sumptuously decorated *mahal* or palaces. Lavishly designed buildings made from red sandstone liberally accoutred with lofty spires and turrets cropped up at many unexpected places in Bikaner. By contrast, the newer quarters of the town were an uncoordinated and overcrowded urban jumble, bursting with scooters, tongas, three-wheeled rickshaws and camel-drawn carts.

I much preferred the rural areas with their bucolic scenery, the villages and houses unadulterated by any signs of western influence, the colourfully clothed villagers, and the bright smiles of the children. But it was a beauty I somehow could not grasp, a fabric that I could not become a part of. Visits to the villages always followed the same routine. I was treated with immense courtesy and respect, seated somewhere in the public sphere, but at a discreet distance from the men. A huge crowd gathered around me, watching how I drank tea and observing my every move. Often I was invited to meet, behind closed doors, the women who were exuberant at the opportunity of inspecting me at close range. Lacking any other means of communication, we usually just exchanged smiles and I fulfilled endless requests for photographs.

On the whole, my research was feeling disconnected and pointless. The biggest hitch was that I never got to see the camel herds themselves, except for occasional sightings of a few animals wandering around in the distance. Although draft camels were ubiquitous in and around Bikaner, and lines of camel carts piled high with fuel-wood and a range of other products, often with their driver asleep, were one of the most characteristic local sights, breeding herds remained elusive. This left no opportunity for cross-checking the information that people proffered. There was no means of validating the number of animals owned, let alone the relative proportions of male and female animals, the age profile of the herd, calf mortality, reproductive performance, and any other scientific parameters necessary to gauge the economics of camel breeding. To acquire solid data about free-ranging camels, one would have to adopt the methods of a wildlife biologist, I mused. But this was entirely out of the question since I had neither the necessary equipment nor training. And, in any case, this was a sensitive border area where a foreigner could not move around at will through the landscape, but had to stick strictly to specified roads.

My research approach was neither that of an anthropologist, nor of an animal scientist. The former would have done away with the taxis, lived in a village, learnt the language, conducted participatory observation and interviewed key-informants. The latter would not have talked to the people but recorded measurable aspects, such as milk yields, growth rates, and intercalving intervals on camels that were kept under controlled conditions, just as my colleagues at the NRCC were doing. Instead of pursuing these classic lines of investigation, I was trying to understand the relationship between people and animals, so it needed a different approach. But what kind of approach? This was the big question that would puzzle and haunt me for some time to come.

A saviour arrived, in the guise of a Raika who had recently graduated from Bikaner's veterinary college. His name was Dr Dewaram Dewasi and he was one of only a handful of people from the community that had managed to acquire a university education. Shy and soft-spoken, he came from a sheep-breeding family that he described as quite poor. All his brothers and their families were still migrating with their herd of sheep. Originally, there had been no plans for him to go to school either but, by chance, a neighbour had taught Dr Dewaram the alphabet which he had then practised by drawing into the sand with a stick. Making his way through school and veterinary college had been an enormous struggle, placing a great financial burden on his family, although he had also supported himself by selling milk to the other students. His nature was very different from that of the smooth and omniscient veterinary students with a city upbringing who had accompanied me until then. Because of his background and because of his empathy, people opened up and interviews stopped being stage-plays, they became conversations between equals about topics of mutual concern.

Dr Dewaram immediately answered the question of why the Raika made such a limited use of camel milk. "We Raika have a cultural rule against the sale of milk. For us, it is a gift of god, and if we have it in excess, then we should give it away for free and not take money for it. Selling milk for us means the same as selling one's children. But this rule is not so strict anymore. I was told about it when I was ten years old, but now things have changed. We have started to sell the ghee from our sheep, although camel milk we still do not sell."

Then he emphasised, "Camel milk we always drink fresh and never boil it. It is forbidden in our caste to make curd or ghee from it."

Unfortunately, Dr Dewaram's sojourn in Bikaner was shortlived. He had joined the Rajasthan government's Department of Animal Husbandry and within a few days he received his posting to an animal hospital in Sadri, a small town in the middle of Rajasthan. He invited me to visit him there, promising to introduce me to both Raikas and camels. This is where the story began in earnest.

Chapter 3

SADRI

"The Rehbaris have generally two divisions called the Maru, and the Chalkia. The Maru Rehbaris occupy a superior position. They can marry the daughters of the Chalkias, without giving their daughters in return, and deal only in camels. The Chalkia Rehbaris on the other hand, keep large herds of sheep and goats. They abound in Godwar, and are also known as Pitalias, because their women generally wear brass ornaments."

– *The Castes of Marwar (census report of 1891),*
Munshi Hardyal Singh, Census Superintendent of Marwar

February 1991

"So, you need a good driver. I will see that I arrange one for you," decided the assistant manager of the Ghoomer Tourist Bungalow in Jodhpur, when I had told him I needed to go to Sadri, which was supposed to be somewhere in Pali district.

"Yes," I said, adding, "I certainly do," with a sigh, mentally recalling the series of disastrous experiences with taxi drivers that I had undergone in Bikaner. They never came on time, although even more likely they did not come at all. They always hated going to villages, sometimes pretending that there was something wrong with their car when one was halfway there, and then making a unilateral decision to go back to Bikaner. If one did get as far as a village, they would be uncooperative and sullen, signalling with all the might of their body language that they did not like the "rural areas" and wanted to get back as quickly as possible. Once one completed the tour in Bikaner, there was the inevitable skirmish about the bill. Whatever one had agreed on beforehand, always became null and void. Drivers who had previously pretended to not know a word of English, suddenly surprised me by their amazing facility with figures reaching astronomical heights.

I had reached Jodhpur the day before by an overnight bus from Bikaner. Since I did not know the exact location of the village in which Dr Dewaram had been posted, a taxi seemed the only means of getting there. The tiny slip of paper with his address read just: Dr Dewaram Dewasi, Vet Asst Surgeon, Vet Hospital, Sadri, Dstt Pali. I remembered that he had also murmured something about "Godwar", but foolishly I had omitted to ask him for further details. Hiring a taxi for an overnight trip made me feel like a glutton for punishment, but there was no alternative. If I tried going by public transport, I would get lost and not be able to enquire my way back to civilisation. And once I had linked up with Dr Dewaram I would also need transportation to visit the Raika and their camel herds. A taxi was the only option.

The tourist bungalow was a cavernous, rather unkempt building on High Court Road with rooms ranging from ordinary to air-cooled super-deluxe, according to a velvet-covered signboard with metallic letters displayed in the reception. I had intended to spend the previous night here, but had been waylaid by somebody from the tourism department who had recommended that I stay instead in a guesthouse outside Jodhpur, after I had told him about my interest in camels. He had lured me there by saying that I would be able to meet a ninety-year-old Raika sage revered for his traditional knowledge. It had all been a ploy and I had not been able to find a trace of the Raika, but it had been nice to get out of noisy, bustling Jodhpur. Somebody had advised me that the tourist bungalow was also the place for hiring taxis and, indeed, a fleet of polished ivory-coloured Ambassador cars – the prevailing model of conveyanace for both government officials and foreign tourists – was waiting for customers outside.

"You drink your tea, Madam. I go and find a driver," the manager said and stepped out, while I leaned back in the chair and waited, thinking with some satisfaction of the morning's interview with Komal Kothari, an expert on Rajasthani folklore. I had met him at his residence in Paota. A grey-haired original who had devoted his life to studying and documenting Rajasthan's culture, Komalda, as he was reverently referred to, had provided me with some useful new intelligence, for instance, on the history of the ubiquitous two-wheeled camel cart that was a prominent feature of Jodhpur traffic as well. "These carts are actually quite a recent invention. We never used to have them in Rajasthan – camels were used only as pack animals and sometimes, very rarely, to pull four-wheeled carts. The two-wheeled carts became popular only after World War II. Somebody had the idea to equip the basic ox-cart with used airplane tyres. You see, Jodhpur had one of the first aerodromes in the country and after the war it became a scrap yard for Dakota airplanes. This new type of cart could transport much larger loads than the ox-cart. One can even say it revolutionised rural transportation in Rajasthan, making it easy to reach isolated villages in the desert that were not connected by roads."

Komal Kothari, who obviously enjoyed passing on his vast knowledge to visiting researchers, had also advised me that if I wanted to find out about the history of the camel in Rajasthan, I should talk to the "Bhopas" and he had mentioned somebody called Pabuji as a crucial person, but I had not really understood what he meant. I was hoping that Dr Dewaram could explain this to me. Komal Kothari had also revealed another interesting detail, when I had asked him about the meaning of Raika and Rebari, and whether the two names were synonymous. "You see, in Rajasthan, all castes generally have three names - one honorific, one ordinary, and one derogatory. In this case, Raika is the ordinary name, whereas Rebari is slightly derogatory. Dewasi is the honorific variety, which is why educated Raika take this as a family name."

"I found a driver for you," the manager had come back with a very slight young man in tow whom he slapped on the shoulder. The driver looked unremarkable, except for the blossom-shaped ear-studs that many Rajasthani men liked to sport. He briefly glanced at me to size up his new customer, presumably, and established eye contact. That fleeting look conveyed unusual alertness and, in that brief instant, I may already have sensed subconsciously that this driver would give me a lucky break. "He'll go and get his clothes and will be back in half an hour, so that you can leave by noon," explained the manager, adding, "He's a really good driver. He speaks English."

Exactly half an hour later, a stately white Ambassador droned into the driveway of the tourist bungalow and pulled up in front of the entrance steps where I had been basking in the warm and friendly winter sun. My luggage was stowed into the trunk, the rear door thrown open with a polite, "You sit here, Madam," and I was comfortably ensconced into the cushions of the back seat. Maybe this time I would be travelling in style. Since I was blowing up my research budget on the taxi rental, I might as well enjoy it. In addition, I was ready to discover a new part of Rajasthan, quite different from the area around Bikaner.

Rajasthan literally means "the land of kings". It is the reincarnation of the former Rajputana, a conglomerate of about twenty sovereign kingdoms ruled over by maharajahs. Never formally colonised, these states were known as "Princely India", to distinguish them from British India. Their desert territories were the bulwarks of Hindu India against the Muslim incursions from the west that started with the seasonal plundering expeditions of Mahmud of Ghazni and culminated in the Mughal Empire. This precarious geographic position explains why this area was not dominated by the Brahmins but by the valiant Rajput warrior caste that had cultivated bravery in battle to unprecedented heights. Rajput men were so concerned about upholding their honour that they preferred death to defeat. Their women were in strict purdah and generally not allowed to be seen, but adhered to equally exacting standards of honour. When their men died, they immolated themselves on their funeral pyre, a practice known as sati. When the men lost battles, their womenfolk committed *jauhar* to avoid being dishonoured by the enemy. Although these customs were now a thing of the past and the feudal system had been officially abolished about half a century ago, they lingered on in the minds and values of the people and were still a source of pride.

Arguably, the two most famous and prominent among the former kingdoms were Marwar and Mewar. Marwar means the "land of death" and it is composed mostly of flat forbidding desert. Jodhpur is its capital and the seat of the maharajah who ruled over Marwar. Now we would be driving towards hilly and forested Mewar, which was the domain of the Maharana of Udaipur.

The driver, thankfully, didn't get up to any antics, but steered the Ambassador along at a safe and reassuring speed. A bumpy tree-lined highway took us directly south from Jodhpur, passing through the town of Pali, formerly an important trade entrepot on a subsidiary branch to the Silk Road, but now heavily polluted by the dyeing industries. After well over a hundred kilometres, we veered off the main road, onto a severely pot-holed asphalt track. Enormous grey rock boulders cropped up, strewn across the plain like oversized marbles splattered by a giant. Just then the misty silhouette of the Aravalli Hills became discernible on the horizon. These geologically ancient mountains snake through Rajasthan from north-east to south-west and form the eastern frontier of both the Thar Desert and of the breeding area of the dromedary. Beyond them the humidity is too high for camels to thrive.

The desert of Marwar was now behind us. We had reached Godwar, the transitional zone between Marwar and Mewar, which forms a green line along the foot of the Aravalli Hills. Reasonably fertile and with a milder climate, Godwar had always been coveted by the rulers of both states and, as a result, its history had been marked by frequent changes in ownership. The density of babul and khejri trees palpably increased; yellow-flowered awlia shrubs became abundant, peepal trees appeared and, occasionally, there were even some small, irrigated patches of green guarded by scarecrows. As we came closer to the hill chain, the countryside turned virtually lush with orchards and crimson bougainvilleas billowing over the walls lining the road.

A flock of sheep, accompanied by a haughty-looking shepherd wearing a red turban and waving a bamboo stick, hurriedly traversed the highway. The sun was sinking fast and bathed everything in a warm and glorious light when we crossed a dried-out riverbed and entered Sadri, a small town nestled in a nook of the hill chain. Passing the teeming vegetable market, we found the veterinary hospital, one of the most imposing buildings in town, immediately.

Dr Dewaram had already been waiting and welcomed me like a long-lost relative, enquiring again and again about my wellbeing, complaining that I was so late, and asking of what service he could be. He had another visitor whom he introduced as Vinay Srivastava, an anthropology student from Delhi who was conducting his PhD research on the Raika. Seated on some rickety chairs next to the cattle-restraining stand in the courtyard of the hospital, we sipped our tea and exchanged news about our families and what had happened since we had been together in Bikaner. Enthusiastically, Dr Dewaram and Vinay chalked out a programme of field visits for the next couple of days to show me everything there was to know about the Raika and camels.

Vinay had already undertaken extensive fieldwork here and around Bikaner, besides searching the state archives for historical references to the Raika. He generously shared the results of his research. "The Raika are very strongly represented here in the Godwar area. But they are a different group to the ones you encountered in Bikaner. They are called Chalkia or Godwara Raikas and do not intermarry with the Maru Raika that you find in Bikaner and Marwar. They tie their turbans differently and have different customs. But they eat from the same plate and this is very important in our culture."

I double-checked with him the information provided by Komal Kothari. "Sometimes, the Raika are also referred to as Rebari. Can these two terms be used interchangeably or is there a difference in meaning between Raika and Rebari?"

"The Rebari encompass actually a much larger number of people. Especially in Gujarat, there are very many Rebari who all keep livestock. Raika is the name adopted by the Rebari of Marwar and it carries a connotation of 'camel breeder'. There are many historical references to the Raika and how they served the maharajahs and other Rajputs by means of their camel-related expertise and how they undertook difficult tasks for them. It is a kind of an honorific term, whereas Rebari is considered a bit uncomplimentary. That's why the Rebari of Rajasthan have decided to take Raika as their official caste name. But, actually, the educated Raika have adopted the surname 'Dewasi', as has our Dr Dewaram."

Then he went on, "But the Rebari of Gujarat and the Raika of Rajasthan all have the same roots. This information is available from the caste genealogists, the Ravs. The Ravs have big books in which they record all the newborn children. They travel from one household to another, continuously updating these records. Anyway, according to the Rav, the Raika came to Marwar from Jaisalmer, the most western city in Rajasthan, close to the Pakistan border. And before that they probably came from Afghanistan or Persia. I will provide you with some references, so that you can look this up."

As I found out gradually, there are several different and conflicting versions about the origin of the Raika/Rebari. As Vinay said, evidence for the origin of the Rebari, and when and under what circumstances they came to India can only be pieced together from the records kept by the Ravs, and from oral traditions. It is often surmised that their first foothold in what is now Rajasthan, was in Jaisalmer but that they were originally from Baluchistan. Others opined that they had their roots in Persia.

* * *

I immediately liked Sadri; it somehow felt right, almost like home. No doubt this was to no small extent because of the very warm welcome I received, but also due to some innate qualities of its own. Busy, but not crowded, traditional, but not narrow-minded, it gave the impression of a small universe in its own right. The dearth of hotels presented a minor logistical problem for Dr Dewaram, but it then occurred to him that there was a dharamshala, a pilgrim hostel, at the Mukti Dham. The Mukti Dham was a recently built temple donated by the Jain community and somewhat unusual, since it was devoted not to one particular deity, but the entire

Hindu pantheon. After having checked into the hostel, we paid our respects to each god, and Vinay used this opportunity for another lecture to explain to me the various roles and functions of each god. Shiva, the destroyer, I already knew; elephant-headed Ganesh whom one should pray to when starting any new venture; Hanuman, the monkey god who rescues people from trouble; Sarasvati, the goddess of science and wisdom; black-faced Kali, the goddess of death and destruction; Ramdevra, a local god mounted on a white horse who takes care of the needs, especially of the lower castes.

Sadri had no restaurants. There was only one little hole in the wall, which barely had room for the three of us in addition to the fireplace on which the meals were prepared. There was only one menu option, served on a steel plate: *jarri roti*, a massive millet chapatti, on which was poured a thimble of ghee, a small bowl with vegetables in a red-hot watery sauce and a fleck of perniciously hot chutney which set my mouth on fire, severely testing my determination to eat everything that I was served. It was all pretty overwhelming and I retired early to my tiny room in the dharamshala, a cold cubicle with walls painted blue, a clanking iron door and nothing but a bed with a scratchy blanket and a single sheet that had been used before. Before I could even write up my notes, I fell into a restless sleep with wild dreams in which the various gods caused plenty of commotion and turmoil.

I woke up to the plaintive, cat-like meowing of peacocks. A male and several females were dancing and courting on the lawn in front of the temple. A temple servant brought me a bucket of hot water for my morning bath and, after a cup of tea, we drove to Latada, a sprawling village centred on a big open square, the *aakra*, where the cattle assemble each morning, but which was empty at this early hour. From this, a number of small alleys radiated leading to the various caste quarters. In one corner there were a few multi-storeyed brick houses belonging to the affluent *baniya* community, but most houses consisted of only one or two rooms.

Five of the eighty Raika families that lived here kept camels, Dr Dewaram explained, as he led us along a narrow pathway winding through thorn brush enclosures. "I know a Raika here whose name is Savantiba. I think he will be able to tell us a lot."

Savantiba was standing in front of his ochre-coloured hut covered with *kaccha* roof tiles, and welcomed us enthusiastically with, "Ram Ram, *aiye*, *aiye*." His thorn-fenced courtyard was filled with about twenty couched camels, lying closely together, resembling sardines in a tin, and in order to get to him, we had to thread our way between their massive bodies.

Savantiba was tall and thin, even emaciated-looking, maybe about fifty years old, and dressed completely in white, including his turban. Despite the early hour, his intelligent face glowed with delight at having visitors and his eyes sparkled. Exuding authority and wit, he seated us on a hastily brought charpai and a metal chair in a small open shed where guests are received. Dr Dewaram explained the reason for our visit.

Smoke from the fireplace inside the house spiralled to the sky. The wind rustled through the crown of the neem trees above us, and the camel herd in front of us was gradually waking up. Most of the female camels were still lying down, but the male was in rut. He had ejected his pink *dulaa* from the corner of his mouth and his face was covered with foam, but his forelegs were tied together, preventing him from lovemaking. The females ignored him, placidly chewing the cud, but two dark and curly newborn camels were up and about. One of them was darting around adventurously, even mounting his mother, while the other one did not yet quite seem in control of its legs. It nudged its mother's udder to extract some milk, but suddenly its legs faltered and it crashed to the ground.

A half-naked toddler, one of Savantiba's grandchildren, wanted to join us and threaded his way through a number of recumbent camels, using their protruding hip bones as walking aids. Savantiba, Dr Dewaram and Vinay had become deeply absorbed in their conservation. Between taking deep inhalations from a small clay pipe, the Raika explained something with a degree of urgency. Normally, it made me very impatient when I couldn't follow conversation, but right now I was too engrossed in the magic of the moment to care. My thoughts drifted back to vet school where we were always told to look at large animals as potentially dangerous beasts and advised to restrain them with iron chains, putting them in a crush, or even sedating them before going near them. But these camels resembled family members and were treated almost as intimately; nobody was afraid of them. It reminded me very strongly of my first encounter with camels in Jordan.

A boy, maybe twelve years old and wearing an oversized red turban handed me a bowl of steaming tea. It was made from camel milk without water added, a potion very suitable for sustaining you through many hours of herding camels. While Savantiba was cuddling his grandson on his lap with one hand and drinking tea with the other, he ordered the red-turbaned boy to lead the camel calf – the one that had fallen down – over to me. The boy bent down over the calf that was lying on its side, talked to it, rubbed its ribs, pushed it into a sitting position, then helped to uncurl and unbend its impossibly long legs, so that it could stand up. As it slowly tottered towards me, I realised that something was wrong – it could not completely straighten out its forelegs. Savantiba wanted my opinion.

The boy steadied the calf between his arms and chest, while I squatted and ran my fingers over its joints and tendons. "I think this is a congenital deformation about which one can't do very much. But it probably will gradually get better on its own," I said, standing up again. Fortunately, the much more experienced Dr Dewaram seconded my diagnosis. Then he translated to me the gist of the conversation that I had missed. "Savantiba says that there are a lot of problems with this herd, lately. There have been several miscarriages and premature births. Some newborn camels died within a few days, and Savantiba is afraid that this calf, which has problems standing up, may also be doomed. He thinks that the miscarriages may be related to a bout of coughing and pneumonia that this herd suffered from a while ago. Only yesterday, an adult camel owned by his brother died with strange symptoms."

We inspected the body of the camel that had died the day before. Outwardly it looked quite normal, although very thin. It had suffered from violent contortions and thrashed around in a circle before it died as was evident from the imprints in the sand. I had no idea what kind of disease this could be and suggested that we could take some samples and send these to a laboratory for analysis, but Dr Dewaram rejected this idea outright. "We cannot touch dead animals and there is no lab anyway that could do this kind of work. But this is really bad. It means that there will be practically no income from the herd this year," he contemplated. Savantiba nodded his head in agreement.

It was time for us to leave; the herd had to be taken out for grazing and Savantiba had to get ready. We declined his repeated invitations for food, apologised for the delay to his day's activities, and promised to come back with some medicines for strengthening and straightening out the spider-legged camel baby. Thanking Savantiba for his time, I enquired about the name of the red-turbaned boy who had handled the small camel so deftly and at the same time so sensitively. "This is my nephew, the son of my younger brother who owned that dead camel we just saw. His name is Sawaram," he said, adding, "Sawaram is just about to go to Bombay – he will be working in a sweet shop there."

I was shocked. "But isn't he much too young to go to Bombay to work. How old is he? He looks like he is twelve at the most."

"Oh, he is probably thirteen or fourteen. That's right, it's tough, but at least he'll get his food there. We all have to fill our stomachs and there is not much profit to be made from camel breeding these days. Although this boy is really good with animals."

By the time we returned to our vehicle, it was surrounded by a huge number of long-horned cows and a smaller number of black water buffaloes. "This is the *chappa*, the village cowherd," explained Dr Dewaram. "They are waiting for the *gual*, the village herdsman, to lead them out to graze. Almost every family owns a cow and they let them out in the morning so that they can join the chappa. When the chappa comes back at around sunset, each cow goes back to her owner's house. You will find this system throughout Godwar and the gual usually is from the Raika community. Every family pays him a fixed amount of grain or cash."

"And," he added, "these guals know a lot about treating animals, maybe more than I do. There is so much traditional knowledge in my community about animal diseases."

In the Ambassador, we heatedly discussed whether we could do anything for Savantiba, and if yes, what. The only place we could think of that could help us identify the disease was the Veterinary College in Bikaner. But that was about 400 km away and sending a sample did not appeal to Dr Dewaram; he considered it a wasted effort. For the first time in at least a decade I regretted that I had neglected my veterinary skills. They would have come in really handy here. I searched my brain for anything I might have read on camel ailments, but could not latch on to anything that would correspond to the symptoms. I was also troubled by the idea of the gentle Sawaram being shipped off to Bombay to fend for himself. Probably never having left his idyllic village, how would he cope with the noise, the traffic and the crowds? I could already envision him joining the people who slept on pavements.

We made true our promise of helping the camel baby, and it did survive. But Sawaram left soon after without any fanfare, and I never saw him again. Only his photograph of that first day remains.

Together with my congenial friends, I visited more camel herds over the next few days. It was an unusual way of doing fieldwork, travelling by taxi and with two excellent guides. If they could not answer a question off the top of their head, they immediately tried to track down an appropriate local expert. The ambience was perfected by the driver, who took an active interest in my venture and was exceedingly cooperative, never complaining even if we kept him on the go from six in the morning until late at night, nor minding if we took his precious Ambassador off the tarmac road to bump across fields where we suspected camels were. After three days I had finally gotten around to asking his name – Hanwant Singh – and he had proudly explained to me that he was from the Rajput community, in fact, the same lineage as the Maharajah of Jodhpur.

Vinay, who would later become a professor of anthropology at the University of Delhi, not only provided lots of background information about the Raika but also about the other castes that composed the cultural mosaic of Godwar. "The people with the longest history in the area are the tribals, the Adivasi. They include the Grassia, the Bhil, and the Mina. Most of them collect forest products, for instance, medicinal plants, and they distil liquor from acacia trees. The women carry head-loads of dried wood from the forest to the market.

"This is also the home of many traders who have developed big business empires in Bombay and other big cities. These merchants are known as Marwaris and belong to the Jain faith. Although their mansions in the old part of Sadri are locked up most of the year, their community still plays a very important role. For, with their profits, the merchants support religious activities in the area, especially the upkeep of the Ranakpur temple and the construction of new temples. As strict vegetarians, they also support activities for the benefit of animals such as veterinary hospitals and treatment camps.

"Jats and Choudharys are the farming castes. They grow wheat, corn, chilli peppers, okra and sesame, irrigating their fields from wells. The Malis are the gardeners and raise vegetables or flowers. Then there are Kumhars who make pots and burn bricks, Ganchis who extract oil from sesame seeds, and Meghwals who make shoes and other leather objects." Then he added, "If you have time, I will show you how you can recognise all these different castes from their clothes and from their jewellery. Half an hour in the market should be enough."

Early in the mornings, we visited more camel-breeders. Savantiba was not the only Raika who had problems with his herd. Throughout the area, camel herds had been diminished by abortions and deaths. Everybody seemed to have a different opinion about the cause. While Savantiba had declared that this was a totally unknown disease, the likes he had never seen in his lifetime, Rajaram, a white-bearded and very dignified relative of Savantiba, attributed the miscarriages to "*tibursa*". Meaning literally "three years" in the local language, this was the native equivalent of the scientific term "Trypanosomiasis", one of the major camel diseases. Similar to malaria, it is caused by a blood parasite that is carried from one animal to the next by biting flies. The parasite multiplies in the blood cyclically and leads to undulating fever which can result in immediate death or lead to a more chronic debilitation. The Raika know no cure for it, so the traditional way of controlling the disease was to isolate infected animals for three years. If they survived this period, they were considered non-infective and readmitted to the herd. Although the Raika have no effective treatment to kill the parasite, they experiment with many different potions and mixtures that are supposed to strengthen the ability of the camel to overcome the disease.

But the Raika were experts in detecting the disease. All they needed for this was their sense of smell. We were sitting on charpais in Rajaram's courtyard; as usual my two gurus and the owner of the house were talking in the unintelligible local language while I was engrossed in watching Rajaram's wife sweep up camel dung and add it to a big pile in the corner.

"Do you know the sand-ball test?" Dr Dewaram asked me, shifting to English. I looked at him blankly. "This is the traditional way by which the Raika determine whether a camel is infected with tibursa. Rajaram will show you how it is done. I myself also don't know very well. We did not learn this in vet school."

Rajaram walked over to one of the couched camels and slapped it on the croup to make it get up. It arose in that typical three-stage manner with which camels revert from the sitting to the standing position. Then it lifted its tail and urinated into the sand. Rajaram scooped up some of the soiled sand and formed it into a couple of egg-sized balls. He placed them on a ledge, explaining that they had to be left to dry for a little while. After about ten minutes, he broke one of them open, sniffed it and his face took on the concentrated expression of a wine connoisseur sampling a new bottle. Then he handed me the second ball. I applied some pressure with my two thumbs and it crumbled open; then I inhaled deeply and slowly and caught a whiff of something that seemed faintly familiar...acetone, I thought, yes, it smells a bit like acetone and remembered how, long ago, back in veterinary practice, certain cows had fallen prey to a metabolic disorder called acetonemia.

The author of the most comprehensive volume on the one-humped camel, A. S. Leese, Captain of the Royal Army Veterinary Corps and Camel Specialist to the Government of India from 1907 to 1913, described this procedure as something that was unique to the Rebari and that they were employed by camel owners to perform this test before the rainy season. He also crosschecked it with a microscope and acknowledged that it worked, but that both types of examination have the same limitation: they are positive only during the stages that the parasite is present in the peripheral blood, which is not always the case.

Gamnaram Raika, a very dapper young man who gave us loving introductions to each of his camels, had yet another opinion about the cause of the miscarriages, insisting that the abortions were due to lack of food and that there just was not enough to eat for the camels.

The camel owners varied in their outspokenness and we generally only talked to men, the women withdrawing into the houses whenever we turned up. This had to do with Rajasthani mores of behaviour, as Vinay explained to me; in the presence of their men, women are supposed to stay in the background, although, as I learned later, this does not prevent them from negotiating with the agents who come to buy their sheep and goats. Because the men are out all day with the animals, Raika women are often described as the finance ministers of the family. Camel husbandry, however, is a man's business; in all these years, I have met only one woman who herded camels herself. Sometimes the women called me into the house to meet me and check me out in seclusion. Because of the language problem, friendship would take a long time to develop. But the women initially had me in awe, for they were everything I was not. They were doing hard physical labour, they were tied down by a traditional code of conduct, they fulfilled endless orders shouted by their men from outside the house for cups of tea and for food, and they coped with all this enormously cheerfully. On top of that, they were incredibly glamorous. Not only did they wear spectacular brass noserings, but their everyday outfits were stunning, consisting of wide swinging skirts, revealing blouses covered up by an *odhni*, a type of veil worn over the head and shoulders, and heavy silver jewellery that weighed down their ears, covered their arms, clanked around their ankles. In this attire, they would carry water, bring firewood, clean the animal pens, cook the food, ready the kids for school (if these were going to school), cook and pack the *rotis* with a dab of chutney that formed their husband's lunch, and then often go out and do roadwork for eight hours to supplement the family income. Compared with these power-women, I felt infinitely inferior. Just the heat and driving around in the car exhausted me, my inability to converse in the local language and express myself made me feel like a halfwit, and with my sensible clothes and hiking boots, I was decidedly unglamorous.

But for the Raika men too, life was hard. Camels need to spend most of their waking hours grazing in order to cover their nutritional needs. So the herders were out all day in the sun and heat, their entire sustenance consisting of the rotis that were tied into a piece of cloth that dangled from their shoulders. They came back after sunset, then it took time to settle and couch the herd, maybe tend to some injuries, or milk a few animals. So there was time left for little else but a meal, to sit around the fire with the family, and then sleep. This cycle continued year in, year out whether the sun scorched down or the monsoon rains poured. Even if they fell sick, there was no chance for a break, since animals unrelentingly need care, day after day.

The camels were fed either on harvested fields or in the nearby jungle that covered the Aravalli Hills. I was always amazed by how one man could control and keep together a herd of, say, twenty animals. To some extent, natural behavioural patterns of camels certainly help. Studies of feral camels in Australia show that they band together into family groups, which are composed of up to ten females with their children; they are joined by a bull only during the rutting season. When not in rut, the male camels prefer to stay solitary or form bachelor groups. These matrilineal groups remain very stable over the years; the male offspring is chased away by the bull after a certain age and he then joins a bachelor group.

The structure of the Raika herds actually resembled this natural social organisation of the camel. They were composed of female camels, and the young male animals were usually sold in their first year. The fact that female camels form stable family groups and tend to stick together for long-term periods explained to some extent how one or two people could lead large numbers of camels out to graze and keep them more or less together. But family ties were not the only factor. The Raika had a vocabulary of at least five different sounds to communicate with their camels. By voice they could order the herd to stop, to assemble, to start marching ahead, to spread out and feed, and to separate into young animals and mothers.

Many camels also responded to their individual names. The names often referred to certain physical characteristics, such as *Kani* (the one-eyed one), *Jhimpri* (the one with bushy ears), *Dholu* (white one), *Mewari* (the one from Mewar) or *Tikri* (sharp-featured one).

A herder could walk up to all of his camels and, without being tied or restrained in any manner, these would stand patiently while being milked. There was a terminology to classify camels with respect to the ease with which they could be milked. Some of them gave milk just like that, others needed their calves to be present, and still others would cooperate only with one specific person and no other.

The camels generally radiated gentleness and serenity. I never saw any sign of aggressiveness. Even I, as a complete alien, could approach any female camel in the herd, pat her on the neck or rub her shoulder. Some of them would blissfully ignore this, not even batting an eyelid, and continue chewing cud. Others would swing around their long neck in a measured movement and give me a long look from those soulful eyes under incredibly long and curved eyelashes. Camels also love being scratched just behind their short and round ears and if one massages this favourite spot, they visibly enjoy it and return the pressure to indicate that they want more and you should not stop. I stayed away from the males in rut that were keyed up sexually, but nevertheless could still be easily handled by the Raika.

Baby camels, like all young animals, are driven by thirst for their mother's milk, the need to strengthen and test their limbs, and by boundless curiosity. While their mothers are still bracing themselves for a long day of finding forage, the youngsters engage in rounds of playing tag, chasing each other like racehorses, until something arrests their attention and they come to an abrupt halt; within seconds, they shoot off again as if stung by a scorpion. Sometimes they neck-wrestle with each other, almost like puppies, displaying behaviour much more interactive than that of calves or foals. And if you stand still among a bunch of camel calves, if only for a short time, you become an object that absolutely has to be checked out. Chances are that they will position themselves at an arm's distance, probingly stick out their neck, start to carefully nuzzle your face with their nimble lips, sniff your hair, and, if they like your smell, maybe give you a little facial massage. Curiosity gets the better of even the more mature camels. Older camels also exhibit these inquisitive manners if you stand among them, and will venture to give you a tickling and memorable smooch.

After a few days, it was obvious that the information we received was pretty consistent. The average herd of a Raika family was composed of between ten to twenty females together with their offspring and often, but not always, one male camel for breeding. The main purpose of keeping camel herds was to sell the young male camels as work-animals to farmers and cart owners. This happened once a year at the Pushkar Camel Fair. Camel dung was valued as excellent manure with long-lasting effect, taking three years to decompose. It was traded with farmers, either for cash or, more frequently, for grain. Handling the manure transactions was the exclusive domain of the women, who swept it up into big piles in the courtyards. If the camels were staying overnight on somebody's field, the Raika were given tea, flour, and *bidis*, sometimes also cash, in exchange for their camels' fertilising effect. A fourth product was the hair that was shorn once a year at the time of Holi. But finding grazing was becoming more and more difficult. Increasingly scarce grazing opportunities were also the reason some Raika had given up camel breeding. They had either sold their herds to other Raika or had given their few remaining camels to others for caretaking. Graziers charged about Rs 3,000 per year for looking after twenty camels. It was their duty to sell the offspring and give the proceeds to the owner.

One day, while sitting in the Veterinary Hospital, we estimated the income that the Raika made from camel breeding. It could be calculated quite easily. The main return was from the sale of male young animals. Suppose a Raika had twelve breeding females – the average holding in Godwar. Since camels become pregnant only every second year, in any given year, six of them would have calves, of which fifty per cent were male. So there would be three calves to sell per year. Prices for these would range from Rs 1,000 to Rs 3,000,[1] depending on their condition and conformation. The annual income thus would be somewhere between Rs 3,000 and Rs 9,000, provided there were no losses due to miscarriages or deaths of the calves. There would, of course, be additional income from selling dung and maybe from herding camels belonging to others. But there was also expenditure, especially the grazing fees for obtaining access to the forest.

"It is hardly worth it," I said. "While I really like camels, from the economic perspective it does not make much sense. I don't understand why they don't switch to other activities," I added, intentionally being a bit provocative.

Both Vinay and Dr Dewaram looked at me somewhat horrified. "Well, you have to understand, it is their tradition to breed camels," Vinay replied.

Dr Dewaram seconded him. "Yes, it is the Raika's duty to look after camels, they can't just give it up," he said.

"Don't you know the story about the origin of the Raika?" Vinay queried, making me feel embarrassed that I did not.

"No, I have never heard it, please tell me," I replied.

Vinay gave me a professorial look and then began to recount. "The first Raika, named Samar, was made by God Shiva to look after the first camel. It happened like this. Shiva was meditating and his wife, Goddess Parvati, was getting bored. So in order to pass the time, she started playing with clay and shaping animals out of it. She made one particularly strange animal that had five legs. By that time, Shiva had stopped meditating and came to see what Parvati was doing. She asked him to breathe life into the five-legged animal. Shiva at first refused, saying that a five-

1 At the time, the value of the Indian rupee was around Rs 20 to the US dollar.

legged animal would just face a lot of problems in its life. Parvati continued begging, so, finally, he breathed some life in it and said '*Uth*!' (Get up!) The animal got up but, as predicted, it had a lot of problems with its five legs. So Shiva moulded together the fifth leg and pushed it onto the back of the strange creature and it became a hump. With its four legs, the animal could suddenly move around very quickly and started creating a lot of nuisance. Once again, Parvati requested her husband for help. 'Please, give me a man to take care of this animal!' So Shiva, who had just made another man, the Charan, to take care of his bull, Nandi, rolled up some dirt and sweat from his skin and out of this he shaped the first Raika.

"So this is why the Raika cannot just quit keeping camels. They have been *created* to look after the camel. It is their God-given duty, their dharma, and their reason for existence. They are the guardians of the camel and it is the basis of their whole culture."

He continued, "You may have noticed that the Raika sell only two products from the camel: the young male camels and the dung. There are restrictions, or call it taboos, on selling female camels, on selling milk, wool, and products of the dead camel, namely bones and leather. Wool and milk are used only for home consumption. The relationship between the Raika and the camel is not simply utilitarian, but is shaped by religious duty."

"In fact," added Vinay, giving me a stern look, "the seventh of the Raikas' ten dharmas, their religious commandments, prohibits them from selling the milk of their animals. As you have heard from Dewaram, a common adage is '*dudh bechna, beta bechna*', equating the sale of milk with that of children. It is believed that excess milk should be given away for free rather than sold. There are many stories circulating about the misfortunes that occurred to Raika who broke this taboo – either whole camel herds succumbed to death or family members died unexpectedly."

Getting still more professorial, he continued, "You have correctly observed in Bikaner that milk is also not processed. Common belief does not condone this. Camel milk should always be had fresh, that is, without previous boiling as is the case with milk from other animals, although it can be used for making tea or *kheer*."

It was a fascinating story, but I was also sceptical. In a world ruled by money, how could anybody just do things out of duty, be it religious or not, I thought somewhat cynically. There must be reasons why the Raika make use of the camel in this particular way. Historical reasons maybe or ecological. Maybe they had transferred the Hindu veneration of the cow to the animal that was closest to them, I mulled. It would be interesting to know how the Muslim in India related to the camel. Did they have a similar attitude as the Raika or did they subscribe to the more opportunistic view of the Arabs who made use of all conceivable products of the camel? With respect to the taboo on processing camel milk, it occurred to me that this could also have a very rational explanation. As I knew from my study of the literature, camel milk is very difficult to turn into curd, or cheese, or butter. It had something to do with the structure of the proteins, I vaguely recalled.

Nevertheless, over the next couple of days, I paid more attention to the attitude and feelings of the Raika towards camels. So far my interest had been on more technical matters, such as herd composition, management and utilisation patterns, but now I kept my ears open, as much as this was possible with my lack of local language skills, for indications of this special sense of responsibility which, according to my gurus, the Raika had towards their camels.

The next morning itself, one old and gentle Raika named Harjiram with a very long white beard provided some further clues. He lived on what I felt was the best piece of real estate in all of Godwar. His hut was perched on the top of a crag from which one had a magnificent view of both the Aravalli range that spread out to the south as well as the plains of Marwar to the north. His wife had died, his four daughters were married off and his only son was working in Bombay. Harjiram was doing his best to take care of his camels, although he was handicapped by his age and opium addiction. He was a gracious host and while his brother's wife was making tea inside the hut, he pulled out a small and wrinkled plastic bag from the depths of his dhoti and unwrapped a sticky, black mass from which he pinched off a few pea-sized pieces that he offered to us. "This is opium," explained Dr Dewaram. "It is part of the Raika hospitality ritual to offer it. Taking a little bit won't do any harm," he encouraged me and then demonstrated the proper etiquette for partaking opium – folding the hands to a namaste, saluting the Mother Goddess ("Jai Mataji", leaning the head backward, with the left hand in the nape, and then putting the morsel on the back of the tongue and swallowing it.

Sitting on the charpais we relished the panorama and talked about grazing problems, about droughts and diseases. Harjiram also felt that diseases had increased in recent years and he attributed this to the gods being angry and punishing the community. "God is angry with the Raika community because they are selling female animals. Before, we never used to do this, but now it is common practice to sell female sheep and things are becoming worse. Even female camels are sometimes being sold to people outside the community. Where will this lead us? Our female animals have to be passed on from one generation to the next. God is punishing us by sending diseases and droughts," he said, agitatedly puffing on his clay-pipe. "My son, Ghisulal, is working in Bombay; I don't even know what kind of work he does, something to do with stone-cutting. He does earn money though and sends some to me.

So that's fine, but what am I going to do with the camels? I have become old and weak, and every day life gets harder."

His gloomy thoughts were interrupted by his *bhabhi* (brother's wife) who handed him a metal pitcher of tea and three cups and saucers. "Some of my camels have a bad case of mange, can you please have a look at them and tell me what best to do?" Harjiram's eight female camels that had spent the night on a small ridge below Harjiram's eagle-nest were indeed in very sorry shape. Some of them had almost no hair left from scratching themselves and Dr Dewaram worriedly shook his head. "This is bad, and the whole herd is going to be infected, including the young ones. These camels need to be treated urgently; their whole bodies have to be scrubbed with an insecticide or with used engine oil. But that is a lot of work – Harjiram will not be able to do this...."

For the second time in a few days, I regretted having let my veterinary expertise slip. Fortunately, Dr Dewaram knew everything about the treatment of mange, a skin affliction that is caused by mites that burrow into the skin and which is the second-most frequent camel disease after tibursa. There were several options ranging from traditionally used and locally produced oils to commercially manufactured insecticides. They all involved dousing the whole camel and vigorously scrubbing its entire body – and camels have quite a large body surface.

Although I was still caught up in the excitement of finally seeing and learning about camels in the flesh and about establishing a rapport with the Raika, in my subconscious I must have had an inkling that clinically detached research was not possible. Camels were not wildlife that I could observe from a distant and neutral standpoint, and from whom I could dissociate myself once my research objectives had been fulfilled. They came with owners and as soon as I started asking questions, a relationship developed. Or rather, without a relationship, nobody would tell you very much.

Unless people felt you were committed, that you cared for their camels and for them, they were not going to tell you anything worthwhile – that had been the lesson I had learnt in Bikaner. Here in Godwar, people opened up because Dr Dewaram was from the same community and took an interest in peoples' problems and his veterinary skills were much in demand. Research was not possible without sitting together, drinking lots of cups of tea, and accepting hospitality, otherwise people would not build sufficient confidence to tell you what was on their minds. Taking tea, especially, was kind of an acid test; it was the absolutely minimal token to prove that you were not just there to collect data for your own sake, an act that signified that you valued people in their own right and engaged with them according to local standards.

With the relationship and with the knowledge one gained, came responsibility. I am not sure whether at that time I was aware of the dilemma that would put me in later. For I had other responsibilities too: my family. Gary, Jon and Aisha were coming to Rajasthan to visit.

Chapter 4

ANJI-KI-DHANI

"At the beginning of the twentieth century, there were 10,000 camels, forty years ago there were 5,000 camels. Now there are about a 1,000 camels belonging to our village and ten years from now, there will be none."

– Ruparam Raika from Anji-ki-dhani

February 1991

Gary, Jon, and Aisha flew into Udaipur, where I picked them up in Hanwant Singh's car. By the time we returned to Sadri, Dr Dewaram had excitedly made plans for our further "programme". He had decided that I also needed to visit some Maru Raika, especially since they were the ones with the real reputation as camel breeders. By some accounts, the Godwar Raikas had started breeding camels a mere hundred years ago. Before that they had bred only sheep, but when a huge drought came they had had to temporarily migrate to greener pastures and this could not be done without camels. This comparatively short engagement with camels rendered them almost dilettantes compared with the Maru Raikas who had never been anything else other than camel breeders. Dr Dewaram had just been told about a Maru Raika village with several thousand camels and he wanted to take us there. It was called Anji-ki-dhani.

All of us, including Vinay, piled into the Ambassador and drove north on a narrow ribbon of tarmac that ran parallel to the Aravalli hill chain and was entirely devoid of traffic, except for the occasional animals crossing the road. Anji-ki-dhani was a sleepy place where time seemed to have stood still. At the village entrance there was a row of white memorial stones depicting venerated ancestors seated on camels. Right beside it was the *kotli*, a platform built around a stately neem tree and meant for the entertainment of village guests. Some old men who had been napping on it, rolled out blankets and made us sit down; glasses of steaming milk tea appeared from somewhere. Dr Dewaram introduced us and explained the reason for our visit. The blond hair of Jon and Aisha aroused the curiosity of the villagers and solicited a lot of comments. As Vinay translated, none of them had seen foreign children before, and one of them remarked that he had always wondered how white people reproduced and whether there were "small" white people as well. Uncomfortable being the centre of attention, the twins strolled off to see what games the Raika children were playing. Not much later they came running back, proudly displaying a sample of the local toys: small camel figurines made from sun-dried clay. Encouraged by my delight, the other children too handed me an assortment of little camels they had shaped out of mud. Each one of them was different. Some of them were obviously male, others not. On some of them thread had been used to indicate a halter. Then there were some very small figurines representing camel calves.

Meanwhile, Dr Dewaram had found out that none of the camels were in the village or even in close vicinity; they were divided into about twenty herds which were grazing at different places, returning to Anji-ki-dhani only once year, at the time of Holi – a Hindu holiday coming up in less than two weeks – for shearing. A bit disappointed, I was already wondering how to come back on Holi when an elder Raika, with an aquiline nose and a pale yellow turban pushed way back to expose his balding head, tapped me on the arm to get my attention. "Madam, my *tola* is staying overnight not far from here; if you really like, you can visit it in the morning." The others called him Adoji and he exuded a powerful personality, speaking very fast in short, emphatic sentences. It was quickly decided that we would stay overnight with Dr Dewaram's family who lived not very far away and meet at a specified place early the next morning. "You come early, not later than seven o'clock – it is starting to get hot now and the camels go out early to graze. If you come later, they will have left."

For now we proceeded to Pachunda Kallan, Dr Dewaram's home village. He lived in a small, but charming mud-brick house, diligently whitewashed and decorated with line drawings of animals in brown. It housed his parents, his wife and two children; his three brothers – who were on migration with the sheep – had small houses nearby. Dewaram's wife, his two young children and all the female relatives were keen to meet me. Eager to finally get to know some Raika women and make friends, I followed Kamla, Dr Dewaram's niece, into a house just outside the compound. A swarm of girls and women had already been waiting and immediately engulfed me in their midst, talking all at once, examining my clothes, pinching my cheeks, raising their voices hoping to make me understand and elicit not only a smile, but some uttering that they could comprehend. The room bubbled over with excitement.

Another girl stepped through the door, dragging behind her a burlap sack that she opened ceremoniously. It contained kilos of silver jewellery, elaborate pieces for decorating hands and feet, anklets, heavy necklaces, ear ornaments weighing several hundred grams. From a metal chest in the corner came the finest of Raika clothes in a rainbow of colours – skirts, veils, tops. They decked themselves out in this finery and besieged me to take photos. One, two, three photos of each person were not enough; their appetite for new poses and different compositions was insatiable. They shrieked with laughter and burst into screams that verged on hysteria. An ambience as if the lid had come off a pressure cooker – totally at variance from the restrained and dignified atmosphere that characterised the interaction with and between men. Finally, after the film was spent and I was utterly exhausted, Kamla led me back to the haven of the men's section.

The next morning we left before dawn to arrive at the specified place where we found a tall and handsome young Raika in a pink turban waiting for us. Squeezing himself onto the front seat, he introduced himself as Gautam Ram, the son of Adoji, and guided us along a bumpy dirt track that led through an open acacia forest and forked here and there. "The tola is staying at the *bera* of a Chowdhury, a couple of kilometres down this road." A "bera" meant a well and an irrigated field, and pretty soon we saw the telltale tall green trees that indicate the presence of water. We parked the car and scrambled over a ditch onto a sandy embankment enclosing a field to look down on an ensemble of well over a hundred camels spread out on a harvested mustard field. The sun had just emerged behind the Aravalli Hills and was covering the mustard stalks in a silvery shimmer and adding rosy halos to the contours of some of the camels. Most were still resting and ruminating, others were standing on three legs waiting for their footropes to be released. The newly born youngsters were frisking around in small troops, nosily investigating their surroundings. Amidst them were men in bright turbans – neon pink, bright orange, crimson red and white – engaged in various kinds of work. One of them, recognisable by his yellow turban, was Adoji who directed us to the embers of a campfire at the edge of the field. With much ado, he grabbed a bhakal, which is the nomad's equivalent to a welcome mat, and spread it out tidily, patting down the curling corners. He made us sit down and stretch out among the sparse clutter of other nomadic necessities – a couple of battered cooking vessels, ropes, spinning whorls, empty containers of various shapes and undeterminable origin, a few burlap sacks of provisions – and a charpai lent by the farmer who owned the field. Then he shouted for somebody to milk a camel so that fresh tea could be prepared. A lot of patter and prattle in an incomprehensible dialect evolved between Adoji, Dr Dewaram and Vinay, while my family and I could just sit and watch. Aisha and Jon ventured out to have a closer look at the newborn camels. The female camels that had just given birth were lying slightly apart from the rest and they wandered off in that direction. Within minutes, they came back running, having made another exciting discovery. "Mama, come and look, a camel is giving birth!"

Under the shade of an acacia, stood a female camel attended by a Raika who fussed over her and talked to her in soothing tones. Within the span of not more than a couple of minutes, and without any great effort on her part, a streamlined calf – basically consisting only of legs and neck and nothing much else – slid out smoothly and dropped to the ground. By comparison to the numerous cattle births I had attended, it was a very quick and painless affair. The man freed the newborn of the greyish translucent skin it was covered in and then removed the mucus around its mouth, while the mother looked on and then sniffed the calf gently, without licking. Within only a few minutes, the calf already made its first attempt at standing up, but found it impossible to sufficiently synchronise its impossibly long spidery legs. Completely held in awe, Jon and Aisha kept a close watch on the baby from a short distance. After only half an hour, it managed to stand, and stumble a few uncoordinated steps, before once again collapsing like a card-house.

By that time, the rest of the herd had already departed for the day's grazing round. They would come back in the evening, spend the night on the same field, before moving on the next day. As Vinay and Dr Dewaram had found out, this group of herders kept almost continuously on the move, never staying more than two to three days in the same place. This pattern required continuous scouting for new places to make a night halt. Adoji, as leader of the group, was responsible for making the arrangements. He had long-standing relationships with many of the landowners who generally welcomed the camels because of the dung that they left in the field. In return for the fertilisation of their soil, in many cases, Adoji was also able to negotiate for substantial amounts of cash.

At the time of Holi, all the herds from Anji-ki-dhani would congregate there for shearing – a communal event in which all people from the village chipped in their labour. Adoji had forcefully invited us to come back for that occasion and witness all the 2,000–3,000 camels that belonged to Anji-ki-dhani in one spot. We took up the offer and Dr Dewaram and I visited Anji-ki-dhani again during Holi, that exuberant and riotous Hindu festival that signals the end of winter and the beginning of the hot season and is celebrated by throwing coloured powders.

It was at this time that I had the memorable interchange with Adoji mentioned earlier that turned me from a sympathetic observer, keeping a safe academic distance, into an active "stakeholder". For days, his plea to help him and his group echoed in my head. He was certainly right in saying that merely taking photographs was of no benefit to the Raika. But could I organise a camp? Honestly, I didn't know how. I had absolutely no resources and my small research budget was overextended by indulging in a taxi to get me to the camel herds. What could I, an academic researcher, do about the grazing problem? And what was the exact nature of the problem, I wasn't even sure. My response – more to myself than to anybody else – was probably that of any typical academic: we need more data. What was the magnitude of the problem? How many families were affected by it? If we had such information, maybe I could interest an aid agency in the situation of the Raika and they could take on the problem and solve it.

Our efforts to get to the bottom of the problem, resulted in not more than a skeleton of information. The Raika were not accustomed to sitting down and calmly answering questions. We could piece together that they were incensed about some "enclosures" which the government had established in the Aravalli Hills, their traditional summer grazing grounds, and where now the grazing of livestock was prohibited. The purpose of these enclosures was to allow trees to recover and the Raika had been promised that they would be opened after seven years, when the vegetation had regrown. But this had not happened, and anyway, the Raika said, the enclosures were pointless because other people came in and cut the trees, with the connivance of the Forest Department.

We continued the enquiries when we returned to Sadri. Vinay, who had developed an interest in the religion of the Raika, was still there. I prodded him to find out more about the situation and problems of the Anji-ki-dhani people and the camel herders in general. This was not a subject he had paid much attention to in his research so far, but he very kindly took an interest and in the ensuing days helped me talk to various people to solicit information.

There were said to be about 5,000 camels in the vicinity of Sadri. Over the last several decades, it had become progressively more difficult for them to get access to grazing. This was due to the fact that more and more deep wells were being dug, so that farmers could irrigate throughout the year and raise two or three crops annually rather than only once during the rainy season. Fallow land, a major pasture resource, had dramatically decreased. Secondly, earlier all villages had maintained their own grazing grounds called *gauchar*, for their livestock. But for various reasons, this traditional system had been neglected, the gauchar were used for other purposes and were now covered with shrubs that are not palatable to animals, such as the infamous "angrezi babul", an acacia species imported by one of the maharajahs from another country. But the most pressing grazing problem for the camels occurred in the rainy season, roughly during the time from July until September. At this time of year they could not stay in the agricultural areas because crops were grown everywhere. Since time immemorial, camel herds had grazed in the forests of the Aravalli Hills during these months. The forest trees provided reasonable camel fodder during this season. But now the forest around Sadri had been declared a wildlife sanctuary and was part of the Kumbhalgarh Reserve. The access for camels and other herd animals had therefore been restricted.

Bhalaram, a Raika with political ambitions and chairman of the Aravalli Ber Palak Sang (Aravalli Sheep Breeders Association), was one of our best sources. Consulting his notebook, he gave us a run down of developments. "The trouble started in 1975 during the Emergency. At that time, the central government issued a twenty-point programme. One point was the protection of the forest and the establishment of nurseries. That is when they started charging for grazing in the forest, Rs 2-5 per camel, Rs 10 per elephant, Rs 1-1.4 per cow or buffalo. The Forest Department receives an annual revenue of Rs 3 lakh from graziers. The situation has become worse since the World Bank established a programme in the 1980s to develop the Aravallis into a National Park. Then, in 1990, the situation came to a deadlock. The government issued an order banning all livestock from the forests, but without informing people of this new law. When the Raika entered the Aravallis in July unaware of the new regulations, after the rains had started, their animals were seized. There was a big protest. A little later, the government changed, and the Congress party was replaced by the Bharatiya Janta Party (BJP). One of the first things the new government did was to issue an order reopening the forest. But, although the order pertained to the whole of the Aravalli Hills, it did not include the so-called protected parts, which make up about seventy-five per cent of the total area."

Bhalaram had written a letter to the chief minister at the time. The Raika had also lodged a complaint about the planned World Bank programme to the minister of environment who had answered that they should stop keeping sheep or at least reduce them by ninety per cent and instead educate their children.

The Raika were angry about this as well as the status given to wildlife. "The government is protecting wildlife. But what are the benefits of wildlife? Which animal is productive?" They were equally adamant that camels did not do any harm to the vegetation because they were top feeders. Instead they blamed the tribal Bhil and Grassia for uprooting trees and selling them for firewood.

All this information was difficult to validate and put into context. Most Raika got very agitated when asked about the problem. They talked about enclosures that the Forest Department did not open, even though it was legally required to do so. They mentioned outrageous bribes and that their animals were sometimes confiscated. A non-Raika informant held that the Raika were susceptible to bribes by the foresters because practically all of them carry a certain amount of opium tucked under their turban.

The answers to any question were often very disparate; it was hard to take anything literally. But it was clear that the Raika bore a real grudge towards the authorities. To me, it also seemed that they had been given a raw deal and that just to lock them, or rather their animals, out of the forest without providing alternative resources was not really fair. But was there anything I could do about it? Something started nagging me. As an outsider with a global perspective, I should be able to understand the background of these developments better and get to the bottom of this. Also, the comments addressed to me in Anji-ki-dhani, that I came only to take photos, had really stung. Nevertheless, I was only an academic and had no connections to the developmental and aid organisations that might be able to help.

Still pondering on how to take action, I continued collecting bits and pieces relevant to my research topic. One personage that I was especially captivated by was Pabuji, a Rajput hero who, according to local lore, had introduced the camel to Rajasthan. He was also a deity, worshipped by the Maru Raika. Dewaram had shown me a small Pabuji temple in his village. Subsequently, Vinay had given me a small lecture on the significance of Pabuji for the Maru Raikas, detailing that they brought Pabuji offerings whenever a camel-related event took place, such as a camel birth, breaking in a young camel for riding, inserting a nose ring, or leaving for the camel market in Pushkar. Not sure whether Pabuji was a historical person (as he must have been by my reckoning if he introduced the camel to Rajasthan) or a god, I asked for more details. How and from where did he bring the camel to Rajasthan? To which both Vinay and Dewaram replied in unison, "For that we have to ask the Bhopa."

Who is the Bhopa, I asked, sighing, for whenever I asked a

straightforward question, I touched upon a myriad of hitherto unimagined phenomena. But I suddenly remembered that Komal Kothari had also referred to them.

"The Bhopas are people who know the whole story of Pabuji. They are his minstrels or his priests and have a long cloth scroll which depicts the various episodes in Pabuji's life. This cloth scroll, called *parh*,[1] is really a movable altar and can be unfolded only during the night. We will see whether we can arrange for you to see it."

It sounded simple. Through the grapevine, Dr Dewaram soon identified a Bhopa living in a village near Sadri. The Bhopa, however, did not consent to just unrolling his parh, but wanted to give a proper performance with song and dance, accompanied by his wife, the Bhopi. He suggested a village where they could act out the story during one night – in fact, in that village a camel was sick and the owner had already approached him to perform hoping to get on the good side of Pabuji, but was not really willing or able to pay for the recital.

Reciting the whole story would take about fourteen full nights, Vinay explained. So we needed to select one particular episode from Pabuji's life – he suggested we should restrict ourselves to the chapter in which Pabuji brought the camels, or more precisely the "red and brown she-camels" to Rajasthan.

The performance was fixed to take place in Bhadras, on an open space surrounding the village shrine. Hanwant and I went to pick up the Bhopa and Bhopi in the Ambassador. They lived in a tiny hut and judging by their worn clothes, they were really poor. The prospect of sitting in the taxi almost overwhelmed them, but finally we had stowed both of them as well as their movable altar

1 Often also referred to as *phad*. However, our Bhopas always use the word *parh*.

into the car. When we arrived at the venue at dusk, there was standing room only. The temple platform and steps as well as the narrow verandas of the low houses bordering the square were lined with people, especially children. An enterprising tea-maker had already wheeled along his equipment on a pushcart and was selling his ware. It seemed as if the whole village had assembled, eager for the spectacle.

The sun had already disappeared, so the foldable temple could be safely unrolled and set up by means of the two long sticks at its end. It was dominated by an image of Pabuji wearing a red robe and a yellow turban in its centre surrounded by a mosaic of other scenes representing his adventures - his black mare, Kali, mounted elephants, cavalcades of horse-riders, and a string of orange-coloured camels. The Bhopa changed into a slightly tattered but still natty white shirt-coat adorned with an appliqué of red cloth stripes, tied on his ankle-bells, and adjusted his colourful turban while the Bhopi fastened her see-through faded red veil over her face and lit a small oil lamp shaped like a soup ladle. The Bhopa then tuned his *ravanhatto*, a fiddle-like instrument, and with some bold strokes of the bow, which also had small jingling bells attached to it, arrested the attention of the audience. He would dramatically recite a few verses then sing a few lines accompanied by the ravanhatto. At the same time, he also kept stepping back and forwards rhythmically beside the parh while the Bhopi would illuminate certain relevant sections of the parh with her oil lamp and sing his refrain.

The effect of the music and the mix of song, dance, and recital was spellbinding, not only for me but also for the children who sat there totally engrossed, their shawls tightly wrapped around them. I could not understand a single word and had to get the details later from Vinay who had tried his best to record everything, although the archaic language made this difficult even for him.

> During a visit to Pushkar, Pabuji arranged the marriage of his niece, Kelambai, with Gogaji Chauhan from Sambhar. The marriage took place shortly afterwards and all relatives gave the usual presents, only Pabuji promised something unusual: red and brown she-camels. Although Pabuji had heard about red and brown she-camels, he did not really know where to get these, and his niece was getting quite impatient for the promised gift. Pabuji therefore sent out his follower, Harmel Raika, to Lanka whose King Ravana was said to own camels. Harmel Raika dressed up as a *sanyasi* (or monk) and reached Lanka after three days. He was captured by Ravana's soldiers and he asked them for some milk. They replied, "We don't have cow milk; we only have milk from red and brown she-camels." After some further adventures, Harmel Raika returned to Rajasthan and told Pabuji about the camels. Pabuji put together an army, defeated Ravana and brought back 700 lactating and 700 non-lactating she-camels.

So, according to this rendering, a Raika had been instrumental in bringing the camel to Rajasthan. His existence in Rajasthan preceded the camel. How did this square with the myth of origin that Vinay had related to me earlier in which the Raika had been created AFTER the camel? Was there a grain of truth in either of these legends?

* * *

By now it was the beginning of April. Temperatures had soared, my mind had become frazzled. In order to rearrange my mental components, I escaped to the much cooler climes of Ladakh. Between trekking, I devoted myself to learning Hindi with the help of a book. My fellowship was practically over, but I wanted to make one "final" trip to Rajasthan to say goodbye to my friends and companions there. And to lay to rest the nagging guilt that I should do something about the problems of the Raika.

For this short trip, and because I still had some Indian currency that could not be changed into dollars, I decided to grant myself the luxury of hiring a taxi. Experimenting with my nascent Hindi and drawing careful letters in the Devanagari script, I sent a postcard to my favourite driver, requesting his services. Hanwant Singh responded by telegram with "my car booked for you" and was awaiting me at the airport in Jodhpur when I arrived there on a hot and sultry evening in June. We drove to Sadri to talk things over with Dewaram. What could we do for the Raika? The grazing/forest nexus certainly seemed totally intractable, but he suggested that he would like to set up a welfare society for his community. "My caste is very backward and needs upliftment." How this society would work remained open; according to Dewaram, women should be given some support, taught about hygiene and provided with income-generation projects. I, for my part, insisted that the camels should be given their medicines. I left Dewaram all my remaining rupees and he opened up a bank account in Pali.

From Sadri, we headed north to Bikaner so I could pay my final respects to Dr Khanna at the Camel Research Centre and thank him for his support, as well as hand him a copy of the report on my research. From there we took the route to Jaipur. Dr Khanna warned me that no conveniences were available on this long stretch and provided me with mineral water and other supplies.

It was so hot now that just sitting in the back of the Ambassador and being driven around was an utterly exhausting task. Outside it was hot as a furnace and one never stopped feeling parched. Stopping at a roadside dhaba for a cup of tea made with rancid buffalo milk provided little respite. My mind had ground to a virtual standstill.

At night in my hotel room, I reflected on the local culture and customs, which were still as alien to me as at the beginning – this somehow made things seem even worse since, by now, I should have absorbed something of it.

My Hindi had made little progress, or seemed inapplicable in Rajasthan. Being still dependent on translators for even the simplest transaction, I felt like a dumb-mute idiot since I was still unable to throw in an intelligible local word here and there, except for *theek hai* – meaning "it's okay". It particularly bothered me that this language did not provide for the little niceties so important in other cultures. Certain standard phrases just did not exist. There is no real Hindi equivalent for a casual "thank you", only the stilted *dhanyavad*, whose use appears to be restricted to flight attendants. Nor is there a phrase for "you are welcome". There is no universal word for "hello" – greetings are caste-specific. Bikaner Raika greet each other with "Ram Ram", Rajputs use "Jai Mataji" or "Jai Shankarji". A specific word for goodbye is absent. According to the phrasebook one can say "namaskar", but that certainly does not seem appropriate in the rural circles that I interacted with. Even the words for yesterday and tomorrow are the same, tellingly I found. Time here had its own particular way – it did not pass at a steady pace, but in leaps and explosions. For days and weeks, nothing happened, then suddenly everything at once.

Another matter I had not come to terms with was Rajasthani food. It was laced with so much red chilli that a single bite was usually enough to set my mouth burning. The chapatis were immersed in so much ghee that I found them indigestible. Asked by my hosts or in any dabha about "which kind of vegetable would you like" seemed totally pointless – everything tasted the same anyway. The only food I could stomach in Rajasthan were bananas and Parle biscuits. And the tea; the endless cups of tea were the one thing that kept me going.

Rajasthani etiquette represented another interesting topic. I had learnt that form was all-important and that display of feelings were frowned upon. Dr Dewaram had explained the reasons for this to me. I had been surprised that nobody ever showed any emotions. For instance, when he met his family after a long absence, neither his wife nor children would rush out to greet and hug him. Rather, his wife would continue to go about her work without even an acknowledgement of his arrival. Did nobody have any feelings around here? I instinctively knew that this was not so, but certainly could not figure it out. Dr Dewaram had explained to me that in traditional Raika culture, close relationships within the nuclear family were scorned upon, because they would work against holding together the larger unit of the extended family or even the caste. Children did not belong to their parents, but to the whole community. To gloss over excessive intimacy, children did not even address their father as "father", but rather as "uncle" (*kaka*). Dewaram also admitted to regret that he had little opportunity to build a close bond with his own children, as he was not allowed to even talk to them in the presence of any elders, meaning practically all the time.

Why would I want to come back to such a strange place for more? Yet in spite of the multitude of unfathomable things, or maybe because of them, I was now even more intrigued by Rajasthani culture than at the beginning, and felt an overwhelming desire to be part of it and not just as an outsider. Among my assets here I did count my driver. Although he said very little and I still knew almost nothing about him beyond his name and the fact that he was a Rajput, his car was a refuge for me. It had become a moveable base to which I could always escape if attentions of villagers became too much or crowds of children got out of control. He was also painfully shy. Unless we were alone in the car, he would never speak to me directly and would enquire about my wishes only in third person. Whenever we left the car he would avoid any proximity, as if it embarrassed him to be seen with me. If we stopped at a dhaba for tea I would naturally choose the chair next to him to sit on because that's where I felt safe amidst the people staring at me. In most cases this would prompt him to get up and sit on another chair just to put some distance between us. I felt hurt by this but, on the other hand, he was always there when I needed him. If I ever got into trouble or somebody gave me a hard time, he would just magically appear from nowhere to get me out of harm's way. Just like me he seemed to be observing everything from a vantage point outside of what was going on. I felt he would go with me wherever I wanted and I knew that I would be safe. This circumstance was one of the major factors nudging me to continue.

My final act in Delhi was to ask whether I could return in November for my remaining fellowship month to see the famous camel market in Pushkar.

Chapter 5

PUSHKAR

> *"Camels are looked upon rather as members of the family than as dumb animals; they plough and harrow the ground, bring home the harvest, carry wood and water, and are both ridden and driven. Their milk is used both as an article of diet and as a medicine; fair profit is made from the sale of their wool, and, when they die, their skin is made into jars for holding ghi and oil. The riding camels bred in these parts are probably superior to any others in India, and the best of them will cover from 8 to 10 miles in a night when emergency demands speed."*
>
> – *The Imperial Gazetteer of India.* Provincial Series Rajputana, Calcutta, 1908

November 1991

Every year in autumn, ending with the full moon of the Hindu month of Kartik, a gigantic camel and livestock fair (*mela*) takes place in the small town of Pushkar that is spread around a holy lake. The auspicious full moon attracts hundreds of thousands of Hindu pilgrims who come to take a bath and obtain salvation in its sacred waters at full moon, but it also has become a fixture on the tourist circuit. This mela is the high point of the camel year for the Raika. It is here that they sell their crop of young male camels, where they hope to realise the whole year's profit all at once. If the mela is slow and there are not many buyers, it is a disaster, because the camels have to be brought home again and kept for another year, before realising any profit. If the mela is strong and demand exceeds supply then the Raika go back home with wads of money and small gifts for their families in their pockets.

I had fought hard for an extension of my grant by another month in order to return to India to witness the Pushkar mela, arguing that without witnessing this seminal event in the annual cycle of the camel herders, my research would not be complete. Leaving the family on their own in California had required complicated arrangements, but my month-long stay would also allow me to pursue two other points on my agenda. For one, I had discussed with Dr Dewaram, at length and by letter, his suggestion of setting up a society with the goal of working for the benefit, or – as he called it – the upliftment of the Raika. A society that could pursue grazing rights and raise awareness about how the Raika were being squeezed out, and that could undertake educational projects and other good works. As had become evident from my interaction with aid agencies in Delhi, a formal structure was needed in order to generate or accept any funds; it was the prerequisite for support by any charity or development agency. Naturally, this society should be composed of the Raika themselves.

Secondly, I wanted to find some answers to the question that had occupied me almost from the beginning: why did the Raika make such restricted use of the potential products of their camels, and hardly exploited their capacity for food production? Why did they have such a different relationship to this animal than, say, the Bedouins or the Somali? One way of approaching this question was from the historical angle. At what point in history, and hence, in which kind of economic, political and ecological setting, had the camel made its entry to Rajasthan? The camel had been domesticated in southern Arabia at least 4,000 years ago, but by what time had it dispersed to India? This was another question on which the literature was silent or could not provide incontrovertible evidence. Intertwined with this question was the query about the origin of the Raika. Had maybe both of them come together? Or did the caste have local roots and develop in response to the need to have a professional class to look after the camel? Vinay had already drawn my attention to the contradiction between the Raika myth of origin and the Pabuji epic. In the former, the Raika is made to take care of the camel, i.e. appears on the scene after the camel. In the Pabuji epic, Harmel Raika is sent out to find the red-and-brown she-camels. So according to the latter story, the Raika preceded the camel in Rajasthan. Could any version of these renderings of events be corroborated with hard facts?

I had found an article listing depictions of the camel in Rajasthan's art and architecture, and I wanted to verify their existence and dating, as well as photograph them. From the analysis of camel objects I had undertaken during my doctoral research, I knew that so-called "camel statues" or representations often were very much a matter of the interpretation of the beholder and could just as well be called dolphins, cattle or any other large mammal.

Besides the historical perspective, there was the cross-cultural angle. I had heard that one group of Muslims, the Sindhi Muslims – named after Sindh in Pakistan – also bred and kept large numbers of camels. Did they have similar restrictions as the Raika? Or did they follow the same customs as Muslims in other parts of the world and relish camel meat? What did they think about processing camel milk – did they also abstain from making curd and ghee and insist on using it only fresh? Or was it just impractical to process camel milk?

* * *

Hanwant, whose taxi I had booked by letter, was waiting faithfully for me at the airport in Jodhpur. He rushed me through the general pandemonium and past the crowd of taxi drivers looking for a fare, and quickly transferred me into the sanctuary of his Ambassador. I had arranged to meet up with Dr Dewaram in a small hotel near the railway station, but he was nowhere to be seen. Hanwant checked me in and saw to it that all my creature comforts were satisfied.

"I will go and search for Dr Dewaram. You just take your rest, Madam. I will be back later," Hanwant reassured me.

"Take your rest" was a phrase that figured big in the vocabulary of my Rajasthani friends. I had heard it so often that I had come to loathe it intensely, never being sure whether people actually thought I needed a rest, or whether it was just a convenient excuse to go about their business without dragging me along. Probably both considerations were involved. Hanwant was very proud to be a Rajput and according to Rajput etiquette, ladies had to be kept safely and virtuously inside the house, while the men marched into battle and eliminated all the problems.... Undoubtedly this facilitated my life on many occasions, but sometimes I also felt left out of the action, as in this instance.

Hanwant dutifully checked back with me later, reporting that his mission had been unsuccessful, with Dewaram nowhere to be seen in Jodhpur. "Maybe he will come tomorrow, don't worry. I brought you some biscuits and bananas," he consoled me. "You need anything else, Madam?"

Although I was ready to go into battle, my army obviously still needed to be assembled. Patience was in order and was eventually rewarded. I spent the evening in my stuffy, windowless room chalking out an itinerary through Rajasthan that would take in as many camel-related monuments and sights as possible. Next morning while I was still taking my "bed tea", the phone rang and the receptionist announced, "A man has come for you."

It was Dewaram accompanied by another Raika, a middle-aged man who wore a yellow turban and exuded energy. "This is Bhopalaram from Khara Bera. You must have heard about him. He is a famous Raika leader and president of the Pashu-Palak Sangh, the Animal Breeders' Association."

Yes, indeed, I had heard Bhopalaram's name many times. Though he was without official political function, he was very much at home in the corridors of power in Rajasthan's state capital of Jaipur. Bhopalaram was pressing for the rights of his caste and animal breeders in general. He was said to have the ear of the chief minister of Rajasthan, Bhairon Singh Shekhavat. Although illiterate himself, he always carried a big file from which he would pull out letters he had exchanged with various government agencies, especially the Animal Husbandry Department.

"I have brought Bhopalaram because I have arranged for a Raika meeting at Pali today starting at ten o'clock," Dr Dewaram explained.

We grabbed a quick breakfast of parantha and curd in the hotel, then we were off to Pali. En route, we discussed the name we would give to the society that was going to be founded and came up with the idea of naming it "Raika Awareness and Indigenous Knowledge Appreciation Society".

Having such a key informant at hand, I also utilised the opportunity to quiz Bhopalaram about the roots of the Raika. He was expansive about the topic. "We originally come from near Jaisalmer, a place called Lodorva. The first Raika to come to Jodhpur was Asuji Raika. He was born there at the time of the rule of Ghazi Khan. Then there was a major drought, so Asuji left for Marwar which was then ruled by Raja Sur Singh in Mandore. Asuji was very experienced with camels, so Sur Singh put him in charge of his camel department, the *suttarkhana*. Asuji proved very successful at managing the camels, for instance, he knew about the prevention of infectious diseases. He gained the confidence of the raja who rewarded him by allowing him to bring the rest of his caste and giving them some land to settle in Jodhpur," Bhopalaram paused for emphasis. "So this is how the Raika came to Jodhpur. But the story is not finished here," he glanced at me, making sure that I was following his story, and went on.

"After some time, another raja came to power. Once when he went for a walk, he witnessed a lion attack a sheep herd and try to get away with a lamb. But the mother of the lamb was so ferocious that the lion withdrew and had to leave hungry. When the raja saw this, he thought, 'This is a piece of land where heroes are born. I think this is where I should build my new palace.' So the raja asked who the owner of the land was and learnt that it belonged to a Raika. Then what did he do? He sent his wife, the rani, to make friends with the Raika. The rani asked the Raika to become her 'dharam bhai', her adopted brother. Feeling honoured and proud, he willingly agreed. After she had tied the *rakhi* around his wrist, signalling that they were now brother and sister, the Raika asked, as is the custom, 'What kind of gift can I give you?' To this the rani responded, 'Please give me your land.' This the Raika could not refuse and gave her the land. And that is why there is an area in Jodhpur called 'Raikabagh', and even a railway station of that name." Bhopalaram looked at me again searchingly, as if inviting my comment on the naïve nature of the Raika and how they were so easy to take advantage of.

In the meantime we had reached Pali. The meeting had been called in a hostel belonging to the Raika community and Dewaram had obviously engaged in comprehensive preparations, organised a loudspeaker as well as tea and food – more biscuits and bananas. Although it was already well past ten o'clock when we arrived, nobody had turned up yet. Gradually, over the next few hours, about forty Raika men trickled in and seated themselves on the rugs that had been rolled out. By around two o'clock, Dewaram opened the meeting with a long speech. After he had finished, he handed over the microphone to Bhopalaram who stood up to deliver a long sermon, progressively working himself into a frenzy, his voice rising to an almost feverish pitch and his sentences turning into short and agitated exclamations – his demagogic talents were obvious.

My own little speech in which I elaborated that the Raika should be proud of their traditional knowledge and that there were similar people in other parts of the world with similar problems was duly translated by Dewaram, but fell flat compared with Bhopalaram's fierce rhetoric. Finally, when just about everybody who was present had made a little speech, donations started to be collected. People pulled out their money and gave it to Dewaram and me. I was not happy about this, because it certainly added to our obligations. At the same time, no effort had been made to create a formal society. It meant that Dewaram was burdened with more money, while there were no officers or a board that could decide how to spend it, nor, of course, a memorandum of the society's goals. But that could be sorted out later, I hoped – now it was time to embark on our whirlwind tour of the Great Indian Desert, the Thar.

Our team, composed of Dewaram ("Doctorsaab"), Hanwant ("Driversaab") and myself ("Madam"), set off in the trusted Ambassador heading in a straight line west from Pali. The Thar is known as the most densely populated desert in the world. In all fairness, although the white sand lends it the character of a desert, average annual rainfall amounts are much higher than in, by comparison, the Arabian Desert. The most prominent physical characteristic feature of the Thar is its extensive tree vegetation, which provides excellent camel fodder. The most famous tree is the khejri, a stunted and ragged-looking type of acacia whose leaves are high in protein and whose pods are one of Rajasthan's culinary delicacies.

The Thar Desert is vast and the Muslim armies that have invaded India from the west in regular intervals since the tenth century to plunder its riches had to cross it. The first of them was Mahmud of Ghazni in Afghanistan who undertook a total of seventeen raids into India between 979 and 1025 AD and sacked the Hindu temple at Somnath, robbing it of its idols said to be made of pure gold. For his incursions he needed camels to carry water. When preparing for the trek in Multan, he equipped each of his 30,000 soldiers with two camels for carrying water and, in addition, readied another 20,000 camels. In order to procure so many heads of camel, the existence of extensive camel-breeding operations was a prerequisite – we can conclude that these existed in Afghanistan at the time. But what about India proper? This was what we were trying to find out.

Our first piece of substantiation to be examined was a small group of Shiva temples at a place called Kiradu, near Barmer. They were adorned with friezes of camels engaged in copulation and carrying loads. Firmly dated to the twelfth century, this corroborated that, at this point in time, one-humped camels were used for caravan trade through the Indian desert. This, of course, was nothing new, considering the Muslim invasions. There was a big difference between camels being brought in from the west by invaders or traders and the actual active adoption of production of camels. It was the onset of breeding activities that interested me.

Apart from that, I did not really have much of a game plan. The idea was to meet Sindhi Muslims, but I did not have a clue where they were settled.

"Oh, they live near Jaisalmer in the desert, go there and you'll find many," had always been the answer to my query as to where I could meet them. But the desert was big. As it turned out, this lack of precise directions was no obstacle for my small crew and just added a tasty bit of challenge and adventure.

After a night in a dingy hotel in Barmer, where our enquiries did not meet with success, we vaguely headed towards Jaisalmer. Driversaab and Doctorsaab, rivalling in being useful to our quest, stalked down each and every person innocently walking along the road. "From which village are you?" was always the first question, followed by, "What is your name?"; "So you are from that and that caste?"; and finally, "Do you know any Sindhi Muslims?"

Although this was a desert and very sparsely populated, we managed to cover some ground nevertheless, and to get glimpses of how the camel was being made use of, how it generated income and was basically indispensable to the people of the Thar. Differing from the situation in Godwar where only the Raika base their existence on camels, here it was society at large, ranging from the lowest to the highest caste, that depended on them. While the Raika, as breeders, had herds of female camels, here people owned one male camel that they put to work and from which they could earn a livelihood.

It started with a small caravan of four-wheeled camel-drawn carts that belonged to Bhils who are classified a Scheduled Tribe. They were on their way to Mehsana in Gujarat to earn money by means of their camel carts. It would take ten days to get there, but the money they could earn by hiring out their carts for transportation was well worth it. They were not breeders and had bought their camels from other castes, and no, they didn't know any Sindhi Muslims.

The next unsuspecting citizen, a young man with a turban walking along the highway in the same direction we were going and minding his own business, was able to help us:

"No, I don't know any Sindhi Muslims, but I can show you a village with lots of camels. There you can get information."

"Kindly come with us and show us the way to that village," Hanwant had already opened the door and beckoned him in.

"Okay, okay," he said and willingly complied and directed us to the village of Indroi which was hidden behind a flat sand dune.

The first sight was a well surrounded by a throng of women waiting to fill their earthen and metal pots with the day's water requirements. The well was powered by a camel walking rhythmically forwards and backwards to pull up, pour out, and refill a huge black rubber container spouting with water. When we stopped and got out of the car, the male half of the community swarmed from the houses, while the women scattered. After a quick exchange of introductions, it became evident that this was basically a village of Rajputs who belonged to the same lineage as Hanwant, so our chance reconnaissance immediately took on the air of a visit by a long-lost relative. The treatment we received would have done any Mughal emperor proud. In a pleasantly cool *jhoopa* made especially for entertaining guests we were urged to stretch out on charpais and relax. Embroidered pillows were propped under our heads, we were served water, tea and biscuits, and then further stops were pulled to entertain us in style. First of all, a horse decked out with a jauntily decorated bridle and a saddle was brought for my amusement and photo-opportunity. What else could sweeten our stay more than a taste of the local music? When the conversation touched upon the Sindhi Muslims, our host proffered, “Yes, we have some Sindhi Muslims here, although, they are not camel breeders. But they are good musicians. Would Madam like to hear some music?” A rug was spread under a tree and three Sindhis with multicoloured turbans sat down, tuned their instruments and gave an impromptu concert.

They may not have been camel-breeders, but they exposed us to a further facet of the human–camel relationship, its association with romance and longing, as a vehicle for bridging the distance between lovers that are apart. “Moomal and Mahendra” is a Rajasthani love epic in which the camel plays a central role. Moomal was a princess of Lodorva who loved Mahendra, the prince of Umarkot. They were not married, but could not bear to be apart for even one night. With the help of a speedy camel named Chikal, Mahendra was able to cover the 200 km that separated them every night and manage to be back in Umarkot by morning. One day, Moomal was visited by her sister who dressed up as a musician to gain access to the bedchamber to catch a glimpse of the mysterious prince. Mahendra was delayed and the sisters fell asleep waiting for him. When Mahendra finally came and saw Moomal lying together with a man, he suspected her of betrayal, rode off and soon succumbed to a heart attack. When Moomal heard this, she also died of a broken heart.

Listening to the heart-rending sounds, I was suddenly overwhelmed with empathy for all the women in Rajasthan, especially the Rajput women who were more or less closeted at home, and had to cope with the long absences of their husbands. Here, in the rural areas, very few men could find local employment. They went away, to Bombay or another city, and their wives often had little idea of when they would come back and how they were faring. They had to spend so much time waiting, waiting, waiting, and listening for his footsteps or the vehicle that might bring him back. Somehow, I had an inkling that this largely unfulfilled longing made the love stronger and togetherness sweeter.

As if he had read my thoughts, our host invited me to meet the ladies who had assembled in another jhoopa enclosed by a high wall to receive me. All this beauty, all this glamour sparkled even in the darkened hut. Faces were coyly unveiled, alluring eyes examined my unglamorous outfit, questions were asked about my children, the whereabouts of my husband, my relationship to the two men accompanying me. Guiltily, I understood that that they too would like to travel and see places. And that I should come back soon, for another visit.

We continued our expedition and, by early afternoon, somehow ended up at a Raika dhani composed of about thirty houses. Dewaram struck up a conversation with an elder Raika who immediately invited us in, maybe because he felt like having some company. Instead of just giving an order to somebody inside the house, he made the tea himself. While he stoked the fire and stirred the brew, he kept talking, explaining that this was the westernmost Raika settlement in Rajasthan. Earlier, there had been more Raika settlements in the area, but people had wandered to the east. Most families in this dhani owned half a dozen or so female camels for breeding, but goats were the most important type of livestock. Droughts were frequent – every three or four years the people were forced to migrate south deep into Gujarat in search of grazing for their herds. "We have too many people here. The kair used to be so dense that one could not pass through it; now it is hardly there anymore," he lamented. Dewaram gently steered the conversation towards camel milk and whether it was processed in any way. Could curd be made from camel milk? From the look our host gave us, it was clear that he considered us mightily uneducated.

"Don't you know *why* we can't make curd from camel milk?"

he said. "According to the story, the thakur wanted Ratna Raika, who had three camels, to fetch his son's wife from her *pir*. So he sent the midwife out to give this message to Ratna Raika. When the midwife came to Ratna Raika's house, his mother was making curd from camel milk. For some reason, the thakur's message was changed to, 'Your camels have destroyed the thakur's garden and he wants to punish Ratna Raika.' When the mother heard this, she cursed the camels. From this day on, camel milk never curdled, and camels also started suffering from mange and tibursa."

Dewaram had his doubts about this story. "I don't think this story is correct. Actually, Pabuji said that camel milk should not be curdled because it is most valuable in a raw state and can cure many diseases. For this reason it should not be altered."

By early evening we reached Jaisalmer, once an isolated outpost and trading centre in the middle of the desert, but now bustling with tourists. Jaisalmer consists of a glorious fort that is fashioned out of yellow sandstone and surrounded by a maze of little alleys, although the ubiquitous banners advertising camel safaris now detract from its medieval air. We used it as the base for our explorations during the next couple of days.

Despite an intensive search, Sindhi Muslim informants remained elusive here too. In the village of Marudi Rathore, Rajputs were heavily into camel breeding, following the same free-ranging system of camel breeding as in Bikaner. One of them let us into the secret of a traditional system for treating tibursa, but we will not divulge the recipe here. Achla was a Raika dhani with a 1,000 camels. Until 1947, the Achla people had looked after as many as 4,000 camels belonging to the Maharajah of Jaisalmer, Jawahar Singh, one of whose ancestors had fetched Raika from Jodhpur for this purpose. Even now, the maharajah retained a few camels and would regularly give them some money for this.

Because of this association, their camels were still adorned by the brand mark of the Bhatti Rajputs, a bell-shaped symbol on their flanks. Here, too, the camels ranged free for most of the year. However, they were attached to the local well and would return there frequently.

In Mohangarh, we made some headway. It was a dusty place about 4 km from the Indira Gandhi Canal that brings water from the Punjab to turn the desert green, a project which has caused extensive ecological change or, as some say, ecological damage. In some places, waterlogging has set in and malaria has become common. Land that was previously common property and available for grazing had become privatised, often by business people from the Punjab and not the original inhabitants.

Sitting next to the remnants of an old fort, and over a cup of tea, we talked to two Sindhi Muslims and one Rajput, both of whom bred camels. The Rajput made an important point about curd made from camel milk. "Nothing bad will happen if you try to make curd from camel milk. But camel milk just does not curdle. Fifty-four years ago we had a big drought and all the cows died. At that time, we had only camels, so we tried to make curd from camel milk, but this did not work."

Kamal Khan was a Sindhi Muslim from Bhala, a village located about 45 km to the north, very close to the Pakistan border, and scheduled to come into the canal command area. He praised the camels from his village but also conceded that things would change. "The camels from Bhala are famous for their good looks, smooth gait and sincere nature. They cost up to Rs 15,000."

Both confirmed that they let their camels run free.

"Does it not happen that they get lost? Don't they sometimes run across the border?"

"Yes, Madam, sometimes our camels get lost. If the camels cross the border, then we tell the Border Security Force and they get in touch with the people in Pakistan. They always send them back to us," Kamal Khan replied.

"Does this happen often?"

"No, Madam. Our camels are used to certain wells and return there regularly. Every time the female camels come to the well, we milk them. At that time, we also try to tame the young ones. We give them special treats, they remember that and always come back."

"Do you have a big disease problem?" I wanted to know.

"Our camels sometimes suffer from a cough or diarrhoea, as well as mange and ringworm. But tibursa is no problem, because it is very dry here and there are no flies. Maybe this will change due to the canal. When the canal comes, we will sell most of our camels because we will get land. Then we will keep only three to four for work and feed them with fodder."

Who would breed the camels, I wondered. If everybody just wants to have working camels, and nobody wants to breed them, or there is no land for breeding herds, then there will be a problem, I thought.

We needed to head back to Jodhpur, since the Pushkar Fair had already started. Time was pressing, but we could not resist the temptation for a detour to Kolumand, the native village of Pabuji, the Rajput hero, at whose instigation the camel had been brought to Rajasthan as a wedding gift for his niece. Hanwant was most keen that we go there since Pabuji belonged to the Rathore clan like him and therefore qualified as a distant relative. For me too, Pabuji had developed into a knight in shining armour, although I had some difficulties grasping that he had actually been a historical person. After all, he was worshipped as a god by the Raika – another one of these cases where the earthly effortlessly mutated into the divine.

Going to the place where Pabuji had been born and where he had ruled as a thakur, somehow gave me a feeling for the life he had led and the soil that had shaped him. He had been a feudal overlord, but his fiefdom had been barren. In the epic he had come across as a very urbane and witty character, but he must have led a life of scarcity, interspersed with brief spells of plenty during good monsoons. There was a small temple in red sandstone with a devotional *stela*. It was surrounded by an *oran*, a divinely protected area where the cutting of trees was not allowed. The remains of the well at which the cows were stolen for whose protection he gave his life, were also to be seen.

During a flying stopover in Jodhpur, I was lucky to catch up with Professor Zahurkhan Mehar, a Sindhi Muslim by caste, historian by profession and collator of all kinds of camel lore.

"There are three kinds of Sindhi Muslims. One group are the Mehars. Our ancestors came into the country together with Muhammed bin Qasim when he conquered Sindh in 711 AD. Then there are the Siyars of which there are two groups, the Manganiyars and the Kallars. These people were originally Hindus and they converted to Islam during later Muslim rule."

"As a historian, do you know when and how the camel first came to Rajasthan?"

"Yes, certainly! We Mehars were very much involved in it. In the fifteenth century, there was a Mehar named Sayra Baghani, who lived in the village of Lankia which is 12 km north-west of Umarkot. Do you know where Umarkot is?"

"Yes, I know it is in Pakistan. The Mughal Emperor Akbar was born there."

"Correct. Now Umarkot is in Pakistan, but at that time it still belonged to Jodhpur, or rather to Marwar. You must have heard that Pabuji Rathore was looking for some camels to give to his niece as a wedding present. One day, his charan told Pabuji that Sayra Baghani had some camels. Do you know what a charan is?"

"I think so. He is some kind of storyteller and genealogist who worked at the courts of Rajputs."

"That's right. So Pabuji went to Lankia to steal the camels. Sayra Baghani found out about this and there was a big fight between them. Just as they were about to kill each other, the charan exchanged their turbans. Do you know what that means?"

"No, I don't."

"Well, it meant that from now on, Pabuji and Sayra had to consider themselves brothers. They stopped fighting and became friends. Sayra wanted to give the camels to Pabuji as a gift. But Pabuji refused as he did not have anything to give in return. So Sayra Baghani said, 'Why don't you give me your charan?'

"Pabuji agreed and gave his charan to Sayra Baghani. This is why even today, the charans work for both Hindu Rajputs as well as Muslims."

Professor Mehar went on to tell me more exciting tidbits about camels and Sindhi Muslims. The typical occupation of the Sindhi Muslims had been as *katarias* or caravaneers. But because a kataria usually owned only one camel, this had not been rated very highly. It was better to be a *gantawala* – somebody who used camels to transport wood. Another camel-related job was the *shutar sawar* – a camel-mounted messenger posted in police stations. Then there were the Mirdhas, the royal messengers who had usually been of the Chowdhary caste. In order to test my knowledge, he gave me another quiz question. "Madam, do you know where the best camels in Rajasthan are to be found?"

"No, I don't," I had to admit my ignorance.

"The most famous camels in Rajasthan are from a village called Nachna, not far from Jaisalmer. The Nachna camels were once so well known that all camelwallahs took the oath of Nachna. They said, 'I swear in the name of the tola of Nachna.' You must go to Nachna one day and look at the camels there!"

Promising that I would do this when an opportunity arose and mentioning that it would be nice if he could accompany me, I thanked him for his time and information.

We needed to get to Pushkar, but Dr Dewaram insisted on squeezing one more point on to the agenda. A Raika wedding was going to take place in a village en route – as on all such occasions, the festivities were going to be held in the middle of the night. "Actually, it is not a wedding as much as an engagement," Dewaram said, elaborating that Raika children are wed or promised to each other while still in their infancy. But only when the couple is well beyond puberty – usually when they are in their middle twenties – do they actually start living together. At that time, there is another, smaller, ceremony, called *ana*, which signals the departure of the girl from her parent's household to her in-laws' place. Even then the transition is step by step – she will spend only a few days there, then return to her native village. Over the years, the periods she stays with her husband gradually become longer, but she will go back home for the delivery of her first child.

Yet, the main celebration is at the time of engagement. Because of the expense involved, all the unmarried girls of a village undergo this ceremony together. Tonight, eleven couples would be betrothed. Child marriages had been banned by the government and were illegal; therefore, there was always much risk of a raid by the police. No foreigner or other outsider had ever watched such a ceremony. But, because of my active involvement with the Raika community, I would be allowed to attend.

Although I was extremely keen to witness a wedding and very excited about the opportunity, I also felt somewhat uneasy. "If it is a closed occasion, I don't feel I should intrude."

"Don't worry – just do as we tell you. Everything will be fine."

We arrived at about nine o'clock at night. It was pitch dark and difficult to get oriented. I could make out several parked tractors and sensed lots of people milling around – only men, of course. The marriage ritual was not going to start until the early hours of the morning.

"Come, eat something and then you can rest until the ceremony takes place," said Dewaram, leading me along a narrow path winding through high thornbrush fencing to a house where about ten men were huddled around a fire, wrapped in blankets from head to toe. Four others were stirring huge cauldrons the size of a turned-over sun umbrella with enormous iron spatulas as long as broomsticks. Inside was a dark gooey mass, *lapsi*, a sweet dish made from cracked wheat, ghee and molasses that is the standard menu at weddings and all other social gatherings.

Trying to make myself as small and unobtrusive as possible, I hunched down next to Dr Dewaram who got involved in a long conversation, occasionally glancing over to me to see that I was all right. I stared into the flames of the fire, looked up into the sky for shooting stars, tried to pick up the gist of the rather solemn chatter around me and drifted off to sleep. Time passed and Dewaram announced, "We proceed", and led me deeper into the village, pushing through the dense crowds which had formed. I caught a glance of a courtyard where a camel was being decorated with all its finery – the whole array of colourful ornaments, including necklaces, chest cover, saddle, ankle chains that compose the camel attire on special occasions. Dewaram pressed still deeper into the hub of the commotion. Six boys ranging from a babe in arms that could hardly sit up on its own to a mature teenager were seated on a bhakal. They wore tinselled turbans in a range of pinks and red, had their eyes rimmed with kohl, their faces covered with a sparkling powder, and swords by their side.

But these glamorous effects were belied by their serious faces and the nervous way in which they pressed handkerchiefs over their mouths. A pundit was placing a tikka on their forehead, then they were led away I presumed to meet their brides of whom I had seen no hint so far. Suddenly, I became the centre of attention. People were staring at me, the only woman and white-skinned at that. I sensed irritation at my intrusion, even hostility building up and urged Dr Dewaram to leave. He insisted that we stay to observe the next point in the procedure in which the bridegrooms were mounted on camels and had to touch the *toran*, a ceremonial archway made from wood, with their swords. But I had had enough and put my foot down.

Somebody accompanied us back to the car. We woke up "Driversaab", giving him directions to go to Pushkar. Stretching out on the back seat, the drone of the Ambassador plying along the highway immediately rocked me to sleep and when I awoke it was broad daylight. Hanwant had stopped at a roadside dhaba for tea, Dr Dewaram was still sound asleep in the front seat. Hanwant looked up from the paper he was reading, keen to find out my impressions about the wedding. I did not really want to go into this and switched the topic to Pushkar, which was not far from here.

"I want to buy a camel at Pushkar."

"You want to buy a camel at Pushkar? Aha. Have another cup of tea!" Then, after a pause, "Why do you want to buy a camel?"

To explain the considerations behind this plan exceeded our verbal communication level, so I did not reply. But I could see his brain ticking and trying to comprehend. The idea of purchasing a camel had germinated some time back. It was not that I fancied myself in the role of camel owner (although some of that was also involved), but it appeared to me to be a strategically advantageous move. The idea had slowly crystallised in my mind after I had heard some of the herders describe how they looked after the camels of other people and the varying kinds of benefit-sharing arrangements this was based on. If I gave the camel to somebody to take care of, then my presence would be legitimate. As an absentee camel owner, I had the right to ask questions, I would learn a lot, and people could see that I was really taking a serious interest, not just nosily poking around. It would turn me into an insider, I hoped.

Nevertheless, Dr Dewaram had not sounded all that enthused about what I felt was a brilliant idea. "Why do you want to burden yourself with something like that? It is a big expense and what will you get for it?"

"Never mind, I would really like to own a camel, so please try and help me."

"Of course, if it is your desire, then we will do so," Dewaram had answered resignedly.

I had already informed myself about the prices. I wanted a female camel that would produce offspring and eventually develop into a small herd. Female camels were very reasonably priced, they cost around Rs 3000, the equivalent of about $100. The charges for looking after a camel were also very reasonable – a couple of hundred rupees per year, and the caretaker would be responsible for everything, including the sale of the offspring. It seemed like a great investment that would help establish rapport with the community and even produce some scientific data on camel-herd growth. I would experience the trials and tribulation of a camel-breeder, watch my camels multiply over the years...the prospect was extraordinarily attractive.

We reached Pushkar in the afternoon. After passing congested and polluted Ajmer, the road took several hairpin turns to scale a steep mountain from where there was a remarkable view of a wide sandy plain, in the middle of which lay Pushkar. Normally a sleepy and contemplative place where Hindu holy men harmoniously coexist with western hippies, it hustles and bustles with thousands of Hindu pilgrims, livestock vendors and buyers, and foreign tourists during the ten days leading up to the full moon of the Hindu month of Kartik.

We had come later than planned and the fair was reaching its peak. After having paid our tax at the tollbooth, the Ambassador was enveloped by the human masses threading their way through the main thoroughfare and could barely inch along. After half an hour, a parking lot for "tourist vehicles" appeared and we were able to continue on foot.

Although the first impression was one of pandemonium, the fair is, in fact, an outstanding feat of organisation and logistics – how else could the tens of thousands of visitors and equal numbers of camels, cattle, horses and other incidental animals be accommodated, fed, watered and their litter sanitised over a period of more than a week? The mela grounds comprise several well-defined areas. There is the amusement part where one can see a family circus, watch magicians, ride the ferris wheel and visit an exhibition of oddities – such as a goat kid with two heads preserved in formaldehyde. This part is usually so crowded that one has no choice but to move on with the human stream. By comparison, the area designated for tourists is an oasis of peace, but tea and food are at least twenty times as expensive as the places where the local people go. There is a big stadium, where performances and livestock shows are on offer. There are tented bazaars with rows of shops selling all the requirements for rural life – wooden pitchforks with two, three, four and five tines, feeding baskets in all sizes, saddlery, bells, camel ornaments, blankets, iron tools, and, of course, any number of makeshift restaurants and tea stands. There is a veterinary hospital and a place where all changes of animal ownership have to be registered and statistics about the purchase prices are calculated. There is a public address system, which makes announcements about lost children and events in the stadium, but most of the time blasts out religious songs. The part that interested us was the area of sandy hills at the periphery where the Raika and other livestock sellers were camping amidst their camels, horses and bullocks.

I followed Dr Dewaram who was trudging ahead of me. Moving around in the deep sand in the scorching heat and the blinding sunlight reflecting from the white sand was exhausting, and I huffed and puffed to tackle a little hillock covered with camels. Many of them had small red ribbons tied around their tails, indicating that they had already been sold. From the top of the hill, one had an excellent overview of the livestock area which spread out endlessly, and Dr Dewaram immediately recognised some familiar faces. "Look over there, that is the dera of the Anji-ki-dhani people. Every year, they come to this same place and put up their camp on this same spot." Camp in this case meant just a few blankets, a clay pot for water and a fireplace. Dewaram told me to sit there and went off by himself, saying he would make some enquiries about suitable female camels. Somehow I had envisioned that together we would look at a good number of camels, discuss the pros and cons of each one of them, and then come to a measured decision. This way I would learn about the traits that were important in a camel, and about the manner of conducting business. But I realised that was wishful thinking, as I slurped the tea that somebody whom I did not know had handed me.

After half an hour, Dewaram returned with a satisfied smile on his face. "I have found a camel for you. I think it is a good one. It is from Anji-ki-dhani, female, and about four years old. Come and have a look." He led me on a few hundred feet and pointed at a camel. "That's her. Do you like her?"

I tried to put on a knowledgeable air, walked around the camel which looked pretty ordinary to me in regards to colour (brownish) and height (medium), scrutinised its legs and feet, looked it over from all directions. I inspected her teeth. I asked her handler to make her get up and down, walk and trot her, and just as one did with a horse I tried to look her in the eye, to see if something in her personality would talk to me and we would immediately establish some sort of rapport – sometimes this happens with animals. I tried to remember some of the things I had learnt in Godwar about purchasing camels. *Make sure that there is sufficient space between the elbow and the breast pad, that the Achilles' tendon is strong and that the loin region is well muscled. Don't buy a camel that urinates when you look at it, but immediately grab the one that defecates.* At this very moment, she lifted her tail and did just that. So I guess it was sealed. I could not find anything wrong with her; she looked healthy and good-natured.

"What is she supposed to cost?"

"They want to give you a very good price. Only Rs 2,200, special price for you."

"But are you sure there is nothing wrong with her? She is not sterile, is she? Why is she not pregnant?"

"She is not sterile. She is not pregnant yet because she is still very young. She will become pregnant this winter, I am sure."

"I see. So who is the owner? Why is he selling her? I thought Raika were not supposed to sell any female camels – is it not against the caste rules?"

"Yes, traditionally it is, but now times are changing. Anyway, you are almost like part of the community. And the owner needs the money. Raika are very poor these days."

"So who is the owner?"

"You already know him – Adoji from Anji-ki-dhani. We visited his herd and even stayed in his house one night – do you remember?"

"Oh, it's Adoji's! Well, that's fine. If we buy her, then who would we arrange to look after her?"

"I asked about that. Adoji has also agreed that she can stay with his herd. He will charge only Rs 20 per month. I think this is a good arrangement."

Everything appeared to have already been sorted out without me, as usual. I would have preferred to place my camel in another herd than the one it came from. I was paying Adoji Rs 2,200 and then he would take the same camel back with him and even get paid for looking after it. It was a rather opportune deal for him. But the offspring would be mine. Besides, it was take it or leave it – we were late and the majority of camels had already been sold. There were hardly any female camels on offer anyway, only some that were not fit for breeding. So this was actually rather lucky. It would also strengthen ties with the people from Anji-ki-dhani. From now on, I would have a legitimate reason to visit and need no longer feel an intruder. I could just say, "I want to see how my camel is doing."

Just then, "my" camel turned her head around and gave me one of those soulful looks. She would probably be relieved to go back to her familiar place and friends, rather than join a new herd and put up with a lot of harassment until she established her position in the pecking order.

"I will buy her," I announced to Dewaram who had been looking at me expectantly. I thought there would be some kind of ritual confirming my purchase, such as the shake of hands that settles a deal in Europe. However, this did not seem to be the case.

"Congratulations! Now we need to tie a red ribbon around the tail. We also have to get a paper from the mela administration, so that your camel can leave Pushkar. Do you want to purchase a halter or head collar for your camel?"

"Yes, I certainly do. By the way, I am going to call my camel 'Mira'."

The various hangers-on who had followed and observed the transaction seemed to be amused by this idea. It was not one of the standard names the Raika bestowed upon their camels. Mira, respectfully called Mirabai, was a medieval saint whose poetry praising Lord Krishna had made her famous across all of northern India. She seemed to be the one famous woman in the history of Rajasthan, the single female person that had not remained anonymous, but dared to overstep social and caste conventions and ended up becoming almost a deity.

We tied the ribbon and purchased a colourful halter for Mira. She looked good in it and I affectionately patted her neck. Then I left her in the care of Adoji's group who would be leaving for Anji-ki-dhani that night. I would try to catch up with her about a week later. Dewaram was also eager to leave to take care of some urgent family business. We agreed to meet in about a week's time in Sadri to collect some more information on the health status of camels.

In the meantime, Hanwant and I would continue our tour of relevant historic monuments and check out some camel depictions in the eastern parts of Rajasthan. First we had to extricate ourselves from Pushkar which was even worse than entering it. People and vehicles were continuing to stream into the already deluged and bursting town. A layer of exhaust fumes hovered over the road, Hindu devotional music blared from the ever-present loudspeaker system mixing with cries from beggars tapping at our car windows. Between extended standstills the Ambassador could only creep ahead. Strangely undisturbed by the threat of bumps and lesions in his newly acquired car, Hanwant remained superbly composed. As soon as we had fought our way out of the worst mayhem, he wanted to know everything that had happened. "So, Madam, did you buy yourself a camel?"

I told him all the details and ended my story by revealing the name I had given her.

"I named her Mira, after Mirabai, the famous Bhakti saint."

"Mira? That is a very nice name," he said. After a little pause he continued, smilingly, "Actually, you know Mirabai is a relative of mine. She was born in Merta and is from my caste – a Mertiya Rajput. I am also a Mertiya!" He explained that Mertiyas were a *gotra*, a lineage, of the Rathore Rajputs. The Rathores were the most important group of Rajputs in Rajasthan to whom belonged the Maharajahs of Jodhpur and of Bikaner. It seemed nothing out of the ordinary for Hanwant to claim kinship to my two favourite persons in Rajasthani history, Pabuji and Mirabai, persons who had lived about half a millennium ago. This was one of the most endearing aspects and what I liked most about Rajasthan – the way in which past and present, myth and reality were so intricately and inextricably interwoven.

Not such a bad day after all. I had become a camel owner and was learning new things all the time. Contentedly, I leaned back and had a little nap, while we were heading towards Bundi and Kota. Our route followed the Chambal River and meandered through lush landscape and thick green forests. "This area is famous for dacoits – we have to be careful," Hanwant commented. Surely he could not be suggesting that we were in danger of being robbed in bright daylight, I thought, but I wondered, recalling a story I had followed in the newspaper about Phoolan Devi, the Bandit Queen. The Chambal River had been mentioned in this connection. But the only menace we encountered were troops of monkeys leaping through the treetops, sometimes jumping into the immediate trajectory of our car.

Our first destination was a temple at Bardoli, somewhere

near Kota, where I wanted to photograph a sculpture of a camel dated to the tenth century. The Bardoli camel sculpture was tiny – about a cat or lapdog size in relation to the *apsara* or heavenly damsel at whose feet it was couched. A camel it undoubtedly was, but what was the historical significance? Did the fact that an isolated camel was depicted on a temple from the tenth century signify that this animal was known and used in Rajasthan during that period, as the writer of the article would have one believe? Was it not possible that the sculptors had been imported from elsewhere – or that they had just copied this figure from a depiction they had seen somewhere? I was not convinced of the meaningfulness of this historical object for the question I was trying to answer.

Our last stop was Chittor, the enormous fortress which bears testimony to the two only women of fame in Rajasthani history. One of them is the beautiful Padmini, the other one, the rebellious Mirabai. "Make sure you visit the temple of Mirabai," Hanwant impressed upon me, "she is from my caste!"

I meandered through the many buildings and architectural complexes that compose the Chittor Fort. I found the camel statue but it only dated to the sixteenth century when I knew the camel was already very much in use in Rajasthan, so it was not really germane to the question. I paid my respects to Mirabai, and I visited the place where Padmini and 300 other women had committed jauhar, immolation, to avoid falling into the hands of the invading army of Muslim warlord, Alauddin Khilji. I strolled around the women's palace which was in the middle of a lake. The architecture was charming but what would this have meant to women who were locked up inside and had no opportunity to go out, whose fate was waiting for their men to return at some unpredictable time in the future?

My stay in Rajasthan and my fellowship were coming to

an end and suddenly I was overwhelmed with unfathomable sadness at the thought of leaving. Deep inside me there was an ache of a kind I had never felt before. A yearning similar to the longing that I imagined the Rajput ladies, locked up in the palace, must have felt. I pitied them, but at least they had known where they belonged, they were part of life here. But where was my place? When would I be back? How would things continue? Okay, I had bought Mira and thus staked a tenuous claim. But I could not just continue driving around the countryside with Hanwant for ever.

I wandered around Chittor, accelerating my steps while trying to nail down what had taken hold of me and what was attracting me so strongly to India and especially Rajasthan. Was it the feeling of being alive and being among real people with real problems, in stark contrast to the soap opera lifestyle of southern California? Was it Hanwant's loyalty and the feeling that he would keep me safe wherever I went? Whatever it was or was not, it was driving a deep wedge between me and my family. Not emotionally, for I loved them as much as ever, but spatially and in terms of direction. Gary's research in India had not really taken off and he was keen to go back to his long-standing projects in Jordan. Jon and Aisha had been fascinated by many aspects of India but their school experiences had been rather traumatic. So the rest of the family had happily returned to California and had little interest in ever returning to India. I felt a bit like a banyan tree whose air roots had taken a hold at the other side of a brook and were threatening to dislodge the original trunk.

That night I cried myself to sleep and a cloud of depression hung over me when we returned to Sadri. I had extensive discussions with Dr Dewaram on what course of action to take on the miscarriages the camels in the area were suffering from. We came to the conclusion that trypanosomiasis, the blood disease that was transmitted by fly-bites and locally known as tibursa, was a major factor. This was also what the Raika thought and they were keen to have their camels prophylactically treated with a particular drug. I promised that I would try to raise some funds for buying these medicines.

We tried to track down Adoji's herd to check up on Mira, but had difficulties locating it. My time was over and Hanwant dropped me off at the airport. After we had shaken hands, he shyly gave me a gift – a book with a transcription of the Pabuji epic. It was written in Dingal, the ancient Rajasthani literary language, so I could not read it, but I was very touched by his thoughtful gesture.

Chapter 6

THE CAMELS OF NACHNA

"The most famous camels in Rajasthan are from a village called Nachna, not far from Jaisalmer."

– Professor Zahurkhan Mehar, Jodhpur

July/August 1992

It took me about eight eventful months to engineer my return to India. In the meantime, my life had turned upside down. Out of the blue, Gary had lost his position as a tenured professor in San Diego because the whole anthropology department had been slated for closure, due to a fiscal crisis in California. We had moved to my parental house in Germany and needed to make a new start. For people with such esoteric backgrounds as Prehistoric Archaeology and human-animal relationships, this was not easy, but I was optimistic and heartened by the fact that I had been given another research grant which was small but came from the National Geographic Society.

In preparation for my research, I had put a lot of time and effort into learning Hindi from a private tutor and was now in a position to pen letters to my non-English-speaking Indian contacts in a somewhat crooked but legible Devanagari script. This skill came in handy in order to pursue my promise to the Raika to supply them with the medicines they so desired for their camels. To this end, I had entered into a hectic exchange of letters with Bhopalaram and Dr Dewaram.

One of the major problems was the fact that the medicine was not available in India, nor, my researches revealed, anywhere else. A veterinary friend had put me in touch with the Institute of Tropical Veterinary Medicine in Edinburgh. According to experts there, pharmaceutical companies had stopped manufacturing the traditional trypanocidal drugs, most likely because of insufficient economic returns. Camel people are poor in most places, except maybe in the Arab countries where camel racing is big business and there are petrol dollars. However, I was also informed, a French company had just brought a new product on the market. This had no prophylactic properties, only curative ones. Not exactly what we were looking for, but probably better than nothing. Unfortunately, my enquiries with them revealed, "Sorry, our product is not registered for the Indian market, we can't help you."

Before I could engage in wild fantasies about somehow smuggling the stuff into India, I received a letter from Bhopalaram, informing me that an Indian company had once again taken up production and that he had contacted them. Within days, the company notified me that they would be able to supply 10,000 vials at Rs 79 each:

> As a pharmaceutical manufacturer it is our moral responsibility to support and assist scientists like you. We would like to contribute to such a noble cause. As you are aware, there is a tremendous demand all over the country for this product and we cannot reserve 10,000 vials for you for an uncertain period. Our above subsidised offer would in all fairness, be valid until 31 July 1992. We have asked

> Dr Dewaram Dewasi and the Honourable Bhopalaram Dewasi of Luni to send their requirements to us without further delay. We are sure you will help us in helping the farmers of Rajasthan. We hope you appreciate that we are considering this project on humanitarian grounds only and not merely as a commercial proposition....

The price for 10,000 doses, therefore, amounted to about $ 30,000. Where could I get this kind of money? This was far more than I had let myself in for. I found a British-based charity that was interested in helping, but requested additional information about the scope of the problem. So I wrote back:

> The area that we are concentrating our efforts on is the district of Pali (about half way between Udaipur and Jodhpur, if you look at a map of Rajasthan). According to the last available livestock census (1988), the camel population of Pali is 19,000. By our own estimates this figure is inflated - there are probably no more than 10,000 camels in the area now. According to a survey we did in November, about half of the camels are infected with trypanosomiasis (locally called surra - or tibursa); this is based on information provided by camel owners who diagnose surra from the smell of the urine. The health status of these herds is often abysmal; in some of their herds 100% of pregnant camels had aborted (towards the end of their pregnancy) and owners ascribe this to trypanosomiasis. This high rate of abortions is apparently a new phenomenon that has skyrocketed in the last few years. Whether this is really due to trypanosomiasis is another question; I am worried about brucellosis, although according to local veterinarians this disease does not occur. The second problem is mange with which about 50% of the animals are infected, followed by ringworm.
>
> At least partially responsible for the situation is probably

> the bad nutritional status that predisposes animals to diseases. The latter is caused by the rapid disappearance of pasture resources due to the expansion of irrigation agriculture, etc.; the summer grazing grounds in the Aravalli have been closed down to graziers to be converted into a wildlife sanctuary. This has forced camel owners to take their animals into areas to the east where humidity is high and surra-transmitting flies abound. In general, these Raikas are excellent herders – they really care about their animals but they just don't know how to find pastures for them, and they are absolutely desperate.
>
> Herd sizes are from 20-100 animals, averaging 40-50; the smaller herds are village based, the larger ones are migratory. This means that there would be about 200 herds needing treatment. The infrastructure is good in this part of Rajasthan, so getting to the herds would be no problem. In June, i.e. just before the rainy season (July/August), they are all concentrated in the vicinity of the Aravallis...

I was fervently hoping the charity would arrange for some kind of emergency assistance exercise, relieving me of my responsibilities. But things were not that easy. They had different ideas about how to help the Raikas. In their work with pastoralists in Kenya, they had developed the "village-animal healthcare" concept. This basically involved giving training to local people in the treatment of minor diseases, usually with herbal medicines. It did not make provisions for a major prophylactic campaign as seemed necessary here. Before getting started at all, they wanted to do a detailed survey, not just about the disease situation but about the socio-economic status of the Raikas. This, of course, would take time. The person in charge wanted to come to India and see for himself, before making any commitments.

This did not help me with the promises I had made to the

Raikas. But there was nothing I could do. Letters from Bhopalaram further added to the pressure:

> Sister, I want to inform you that we have about 60,000 camels in Rajasthan and about 4-5000 camels die every year due to non-availability of above product. Because the product is very costly and our poor breeders cannot afford it. As you know, we usually give this injection to our camels before rainy season for prevention and now the season is approaching very near so we need these injections at the earliest. Sister, I welcome you once again to India on behalf of all our breeders. I request you once again to please do the needful for financial help.

This was a tall order – 60,000 camels and I was supposed to supply them all with injections? Did people think I had supernatural powers?

Since no charity could be moved into immediate action, the only thing I could think of was to do a private fundraising campaign among my friends in Germany, so as to not arrive in India totally empty-handed. Thanks to their generosity, I collected enough money to buy a few hundred doses.

But distributing medicines was not the official purpose of getting back to India. It was supposed to be research, this time to be focused mainly on the Sindhi Muslims and their relationship with the camel. How did they relate to their camels in comparison to the Raika? Did their communities eat camel meat like other Muslims around the world?

When I arrived in India on 13 July 1992, the monsoon was in full swing. The rains had been generous this year. After the usual preliminaries in Delhi, my first stop was in Jaipur to pick up the medicines. When the plane dived through the cloud cover, there was only a slight drizzle in the air, but the state of the roads leading from the airport into town attested to a massive recent downpour. With at least five inches of water on the ground, the taxi just lurched from one pothole into the next. I had barely checked into the Gangaur Tourist Bungalow when the phone rang, announcing the agent of the pharmaceutical company.

"Madam, I am here, Mr Singh from the drug company."

"Oh, hello, I just got here."

"How are you, Madam, did you have a good journey?"

"Yes, thank you."

"Madam, you made that order. When do you want to pick up the medicines?"

"I think I should wait until tomorrow. I am waiting for my taxi from Jodhpur."

"Oh, Madam, the expense – very costly to have taxi from Jodhpur!"

"But the driver is my friend and I have to go to Jodhpur anyway."

"Well, Madam, as you like. I will check back with you later, after 8 pm and we can set a time."

Shortly afterwards, Hanwant turned up, looking somewhat wan but otherwise in fine fettle. In his company, I felt immediately on firm ground, able to handle cheeky drug salesmen.

"How have you been?"

"I have been fine".

"How is your family?"

"They are fine."

"How is your taxi business going? Did you have a lot of work?"

"Madam, it is off season now – no tourists are here and I have not been busy for the last three months. I have been in my village."

The next day we managed to get hold of 384 doses of medicine, although in not very straightforward dealings by the company representative. Thinking that my pockets were lined with gold, he wanted to push a much larger number on me, and

I had to resolutely refuse this. When we wanted to collect the vials, it turned out that he did not really know where they were stored and it took hours to locate the godown. By evening, I was so fed up with everything that I had an overwhelming urge to get out of Jaipur as quickly as possible. The drug representative was desperate to stop us. "Madam," he said, "it is very dangerous to go by road – the road is flooded and you will get stuck. If you take my advice, do not go." I forwarded this message to Hanwant, who seemed fairly unconcerned. "This is a national highway – maybe there will be a lot of rain, but we will not get stuck."

We left in the evening; I went off to asleep on the back seat, trusting Hanwant to get me safely to Jodhpur. I slept almost all the way through, only waking up a couple of times when the car stopped at tea-stalls. Peeping through the darkened window of the Ambassador, I could see Hanwant stretched out on a charpai smoking a cigarette. We got to Jodhpur at 3 o'clock in the morning.

I looked up my contacts. Komal Kothari, who was my official research affiliation during this trip, was enthused about my project and spontaneously offered to accompany me to Jaisalmer to interview Sindhi Muslims. Dr Dewaram turned up at the right place and the right time. After all these preliminaries were sorted, we set off for Sadri. On my previous sojourns, the Aravalli Hills had always seemed fairly barren and exposed with mostly leafless trees defiantly clinging to steep parched slopes. Now the monsoon had transformed the landscape into a lush jungle complete with mist-covered peaks – everything was green, the plant life bursting with energy. One could virtually see seeds sprouting and hear flowers exploding. An environment more suitable for research on gorillas than camels, was my overwhelming impression.

I put up at the Shilpi Tourist Bungalow, right next to the Ranakpur temples, and surrounded by noisy flocks of green parrots, courting peacocks and troops of monkeys. The landscape was dotted with black umbrellas - nobody, neither camel herders, nor ox-cart men, nor plough men seemed to be without this essential prop. My camel, Mira, had become a local celebrity - everybody in the area knew her and referred to her by name. Before even seeing her, I was told from several sides that she was not pregnant; purportedly, she had had an "early" abortion in the first months of her pregnancy. I wondered if there was something wrong with her and whether that was why she had been sold to me. We tracked down Adoji's herd in the jungle below the Parshuram Mahadev Temple. Definitely, Mira was not in good hump and in dire need of veterinary care, which Dr Dewaram administered immediately.

We then spent three days distributing medicines in Latada, Anji-ki-dhani and other places. The vials were handed out against information on herd size, number of abortions and other disease problems, which we meticulously recorded in long lists in triplicate. Every camel owner testified by thumbprint that he had received the medicines. Suddenly we were immensely popular. People totally changed their behaviour towards us. No more of the previous stand-offish attitude, everywhere were big smiles and expressions of gratitude. I learned more about Raika customs and expanded my circle of friends. One of the more notable new acquaintances was Shivlalji, a self-styled Raika photographer whose otherwise rudimentary English vocabulary included such terms as "reverse light", "aperture", and "zoom lens". While his official job was selling life insurances, his true passion was "Raika dress photography" and there was no way our three-person team could escape this ordeal. Madam had to be recorded for posterity in full Raika regalia, consisting of a *ghagra* (skirt) made out of nine metres of heavy cotton, *kanchli* (blouse), odhni, plus all the jewellery Raika women routinely wear. The entire upper arms are covered in plastic rings fixed by a tied rubber band above the elbows, the lower arms in a succession of various other types of bracelets and bangles. Massive silver anklets, ear adornments so heavy that they act as ear stretchers, and a bobble on the forehead complement the outfit. The hair has to be viciously pulled back, so that not a wisp lurks out under the odhni. In order to create the proper impression, the odhni has to be held in a particular coy way. I looked awful in this outfit. The same was, fortunately, not true of the two men. Both of them took turns dressing up, their attire completed by a big sword.

The man from the British charity came. We introduced him to the camel herders, plied him with camel milk served in the folded aak leaves which the Raika use for cups, and familiarised him with the lay of the land. He was charmed and interested, but wanted more information to make sure that the Raika really were needy before committing himself to any support. He also cautioned that there needed to be a society registered in India that would serve as the official implementing agency and take responsibility for the funds. We told him about RAIKAS, although this did not yet even exist on paper. It was Dr Dewaram's task to move the matter further, but his plate was a bit full at the moment. He was under a lot of pressure from his government job. In the meantime, he had been posted away from Sadri to a veterinary hospital close to his native village, in order to be nearer to his family. His wife had not liked living in the Sadri Veterinary Hospital - without the extended family around she had felt lonely.

On the way back to Jodhpur, we drove via Pachunda to drop off Dr Dewaram. The ladies of the house insisted on giving me henna treatment, part of the Raika hospitality ritual. The area around Sojat is famous for *mehendi* and Dr Dewaram's family is among those cultivating it. Undergoing this beautifying ritual is quite awkward. Dr Dewaram's niece, the irrepressible Kamla, made me lie spread-eagled on a charpai. The girls rolled the henna paste into little balls and threads, then pressed them onto my hands and feet to create the simple designs that are a rustic relative of the elaborate patterns common in the city.

The stretch from Pachunda to Jodhpur took about two hours' driving time. Hanwant made another attempt to talk to me in Hindi, and this time it worked. In English, our conversation was usually pretty monosyllabic or consisted of isolated sentences at most, our companionship based on shared silences more than anything else. Surprisingly, by now my broken Hindi was sufficient to keep the chat going for almost the entire time. He told me about his family, his wife, and his children's school problems. His son had not been given admission to a good school, so Hanwant had to make a "donation" in order to get him in. His wife had attended school only up to Class 4 and was, therefore, not functionally literate and could not help the kids with their homework. He enquired about my family and I confided that we had moved to Germany because my husband had lost his job. "If one way is closed, God opens up another one," was his comment.

With our charitable mission finalised, it was now time to get going with my research project on Sindhi Muslims. I had learnt a little more about them since what Professor Mehar had told me and knew that they were concentrated in the Jaisalmer area. Only three weeks were left and I needed a translator. Various people had indicated interest, but suddenly they were all busy with other things. Initially, I had banked on Dr Dewaram who had signalled his consent, but now he was in no position to get leave. I reported my problems to Komal Kothari, whose failing health prevented him from coming himself. As always, he was eager to help and waved over a young man who had been hovering around. "This boy will help you. He has some experience."

The candidate, a smooth and beautiful young man with a very artistic hairstyle, spoke perfect English and recited his experience, dropping the names of quite a few famous researchers. We agreed that he would go back to his village and pick up some of his clothes, so that we could start for Jaisalmer early the next morning.

But by noon the next day, he still had not returned – maybe he had bigger fish in the sea, or older friends than Madam. Impatience was getting the better of me, especially since the taxi was already hired and I had to pay for it. Would it not make more sense to try to find a translator in Jaisalmer itself? Fed up with waiting and cursing all unreliable aides, I gave orders to my driver to just steer the vehicle to Jaisalmer so that we could try our luck by ourselves.

Hanwant gave me a surprised, questioning look. "We don't have any translator, Madam?" he asked.

"No, we don't, let's just go and see how far we get."

"*Theek hai*, Madam, *chale*."

Secretly, I was also banking on the option that, if worst came to the worst, Hanwant himself might be pressed to take over the role of translator. I could understand his Hindi and if he translated the local Marwari into Hindi, we would be able to get by. He also had a knack of getting people to open up. So far, he seemed to have been restrained by an invisible border that separated simple "drivers" from the more elevated caste of "translator" and "research assistant". But now, with nobody else being around, he would just have to step to the fore and help me collect data.

Before departing from Jodhpur, there were a few errands to run. One of them was to change money. The bank manager, who by now had a vague idea about my interest in camels, motioned me over.

"So where are you going today, Madam?"

"I am off to Jaisalmer."

"Really – well, I used to be posted in Jaisalmer. Check out the camels from Nachna. They are famous!"

"Famous, in what way?"

"I don't know. But many times I have heard people speak

about the camels from Nachna. I think the Nachna Thakur used to have a famous tola. He was my friend, remember me to him."

Nachna. There was the name again. I recalled that Professor Mehar had also referred to the camels of Nachna and that all caravaneers used to speak an oath in the "name of the camels of Nachna".

It was well into afternoon by the time we rolled out of Jodhpur. It was excruciatingly hot – nevertheless, the supposed desert was green almost all the way to Jaisalmer. I checked in at the Moomal Tourist Bungalow because one of my Jodhpur contacts had equipped me with a *chithi* to the manager, no doubt informing him about my considerable importance.

In the morning, I met the manager and handed over the chithi. He took his time scrutinising it."So, Madam, you want to go on a camel safari?"

"No! I am not a tourist. I am doing research and want to collect some information on camels. I would like to talk to some Sindhi Muslim camel breeders."

The manager promised he would make enquiries and arrange a selection of informants – but this would take until evening.

This left me time to find out about how to get to Nachna. I knew that it was in a restricted area – like all the area around Jaisalmer and that one needed a permit. We headed for the appropriate permit-issuing office.

I explained my mission to the sleepy officer who gave me a nice smile and seemed quite cooperative at first glance.

"So you want to go to Nachna?"

"Yes, I do."

"But, Madam, there are plenty of camels near Jaisalmer and at the Sam sand dunes. You can book a safari over there. If you want, I can help you – my brother-in-law has a business."

"Sir, I am not a tourist, I am doing research with permission of the Government of India. My research is on camels and everybody has told me that the camels from Nachna are special. Therefore, I want to go there."

"But, Madam, no permit for Nachna has been issued in the last five years."

Among his dusty shelves he searched for and, very surprisingly, located a dog-eared registry that he opened up.

Indeed, the last entry dated several years back.

"But my work is important. It is sponsored by the Government of India. Can you not please make an exception?"

"I wish I could. But, Madam, this is a military shooting zone. Very dangerous. You will most probably get killed if you go there."

There was no room for argument after that statement. I reported back to Hanwant. He was not quite so easily convinced.

"I don't believe this. Shooting is surely not going on all the time. I think, this man only wants money. Try the district collector, he can give a permit."

"Well, let's see. Maybe, it is not necessary to go to Nachna. Perhaps we can get good information here in Jaisalmer. It's likely that the manager has arranged some people."

"As you like, Madam."

"But we have to wait until the evening. What can we do in the meantime?"

"There is a museum here. You go there and have a look, maybe some information on camels is available there."

Obediently, I followed his suggestion and let him take me to the museum – a two-room affair, run privately by a Mr Sharma. Indeed, there were two exhibits that related to camels. One was a small sign proclaiming, "On 26.6.1857, a new postal route from Jodhpur to Sindh via Malani and Jaisalmer was opened. Postal posts were established at every six miles. At every post, two camels to carry the dak were arranged."

More fascinating was an exhibit of "camel jewellery" - an elaborate affair consisting of - at the minimum - a saddle girth, ankle bells, chest gear, necklace, headpiece and reins. The saddle girths arrested my attention. Several of them were on display, elaborately woven from sheep and camel wool, with intricate designs. Mr Sharma noticed my interest.

"These are made by Iser Singh, very famous camel ornament-maker."

Camel ornament-maker? Another profession to do with camels and which Hanwant insisted we follow up - after all, we had time to kill. We tracked down Iser Singh at his haveli. Proudly, he showed us a book entitled, *Ply-split Camel Girths from Western India* centering on his work and written by two American researchers. He also showed us the National Award for Craftsmanship that had been given to him. His saddle girths were exquisite but too pricey for me.

By now it was late afternoon and we headed back to the Moomal-Mahendra to see if the manager had made good on his promise. A fancily decked-out camel was hobbled right outside the building and a man with a colourful turban and significant moustache emerged from the shadow of the wall. He had been waiting for me, as was immediately confirmed by Hanwant.

"This man has been called by the manager and wants to know if you want to go on a camel safari."

"I most definitely don't want to go on a camel safari, I just want to ask some questions about camels."

"Okay, so, what do you want to ask? I will translate."

It promised to be a painful and futile exercise. Trying to have a serious conversation with somebody who thinks you are a customer for a safari while interested tourists look on was not what I had envisioned for my academic research. Still, I had wasted the whole day without getting anywhere significant, my time was extremely limited, so I'd better give it a try. We pulled over three of the white plastic chairs and ordered some tea.

His name was Fateh Khan; he was from a village near Sam and owned two camels.

"Only two camels? I had heard that here in the Jaisalmer area people have huge herds. Is that true?"

"Yes, there are some tolas with 120 camels. But I have only two."

"Is camel milk ever sold here?"

"Oh no, if you sell camel milk, then God will be very angry. We only drink it ourselves."

"What about eating camel meat? "

"No, no never – the camel is our best friend – how could we eat it?"

Fateh Khan seemed really upset and ready to break off the conversation. We steered the conversation towards more palatable subjects and established a list of camel-fodder plants. Then again back to camel milk. How was it different from that of other animals? On this subject, Fateh Khan was quite expansive. The one drawback of camel milk was that it did not last long – it spoilt within half an hour. Cow milk made for the best ghee, goat milk the best tea and sheep milk the best kheer. Buffalo milk was very tasty and made the body strong.

When we got round to discussing where the best camels come from, he immediately mentioned Nachna, followed by two other places – Bhala and Ramgarh. But it was the Rajputs and Muslims who breed them in these places – not Raika.

At this stage, Fateh Khan started to get a bit fidgety and looked at his watch. Sunset was approaching and he had to get to the Sam sand dunes for his business. Wouldn't I also like to come? So many camels to be seen there and I could talk to some other people, collect more information.

Hanwant was also keen that we go. "Madam, this is big tourist attraction," he said. "You should go and see."

I was very doubtful, but, in the interest of team harmony, and also because Fateh Khan wanted a lift and we had taken up his time, I agreed.

My expectations were not wrong. At the foot of some, well, reasonably sized sand dunes, countless camels were paraded around, mingling with mini-buses, tourists, cold drink and postcard vendors. Of course, any kind of dialogue was set, not going beyond, "Madam, you want camel ride? I give you good rate!" Definitely not a research scenario, I fumed to myself, although I valiantly tried to maintain a placid appearance on the outside. Luckily, it did not take long for the red-hot ball of sun to do its duty of majestically disappearing behind the dune and we could go home. Useless, useless, I mumbled to myself, wondering what was the point of all this. It had been a severe miscalculation to believe that after being adopted as a sister by Raika dignitaries, another community would accept me as well. It felt like a déjà vu of the time I first started out in Bikaner. After all, I had found it possible to gate-crash the Raika society around Sadri only *after* having first bought a camel from them, then giving it back to them and paying them to care for it in addition to supplying emergency relief to their camels.

I had no time to go through the same exercise with the Sindhi Muslims.

Still, maybe, something nice would happen tomorrow. By now I was used to the Indian pattern of nothing happening for days, then everything at once.

In the morning, I had another chat with the manager, trying to get my point across. "I am not a tourist, I don't want to go on a camel safari. I just want to talk to some normal people outside the tourist circles."

Quite obviously, he was unused to such requests, but his helpful nature would not allow him to admit this.

"I will arrange a very good guide for you. He can take you to some villages."

What could I do? I had no other tricks up my sleeve. It took only a couple of hours until the new banner of hope showed up. His name was Manu, a short, roly-poly guy, well versed in the tourist trade. He spoke very good English, so I made another attempt to get my point across that I DID NOT WANT TO GO ON A CAMEL SAFARI. Apparently, with some success, for he offered, "I can take you to Rebarion-ki-dhani. There are many Raika and many camels. But today it is too late. We have to go early in the morning, before the villagers go to their fields to work."

"Do you know any Sindhi Muslims?"

"Oh yes, I do!"

"Maybe you can introduce me to some?"

"Sure, come with me, I will introduce you to some."

I followed him through the labyrinthine streets that lead up to the fort. We sat in a tea shop while he talked to some guys, probably convincing them to round up a few Sindhi Muslims. He came back and plied me with interesting episodes in his life as a tourist guide. Pulled out an address book and a bundle of airmail letters. Enquired whether I would like some ganja. "Really good for you, Madam, you will feel much better then. Relax, relax."

While we were waiting for the people he had summoned, he divulged all the details about camel safaris – how they are priced, where they go, the equipment people take. But he also had more pertinent intelligence available.

"Madam, why do you have such an interest in camels?"

I tried to tell him that I was looking at the ways they are used. That in Arabia and Africa, camels are used for food, and that I was trying to find out why this was not so in India.

"Actually, in Jaisalmer, they are mostly used for smuggling. They take gold to Pakistan and bring drugs into India. They are trained to do this all by themselves and to cross the border without any people involved. Sometimes, they carry the goods on their back, but often, they are operated on and carry them in their stomach."

At least this provided an explanation for why people were so reluctant to answer my questions about why they kept camels! Probably all involved in illicit dealings...

By evening, nothing had happened – no further contact with Sindhi Muslims had developed. Manu tried to cheer me up with the prospect of going to Rebarion-ki-dhani. "Tomorrow morning, early, we will go there by jeep," he said. "I will come with jeep at 6.30 am."

Frustrated, but still hopeful, I went to bed.

Next morning, nothing happened. I woke up early, but 6.30, 7, 8 o'clock passed. Being spoiled by Hanwant, I had forgotten my earlier experiences with jeep drivers and that they never turn up...

What else was there to do? Try to get the permit for Nachna? But the DC was only available after 10 am. I decided to follow up on my only remaining lead, the Thakur of Nachna, and check out whether he had any anecdotes about camels. We had already found out that he did not reside in Nachna, but in his townhouse in the centre of Jaisalmer. If I mentioned his friend, the bank manager in Jodhpur, maybe he would be helpful. His place, a multi-storeyed, crumbly building, was easily located. A servant received and seated me in a room with a high ceiling and some rickety but stylish furniture. The whitewash peeled off the wall, but there were interesting old sepia-print pictures to make up for it. Tea was placed in front of me and then the thakur sahib himself appeared. We exchanged some niceties and I tried to explain to him that I had an interest in camels, but not in camel safaris. The subject did not generate a lot of enthusiasm.

We were on firmer ground talking about his noble heritage. The first Nachna Thakur was a younger brother of the Jaisalmer ruler and given the *jagir* in 1786 AD. Later, relations between Jaisalmer and Nachna had soured. I was shown a document dated 1932 which had been given by his grandfather to the political resident – it contained complaints about various injustices done to him by the Jaisalmer state. He demanded a share of the taxes on the goods that passed through Nachna, entitlement to grazing and watering fees on cattle, and also a certain amount of tax on every camel load.

"Might you know somebody who could fill me in on the role of camels in Nachna?" I enquired.

Thakur sahib scratched his head. Finally, he wrote a small chithi and put it in an envelope, saying, "Take this to my *mahajan* in Nachna – he will give more information." With that the audience was over.

Mahajan translates into accountant or bookkeeper. It was quite possible that the mahajan would be able to produce some numbers of camels, their economic role, and so on. But what good would the letter be if I could not get to Nachna?

Permit-wise, the situation seemed pretty hopeless. But, having abandoned any attempts at shaking out anything sensible from the camel safari people, and with no other ideas left, yet feeling obliged to do something – even if only to placate Hanwant who was anxious for action and kept asking about my "programme" – I went and joined the crowd that was already waiting patiently in the antechamber of the district collector's office to make a petition. It was an interesting jumble of characters. Most notable was a fat and hirsute man in a long green *jallabya*-type of garment with the kind of turban that denoted him as Muslim. He needed two chairs to sit on and was surrounded by a strange aura. He was accompanied by two slight underlings who fawned on his every "ahem" and "aw". Then there were two ultra-smooth Bombaywalas whom I had already noticed in the tourist bungalow – they were from a film company and wanted to shoot an advertising spot in the streets of Jaisalmer – and also needed a permit.

The other supplicants were less noteworthy and I wondered what kind of fate had brought them here. There was one veiled and clearly emaciated young woman accompanied by an older man – maybe regarding a marriage dispute.

I was sitting there not because I had any hope, but because I didn't know what else to do. After a couple of hours, my turn finally came and two turbaned servants whisked me into a darkened office where, behind a huge desk, sat a rosy-cheeked young man looking as if he was barely out of college. But, befitting a representative of the Indian Administrative Service, his nature, speech and mimicry were incredibly refined. "What can I do for you, Madam?" he asked.

I hardly dared to tell him my unreasonable request, expecting a rather arrogant retort.

"I would like to get a permit for Nachna. You see, I am doing research on camels and the camels of Nachna are famous. So I would like to go there!"

A faint smile. "Really, I did not know that the camels from Nachna are especially noteworthy. Well, no problem, your permit will be ready tonight!"

He scribbled something on a piece of paper and handed it to me. "Have a nice trip, Madam. Good luck."

I could barely believe it. The whole transaction had taken only about a minute and a half.

Was he serious? He noted my hesitation. "The clerk will issue you your permit, Madam, don't worry."

"Ah, hmm, you mean it is not dangerous to go there because of shooting?"

"No, I would not worry about that, Madam." With that he was already signalling to the peon to call in the next supplicant.

Stunned, I revisited the clerk who could not believe it either. "No foreigner has been there in five years," he repeated. "This cannot be true. Madam, I have been telling you, it is not possible to go on a camel safari in Nachna."

"Yes, it is," I insisted. "You can ask the district collector sahib."

"Well, well," he nodded his head, "Maybe the district collector sahib said yes. But you cannot go there on your own. This is a military shooting zone and dangerous. At the very least, you must take a responsible person with you to keep you out of trouble and to prevent an incident."

I suggested Hanwant. "I have a very good driver with me. He can be the responsible person."

"Tsk, tsk, from where is your driver? From Jodhpur? Then he does not know the area. You must take a local person."

We finally agreed on Manu, the guide, to act as the responsible person and his name also was entered in the permit. It was for one day and stipulated checking in at various police stations on the way to and in Nachna.

Triumphantly, I waved the permit at Hanwant, "Look, what I got!" Now Hanwant started worrying about the condition of the road and whether it would be possible to go there by his car or it would be necessary to rent a jeep. The problem was that the situation changed from day to day because of the moving sand dunes – everything might be clear one day but blocked the next. After making enquiries with various people, he finally decided that we could risk going in his car. He also revealed that he had meanwhile arranged for a jeep for early next morning to make the excursion to Rebarion-ki-dhani that had fallen flat.

So it looked as if the next day would be extremely busy – early in the morning to Rebarion-ki-dhani and on return from there to

Nachna. Indeed, the next morning at 6 am on the dot, the jeep turned up. It took about twenty-five minutes to get there, most of it on a small sand track. Rebarion-ki-dhani was a tiny hamlet consisting of fifteen Raika houses situated on a gentle slope in the middle of the sand desert. Considering that we had never been there before, the people were quite friendly and willing to talk. About half a dozen men sat around on their haunches, passing around a *chillum*, and put us into the picture. They had lived in this isolated spot for seven generations. Their ancestors had come from Jodhpur and settled here at the request of the Jaisalmer Maharajah who needed good people to look after his camels. They also mentioned that earlier there had been about a dozen other Raika settlements nearby. But all of them had chosen to leave the area because of a marriage dispute with the thakur from Lodorva who had requested one of their daughters as dowry. Did they still keep camels? Yes, they did, although nowadays most of their income derived from growing millet, guar, til, moong and watermelon, and from keeping sheep, goats and cows. All their camels, about 200–300 head, were running free, but would soon be caught to prevent them from doing damage to the crops...

Because of the trip to Nachna, we didn't stay too long and were on our way again within less than an hour.

In Jaisalmer we reconnected with Hanwant and packed into his car for the big adventure. We had to backtrack towards Jodhpur to get there. The "responsible person", Manu, was sitting in front deeply involved in a conversation with Hanwant of which I caught only occasional snippets.

We arrived at the first checkpoint for Nachna where I had to sign in. At least there was no sign of shooting exercises and tanks – everything seemed to be quiet on this western front today. The only reason for worry was the piles of sand on the tarmac road that increased in frequency and depth. Although cloudy, it was also hotter than on previous days, well over 100 degrees. About 9 km before reaching Nachna, a bigger sand dune obstructed the road. Hanwant worriedly creased his brow but gave it a try anyway. We got stuck, irrevocably stuck. Our pushing did not make any difference. We were unable to do anything but sit and wait for another vehicle to come along. After about half an hour, two jeeps appeared, approached the sand dune, got stuck for a little while, but eventually emerged on the other side. Hanwant urged both of us to go with them, but I did not want to leave him there all by himself, without even a drop of water in this incredible heat. We argued. He kept insisting, "Madam, you must carry out your programme. I am okay here, don't worry. You do your work, then come back. I will wait here. If we go on by car, we will just get stuck again." Finally, we reached the compromise that Manu and I would take a lift with the jeeps to Nachna, sign in there with the police post, come back to bring him a bottle of water and a few packets of cigarettes, then go again to Nachna.

Nachna was a somewhat depressing place with a ramshackle appearance. By the time we got there the second time, it was raining cats and dogs. We took shelter in the Rajpurohit Lodge and from the intensity of the stares that followed my every move, it was evident that no white person had been here for eons, if ever. At least nobody offered me a camel safari.

Sitting there communally and watching the sky emptying itself out, creates a sense of togetherness even among total strangers, and conversations take their course naturally. Manu translated the gist of what our tea neighbour had to say:

"Life in Nachna had been disturbed by the arrival of the Indira Gandhi Canal, a big irrigation project that was supposed to bring water from the Punjab into the desert. People were happy before the canal arrived ten years ago. But then the Punjabis came and bought all the land. Although there was supposed to be allotment of land for local people as well, rich people came from outside and gave bribes to the officers."

"What about camels? Were they still of importance here?" "Much less than before," was the answer. "Previously, the Nachna Thakur paid wages and food to Raika and Sindhi Muslims for taking care of his camels. But then he sold them to the Maharajah of Jaisalmer and the system broke down. Now there is no grazing land for them anyway. Pastures have come under the plough due to the canal. And almost all their animals have died."

When the rains had tempered and reduced to a drizzle, we marched to the Nachna Fort where the mahajan, the addressee of the letter written by the Nachna thakur, was said to reside. Yes, he was there, an old man with a white turban. He opened up the letter and started reading it aloud. I only needed to catch the words "one tourist lady" to know that again we would have to undertake lengthy – and futile – explanations of what we were there for. No, he did not recall much about camels. Sure, they used to be there, but now there are very few. The thakur sahib might still own some, with Raikas looking after them. Would we like some tea? With that he seemed to have passed his communicative phase and resumed puffing his pipe. While we were waiting politely for the tea to appear, the downpour resumed and more rain came down heavily. We moved our charpais into the gateway of the castle. Mahajan sahib stretched out and fell asleep, snoring heavily and did not regain consciousness even when the tea was served. We gulped it down and took our leave. By this time, the ground was covered with several inches of water. I turned around briefly, feeling bad because we were leaving like that when I caught sight of Mahajan sahib's charpai floating on water like a water lily in a lake.

Had we learned anything new? Was it worth it? Well, we had reached Nachna but, in the process, it had lost some of its mythical character. Its fame for camels definitely belonged to the past. But at least we managed to get there and have a hilarious time.

The slight sense of satisfaction of having made it to Nachna against all odds, however, gave way to immense frustration later in the evening. We spent the night in the tourist resthouse at Pokharan, the site of India's nuclear testing range – a fitting conclusion to a strange day. While I was sitting on a dilapidated cane chair in the small lawn in front of the building and waiting for dinner, depression overcame me. The whole Jaisalmer episode had been more or less useless. It had driven home the point that it was not possible to just go and do some quick research, that first a significant amount of time had to be spent on building up relationships and social capital. Now only a few days were left and I had not come up with any significant new conclusions that I could report to the society that supported my explorations. My research had been a failure. Beyond that, I had no idea what the future held for me and my family. I was going back to Germany and then would have to focus all my energies on finding a job and supporting the household. It seemed unlikely that I would be able to return to India in the near future, if ever. The idea was unbearable. Even though I was bone-tired from the long day, I found it impossible to sleep and kept tossing and turning.

The next morning, when I was settling in the back seat of the Ambassador and we were ready to roll, Hanwant turned around. "Madam, I have a suggestion. There is this charan I have heard of. I think he can help you and you should meet him."

The "charans" were a caste of storytellers, family record keepers and chroniclers. They memorised the history of Rajasthan's royal lineages as well as of Rajput families in general, and passed them on orally from one generation to the next. Even now, each Rajput or Sindhi Muslim family had a hereditary charan who recorded family events – births, marriages, and deaths – in a big book. He regularly visited his client families, to keep track of these developments.

The charan Hanwant wanted me to meet, however, was not working for Rajputs but for Sindhi Muslims. Hanwant had heard about him in his enquiries on the side and expected that he would tell us something about the history of the Sindhi Muslims, including of their connection to the camel and how this animal came to Rajasthan. His name was Tejdan Charan and he lived in a small village near Phalodi.

I felt we were grasping at straws, but any diversion that could delay the return to real life was welcome. We successfully located the village, asked around and found his small one-room house but, of course, the charan was "out of station". Since his job was to record family events, he was travelling most of the time, wandering from one family to the next to document births, marriages and deaths. He had gone somewhere near Jaitaran, east of Jodhpur, his brother reported.

The last location on our itinerary before returning to Jodhpur was Bikaner – I wanted to have another stab at the archives in the Lalgarh Palace, hoping they would reveal in greater detail the military significance of the camel. Although it was in even greater disarray than at the time of my first visit, I found some documents that I had previously overlooked. There was ample information about the Ganga Risala, a camel corps founded by Maharajah Ganga Singh, the ruler who had played a seminal role in World War I and whose idea it was to green the Bikaner desert with a canal – the forerunner of the Indira Gandhi Canal. The Ganga Risala was frequently sent out to support British troops and thus saw service in the China War of 1900, the Somaliland Campaign from 1902 to 1904, in both World Wars in the Middle East, and in Sind in 1941 to suppress the Hurs. After independence, the

Ganga Risala and the Jaisalmer Risala were merged and eventually turned into the 13th Battalion of the Grenadiers Regiment of the Indian Army.

I was intrigued to note that the same problems that affected the Raika camels currently had also undermined the health of the Ganga Risala camels. In the annual report on the Bikaner Camel corps for the year ending 31 March 1910, I found the following passage by a Major Finnis, Inspecting Officer of the Imperial Service Camel Corps:

> It is most disheartening and of great regret to the State and all ranks of the Ganga Risala that the camels have suffered so much from "Surra". There is an improvement now and I hope by the end of this year that it will have completely disappeared. I look forward to seeing the Corps what it is meant to be namely, a mounted corps and not a dismounted corps which now it is, through force of circumstances.

There was an abundance of other references pertaining to camels. Sometimes they had led to fights between Bikaner and Jaisalmer.

> In 1829 AD the Bikaner forces invaded Jaisalmer to avenge the outrages related to the seizure of camels from the Bikaner territory by the Jaisalmer subjects. The Bikaner ruler alleged that the camels were taken away with the connivance of the Jaisalmer ruler. Therefore he despatched forces to punish the Sardars of Jaisalmer, who were implicated in the mischief....

Jodhpur was the last stop, and the return to the real world was now inevitable. Dr Dewaram came to see me in my room in the tourist bungalow and to say goodbye. He wanted assurances that I would be back soon, so I explained to him my precarious situation and family responsibilities. He listened solemnly and then said,

"Madam, I know this professor here at Jodhpur University. He once helped me out and is quite interested in the Raika and even in camels. He is a zoologist. Why don't we go and meet him?"

There was hardly time left. Hanwant had insisted on driving me all the way to Delhi for the cost of petrol. It was going to be a long haul and we needed to start moving, but I could not resist the temptation to put off my departure further.

The professor was at home and received me in his spacious and airy sitting room. A perky little man in his fifties with thick spectacles and clad in white cotton, he had once spent a year in Germany on a scholarship. Although he was a primate specialist, his fascination was desert ecology and he was concerned with the development of the Thar Desert. Sitting cross-legged in the corner of his couch, he listened patiently to the long story about my trials and tribulations in Jaisalmer and my association with the Raika. "Very good, Madam, I hope you can continue your research. I really applaud your hard work and dedication. Is there anything we can do to help you?"

"Thank you, but it will probably be impossible for me to come again. I am heading back to Germany just now and have to look for a job there. You see, I have family to take care of, " I replied.

The professor gave me a quizzical look. "But there are scholarships you can apply for in Germany. I could be your host for a research project! Please look into this!" He leafed through his address book and wrote down the name of an academic foundation in Germany on a piece of paper. Then he accompanied me to my waiting vehicle outside. "Do follow this up! And stay in touch! We will help you!" he assured me and then waved us off.

I was grateful for leaving on a hopeful note. Hanwant wanted to know all the details of my conversation with the professor and then fell into his customary silence. We were bound together more by shared stillness than easy-going dialogue. The rather desolate landscape with scarce and minimalist desert trees sprouting thorns rather than leaves flew by – apparently this stretch had not yet benefited from the monsoon. There was a turn-off to the left, a signboard, and Hanwant suddenly stepped on the brake. "Jaitaran...wasn't this where the charan was supposed to be having some work?" he asked more to himself than to me, for I did not have a clue what he was talking about. "Madam, I think we should try and find him. Maybe we will be lucky."

Before I could refuse or consent, he had already veered off the main road, like a bloodhound hot on the tracks of wounded game. He stopped at the next tea-stand. "Where do the Sindhi Muslims live? Is there a Sindhi Muslim dhani here?" he asked.

"In the next village, after about 5 km, there are quite a few Sindhi Muslim houses," was the answer.

We followed the directions and identified the Muslim quarter on the basis of a mosque and the clothes of the people milling around.

"Have you seen a charan here? A charan from Sankali village, name of Tejdan Charan? We are trying to find him," we asked around.

Some schoolboys came to our rescue. "Yes, he was here about four to five days ago," they confirmed.

"Any idea where he was heading for?"

"He went towards Diravali, I think," said an older woman.

Diravali was the next village. "Has there been a charan here lately?" we enquired there.

"Yes, but he left about two days ago, the day before yesterday, in the morning," was the response.

We continued in the same direction, then faced a fork in the road. No trace of him in the next village, so we backtracked and tried the other tine of the fork. We were getting closer – for in the first hamlet we came across, he had left only that morning. After about 4 km, we picked out the silhouette of a single man walking ahead of us along the road. As we came closer, we could see he wore a colourful turban and carried a satchel. "I think this must be him," muttered Hanwant and leaned out of the window. "Ram, Ram! What is your name? Are you by any chance from the village of Sankali? Yes? Then you must be Tejdan Charan...we have been trying to find you for weeks, searched for you all over Rajasthan, the entire area between here and Phalodi. Sit down in the car, let's drink some tea somewhere!"

Tejdan Charan did not blink or bat an eyelid. Never losing his composure nor uttering a sound of surprise, he sat in the front seat and accompanied us to the next tea-stall while Hanwant explained our ("Madam's") mission to him.

His version of how the camel came to Rajasthan is as follows:

> An ancestor of the Mehars, named Sayra Baghani, lived in the village of Lankia, about 12 km north-west of Umarkot which is in Pakistan today. Pabuji's charan told Pabuji, who was looking for a wedding gift for his niece, about Sayra Baghani's camels. So Pabuji tried to capture Sayra Baghani's camels. The two fought each other and it seemed that neither would relent till death. Pabuji's charan saw this and exchanged their turbans. This meant that they became brothers (*dharam bhai*) and had to respect each other's wishes. Sayra Baghani, therefore, wanted to gift his camels to Pabuji. But Pabuji refused, saying that he had nothing to give in return. Sayra Baghani then asked whether he could give him his charan as a present. Pabuji agreed to this. As the charan was a gift of Pabuji, he is respected by both Hindus and Muslims and, today, charans serve both Hindus and Muslims.

Basically, he had repeated the same story that Professor Mehar had already told me. I asked if he had any idea when this event happened.

He answered, without any hesitation, and like a schoolboy who has learnt his history lesson. "Madam, this was in Vikram Samvat which is the year 1266 AD in your reckoning."

"Was this really the first time that camels were brought to Rajasthan? You are sure that there were no camels here before then?"

"Absolutely, Madam."

"But can you tell me, when and how the camel reached Pakistan?"

"Basically, the camel arrived together with the Arabs who were the ones who domesticated it. And the first Arab to come to Pakistan was Muhammed Qasim, in 711 AD."

Tejdan had an answer for everything we could think of asking him. He was a walking dictionary with respect to Sindhi Muslim history in particular, but also Rajasthan history in general. We could easily spend days with him to benefit from his knowledge and it was a shame that we did not meet him earlier. But we were already several hours behind schedule and the road to Delhi was long and bumpy. With great reluctance we extrictated ourselves from this intriguing encounter, thanked Tejdan profusely for taking up his time and expressed the hope that he would grant us another audience some time in the future.

We should have been elated with our luck, but this was not so. For the remaining twelve hours of our journey to Delhi, we could hardly talk. We had to focus all our attention on manoeuvring the murderous traffic in the capital. With the help of a map, I tried to guide Hanwant to my guesthouse and we found it quicker than expected. I treated Hanwant to a final cup of tea, but he seemed out of his depth, confused by the Delhi traffic. He gulped it down and took off.

Chapter 7

THE EAR-TAG PROJECT

"As the times changed, the Dewasis also changed a little and bought some land and some wells. It became necessary for them to send their children to school. The present situation is that only 10% of my brothers will live off livestock. The others have no animals and their future is in darkness."

– Ruparam Raika's diary

Winter 1993

Back in Germany, my task was to find a job and make a new start. My problem was that I did not fit into any disciplinary pigeonhole. My research record was a mixture of anthropology and animal science, with archaeology and ecology thrown it. This had been no hindrance in the USA where I had been able to teach in an Anthropology Department despite having only veterinary credentials, but in Germany I had become a misfit. I needed to reinvent myself to fit into one particular academic discipline. But which one? I saw no scope in veterinary medicine itself. Animal science seemed more appropriate, but my orientation was too general and a research proposal had already been rejected. Anthropology was most attractive, but there were relatively few opportunities in Germany and I was warned that it would be a dead end. More or less by chance, I temporarily found a disciplinary home in zoology. It was not only the zoology professor in Jodhpur who egged me on, but another one in Germany who offered me an affiliation and the opportunity to teach part-time. The German professor who promoted the subject of "cultural zoology" suggested I subsume my research under this heading and try for my "Habilitation", that uniquely German degree that attests to the ability to teach at a university.

While I wrote a proposal for this, the Indian professor was active at the other end. Due to our brief meeting, he seemed to have developed an avid interest in the camel and the Raika.

Together we organised a conference on the future of pastoralism in the Thar Desert that took place in Jodhpur in early 1993. It was a notable meeting because, besides the usual contingent of scientists and developmental experts, a large delegation of Raika, and even Raika women, participated. At most such occasions, attendance is limited to experts who talk *about* pastoralists but not *with* them. Maybe for this reason it turned into a tumultuous event for some Raika around. Bhopalaram accused the scientists saying that their research did not really address the pertinent issues and their needs. This caused an éclat and the two groups – scientists and Raika – even started beating each other up with their shoes. While I found this terribly embarrassing at the time, in many ways the Raika were right. They also brought out a statement that succinctly listed all the problems that their community experienced.

Statement by Pastoral Federation (*Pashu-Palak Sangh*)
at the Workshop on Pastoralism and Common Property
Resources in the Thar Desert (March, 1993)
(Translated from Hindi/Marwari by V. K. Srivastava)

We propose the following measures for improving the situation of pastoralists:

1. **Grazing problems**
    a. Protection and development of *gauchar*, *oran* and *agor*, and the routes leading to them.
    b. Illegal occupation of these areas should be stopped.
    c. Permission to graze in the Aravalli forest area.
    d. Forest enclosures should be opened after every five years.
    e. Support for grazing on fallow lands after the harvest.
    f. Permission to graze in neighbouring states on minimum charges.
    g. Development of grazing near the Indira Gandhi Canal Project.
    g. Elimination of *Prosopis juliflora* from grazing lands.

2. **Financial measures**

    For the sake of economic upliftment, the prices for animal products should be raised according to the increase in the prices of other commodities. Taxes should be imposed on imported wool, to encourage local wool production.

3. **Management of marketing of animal products**

    Pastoralists are often cheated in the wool markets and made to sell 5 kg wool for the price of 4 kg. Building of cooperatives should be encouraged.

4. **Animal healthcare programmes**

    The pastoralists should be given vaccines and anthelmintics at a reasonable rate. The programmes of the Department of Animal Husbandry and the Sheep and Wool Department should be organised so as to reach the pastoralists.

5. **Shearing**

   The pastoralists should be introduced to new mechanised methods of shearing.

6. **Education**

   For education, boarding schools should be opened and the students given scholarships.

7. **Permission to use arms**

   For protecting themselves during migration, the pastoralists should be permitted to keep licensed arms.

8. **Help to pastoralists during emergencies**

   Pastoralists should be provided help at the time of epidemics, natural calamities, and accidental deaths in encounters with anti-social elements.

9. **Representation of pastoralists in different bodies**

   Pastoral representatives should be invited to voice their opinion in different governmental and non-governmental bodies dealing with the welfare of pastoralists and the marketing of pastoral products.

Dr Dewaram and a few other old Raika acquaintances were there and we had another meeting to formalise "RAIKAS" since so far his efforts in this direction had floundered. One of the participants in the meeting was Adoji. After assuring me that Mira was in fine fettle and this time pregnant for good, he requested a separate rendezvous, so we arranged a meeting at the house of Komal Kothari. While I made my way by autorickshaw to the quiet suburb where Komal Kothari lived, I wondered what kind of favour he was pressing for this time. It did not take long to find out, for he was accompanied by a young man in his early twenties – his son Ruparam. Adoji did not beat about the bush that he wanted me to arrange a job for Ruparam, who was well educated for a Raika, having passed Class 10 and would be an asset for any employer. I had so many connections – I must be able to do something for him! It was really necessary for him to get a job, since, as I knew, they were a poor family and there was hardly any income to be made from camel breeding.

I rapidly scanned through the options. Certainly, I knew no potential Indian employers. But maybe *I* could hire Ruparam – there really were not that many literate young Raika around and surely he must be able to do something useful, such as collecting information and data...this might provide unique insights into the community. Last year, when we had made the first effort at distributing medicines for the camels, I had set up a registered society in Germany, the League for Pastoral Peoples (LPP). Its purpose was to support pastoralists through technical support and advocacy. I was sure that my fellow board members would agree if Ruparam became our local liaison person with the Raika community...our first employee. The idea appealed to me.

But what was Ruparam doing at the moment? "He is working in a cement factory. The work is not good and the pay is low. He is much too highly educated to work in such a job," Adoji explained.

It was a risk, but with the help of Komal Kothari we negotiated a deal. Ruparam became our field assistant, and he was to regularly report to Komal, besides sending me monthly reports by mail. His main assignment was to record the migration route of his father's camel herd, and to document other aspects of camel management.

By the beginning of 1994, my efforts at proposal-writing had paid off. I had been given a long-term scholarship to do research towards my Habilitation, which would qualify me to teach at university level. The fellowship even provided the opportunity to bring my whole family to India. We would set up house in Jodhpur and I could cater to the two most important matters in my life without being torn apart. Although I had some apprehensions about how Jon and Aisha would cope with yet another new school and Gary with being a house husband, it was like a dream come true and I felt all my previous problems could be sorted out.

I arrived in Jodhpur in February and was welcomed by both Hanwant and Ruparam who had been in close touch. Ruparam had the good news that Mira was expected to give birth soon, while Hanwant seemed to be determined to be "at my service", as he put it. He helped me find a house for the family by putting an advertisement in the local newspaper to which the owner of a nice bungalow in Paota replied. I quickly rented the place and readied it for the arrival of the family a few weeks later.

Everything seemed to fall into place, for, at the end of spring, we received the additional good news that we would finally be able to have a real, a proper project for the benefit of the Raika. It was funded by a German charity whose programme coordinator was familiar with the difficult life in the rural areas of Rajasthan and had a sympathetic ear for the plight of pastoralists. It was an exhilarating feeling to be finally taken seriously, to do something with a more official character, and to even have funds at one's disposal. This project had to be administered by a local organisation, and it was fortuitous that my professor had already set up an NGO which could be in charge. The overall goal of the project was to improve camel husbandry so that it once again became a profitable occupation and continued to provide a reasonable living for the Raika. This was to be achieved through action research – the collection of data that would enable us to understand what was really at the root of the Raikas' problems, followed by analysing whether there was any way of solving them.

Another objective was to mobilise the Raika into self-help groups and enable them to take their fate into their own hands. All this had sounded great on paper and made a very convincing proposal. Now, actually putting it into practice was something different. We had to establish a permanent base in the project area, hire staff and, most important of all, ensure the active participation and cooperation of the Raika.

The project was baptised as the Camel Husbandry Improvement Project (CHIP) and provided for a handful of positions, including a veterinarian/animal scientist, a social scientist and a couple of field assistants. Hanwant was to be the project manager. When I had written the proposal I had created this position for him, because he had become indispensable to me in sorting out the myriad of bureaucratic, technical and social problems that characterise day-to-day life in India. He had also proven to be a very efficient organiser and would be good for certain technical things, such as looking after the motorbike and the jeep, arranging supplies, and so on. Although he had already become a sort of security blanket for me, it was not foreseeable at this stage that he would soon turn into the linchpin of the whole operation.

Our first job was to find a field office, a project headquarter somewhere in Pali district. Originally, it had been envisaged that this might be in Anji-ki-dhani, since it was, after all, Adoji and his crowd who had instigated the whole project by persistently asking for help and for medicines. On second thoughts, Anji-ki-dhani was an impractical choice, since none of the camel herds could actually be encountered there, except for a couple of days at Holi and Diwali. Instead, as had become evident from Ruparam's recordings, they were migrating throughout Pali district without a fixed location for about nine months out of the year. Only during the three months of the rainy season did the pace of migration slacken. Then, all fifty or so herds were positioned just outside the forested ranges of the Aravalli Hills, to wander into them for grazing during the daytime.

Once again, it was our relationship with Adoji that precipitated a decision and let us move ahead. His tola had a long tradition of spending the rainy season near the small village of Rajpura, a few miles from Sadri. Located on the main road from Jodhpur to Udaipur, Sadri offered distinct logistic advantages quite apart from having felt almost like home on that first fateful visit three years earlier. So we started looking for an appropriate house to rent in Sadri, an endeavour that immediately revealed itself as a major problem. Although there was no shortage of suitable houses in Sadri and most of them stood empty, their absentee owners would never dream of renting them to outsiders, and especially not foreigners. These affluent property owners going about their business in Bombay or other big cities often belonged to the Jain religion, and were, therefore, very concerned about non-vegetarian food cooked on their premises or about any drinking of alcohol.

We asked everywhere and met polite rejection as soon as we started explaining why we needed a place to stay in Sadri. Camels and Raika? If you want to do something with camels, you should go to Jaisalmer. Here we don't have camels, was the general tenor.

Hoping for a more enlightened response, we paid our respects to a local noblewoman, the Thakurani of Ghanerao. Serving us tea on a lofty terrace of her gently crumbling castle, she graciously offered us her "garden cottage" to rent – a perfectly preserved period piece from the colonial era complete with bulging chintzy sofas hidden under dust covers, a dining table with eighteen high-backed chairs, Chinese vases, and gold-rimmed mirrors. Not very office-like in character, but so atmospheric that I was tempted. Of course, it was way out of the range of our budget – actually, in our inexperience, we had neglected to include house rent in the budget of our proposal. After weeks of searching, we finally managed to track down two tiny rooms on the first floor of a small building whose owner, a Muslim schoolmaster, was willing to let them to us. It was obvious that they would not do once the temperatures got hot – they were tiny, had no ventilation and the ceilings were too low to attach a fan. Nor was there any bathroom. Still, it had to do – at least it would provide a space to store our things, such as medicines, even if it was uninhabitable. The rent seemed pretty steep and we were furnished with a leaflet of draconian rules and regulations. Drinking alcohol and smoking was forbidden in the rooms. The only advantage of the place was its location on the road that connected Sadri with Rajpura.

The next problem to be tackled was hiring of staff, but this was the responsibility of the professor in Jodhpur. An advertisement had to be drafted and placed in an appropriate newspaper, candidates needed to be interviewed. Furthermore, the jeep that had also been sanctioned as part of the project still needed to be delivered. While this was in process, Hanwant and I set off to introduce the Raika community to the project.

The project was designed to address the problems as they had been articulated by the Raika – especially those from Anji-ki-dhani – in countless interviews, conversations and informal meetings over the previous years. Couched in developmental terms, it was aimed at strengthening the community economically – by improving camel husbandry – and socially – by organising them into pressure groups. But the Raika saw everything in much simpler terms. Most of their needs, as perceived by them, were embodied and epitomised in the teeka, the injection that protected their camels against trypanosomiasis. This teeka would stop their female camels from aborting or dying, thereby resulting in a higher birth rate and a larger number of young camels to sell at Pushkar. Their idea of a project was a teeka project in which Madam would give free medicines to each one of them. The teeka was what they wanted from me and they hoped that Hanwant and I would continue to make it available for free.

We had no definite proof that it was trypanosomiasis that was causing the abortions. But since starting the prophylactic campaigns a couple of years earlier, abortion rates had declined significantly, according to what we were being told. It was also clear that while tryps could be diagnosed quite reliably by means of traditional knowledge, the indigenous treatments were not satisfactory. These were very unspecific and included such recipes as preparations of chili peppers or of *tumba* (*Citrullus colocynthis*), feeding one mouse daily for four days, administering sheep milk, or drenching with a swig of donkey dung dissolved in water.

The very old owner of a veterinary drug shop in Jodhpur had once enlightened me about why the Raika were so keen on the teeka. Apparently, this had a long history going back to 1939 when industrially produced trypanocides were first introduced to Rajasthan. At that time, Ummaid Singh, the Maharajah of Jodhpur, had donated the substantial sum of Rs 100,000 to distribute them for free. The Raika had become staunch believers in the benefits of these medicines but, unfortunately, in the 1970s and 1980s, the foreign-based companies who had produced them, stopped the supply. This resulted in severe shortages and trypanocides could only be obtained via the black market, smuggled in from Pakistan.

Of course, there was no possibility of emulating the generosity of the Maharajah of Jodhpur. This was an action-research project in which we had to determine if giving medicines was economically worthwhile. My idea was that we should constitute a test herd which would receive prophylactic treatment against trypanosomiasis as well as other veterinary care, as and when needed. We would then compare the performance of this test herd with that of a control group which did not receive such inputs and calculate whether the added inputs also translated into added profit.

Trying to fathom how this concept could be executed in practice, I had come to the conclusion that the animals that received the medicines would need to be equipped with ear-tags so that we could identify them and collect reproductive data from them. I had tried to explain this idea to Hanwant who had nodded his head in a noncommittal way and without exerting himself verbally. Somehow I had the uneasy feeling that this ear-tag idea would be considered too much of an interference and not go down very well.

Hanwant, Ruparam and I journeyed down to Anji-ki-dhani in the Ambassador which had temporarily been rented by the project. We rolled along the now-familiar highway to Pali and then took a left towards Sojat.

At this moment I felt foreign and tense and when we passed through the alley of old neem trees that forms the final approach to Anji-ki-dhani, I had butterflies in my stomach. Although I had adopted local clothes, picked up Hindi and put in a lot of hard work to bring about the project in response to the continuous requests of the Raika for help, I still felt an intruder and was extremely uneasy about the reaction we would get. As always, a few men were napping on the *kotli*, while a couple of women were moving about, balancing water-filled *matkas* on their head. When Hanwant revved up the diesel engine before turning it off, some of the sleepy figures groped for their turbans and stared at us in a disoriented way. I wanted to give them time to compose themselves and emerged slowly from our vehicle, but after perfunctory greetings, Ruparam rushed us through the narrow alley that led to his father's home.

"Take rest, Madam," he urged me. "I will arrange everything." Then he disappeared to alert the women of the house and set into motion the routine for receiving guests. Following Hanwant's cue, I took off my shoes and stretched out on a charpai. Within minutes, Ruparam returned carrying bhakals and pillows and proceeded to turn the string-bed into a resting place fit for a princess. This hospitality ritual succeeded in making me feel welcome and esteemed, so I began to relax and resign myself to the fact that everything was down to fate and Hanwant's negotiating skills. My role was merely that of an onlooker.

One of Ruparam's sisters brought glasses of water on a tray, followed by tea. Then lunch consisting of *dal* with cloves of garlic and of roti with onion chunks was served on copper thalis. By the time we were wiping up the last bit of dal, two bearded, old Raika had come, greeted us with a namaste, crouched into a corner of the room and filled a clay pipe with tobacco. Gradually, more men, most of them older with beards and prominent, hooked noses that made them look like Afghan warlords, and all of them wearing turbans, trickled in and sat down on the rough camel-hair rugs that had been spread out. Although everybody huddled together closely, eventually the entire floor space was filled up. Some younger men passed out small steel bowls filled with tea, and one older character with a long beard, doled out small morsels of opium.

Hanwant and I sat elevated on a charpai at one end of the room; while Hanwant looked very composed, small beads of sweat ran down his forehead. Suddenly the murmur and mumble in the room turned into silence and all faces were expectantly turned towards us. Quietly and in a comforting voice, Hanwant explained why we had come. He was speaking Marwari, so I could really only understand an occasional word. But I fathomed that his narrative started out with a reference to the bad economic situation of camel breeders in general, to the complaints of the Anji-ki-dhani people in particular, to Madam's past attempts to provide them with medicines. That due to her love for camels and the Raika, we wanted to help them make camel breeding once again profitable.

That we needed their cooperation for this and that there should be mutual agreement. We would provide them with veterinary treatment, but also had to make sure that it was really worthwhile to spend a lot of money on medicines, or whether there were other ways of solving their problems. Therefore, we needed to monitor the effect of the medicines on the camels and see whether it really stopped them from having abortions. We were looking for some camel breeders who would cooperate with us and allow us to record the births, deaths and abortions in their herd, in exchange for getting their camels provided with the teeka. These partners would have to commit themselves to the project by allowing their camels to be equipped with ear-tags.

I was trying to read the expressions on the faces of our audience and felt that most of the Raika had problems grasping this proposition. There were requests for clarification and Hanwant patiently explained again and again. Apparently uncertain what to make of the offer, with a hint of suspicion, the men formed small circles and started discussing among each other. They don't trust us, I thought, and they have never heard of ear-tags. Probably, they don't even know what ear-tags are. Why should they agree to this when, in the past, they received the teeka for free? Like all pastoralists, they would anyway be loath to let outsiders know how big their herds actually are.

But before I could talk myself deeper into this scepticism, Gautamji, Ruparam's elder brother suddenly indicated he wanted to speak and announced that his family was ready to cooperate. There was a brief silence, and then another arm went up. "I also want to participate." Hanwant asked for his name and for his father's name and then wrote this into a notebook. Now there was a general commotion, people got up and crowded around us. "Put my name also on the list!" "My name is Pabudan, son of Ramaji, and please write it down..." Within seconds it seemed as if the atmosphere of doubt and wariness had spun around and our project had turned into a bandwagon everybody wanted to get on. One Raika after another dictated his name, adding his father's too for closer identification. They watched as this was written down, then turned towards me and gave me a respectful namaste. Some of them tried to talk to me and, when I did not understand, attempted to communicate in sign language. I could sense some cautious excitement in the air, but within half an hour, everybody had unceremoniously dispersed.

On the way back, I tried to sound out Hanwant for his impressions and evaluation of the day. "There is more interest than I thought. I hope we will be able to involve everybody," I ventured, hoping that he would share my interpretation of events. He was deep in thought, steering the car around the potholes. "Yes, Madam, there was some interest. But we will just have to see what happens."

A couple of days later, I was having lunch with Jon and Aisha, listening to their adventures with the street dogs and stray cattle that roamed the gully outside our bungalow and to whom they had given individual names. They were just relating their observations of a fight between two bulls called Blue Boy and Rupert when the doorbell rang and Ruparam was standing on the porch with his shy smile. I seated him in the living room, keen to hear news from the horse's mouth and any pertinent developments in Anji-ki-dhani after our departure.

Ruparam did not seem too eager to talk, but gradually divulged that almost all of the people had changed their mind. They felt that they could not trust us, that ear-tagging meant they would relinquish ownership over their animals. They even had expressed the fear that Baiji, meaning me, was doing this in order to take all their camels to Germany. However, his father had trust in us and would also convince the four other Raika in his herding group to participate. We could ear-tag any time we wanted, as long as we would give the ear-tagged camels the teeka at the same time. In fact, his father was quite keen that we give the teeka as soon as possible for the rainy season was approaching and it was best to protect the camels beforehand.

In the evening, Hanwant dropped by and evinced not too much of a surprise about this turn of events. "Okay, we will come as soon as possible," he assured Ruparam.

But we could not jump into action immediately, because we first had to hire a veterinary doctor who could administer the teekas. In the meantime, quite a few applications for the veterinary post had been received, all of them from fresh graduates of the Veterinary College at Bikaner Agricultural University. At first glance, there seemed to be quite a selection to choose from, but when we invited the first batch of candidates for an interview in Sadri, only one showed up. He seemed nice and capable enough, but it turned out that he was a Chamar, from a leather-worker caste and, therefore, despite his academic degree and everything, considered untouchable by other rural people. Hanwant immediately commented that the Raika would not accept a veterinarian from such a social background. I was livid about this – certainly I would not tolerate any discrimination on the basis of caste in a project I was involved in and I was upset and extremely disappointed with Hanwant whom I had so far judged to be a tolerant person, above such petty and archaic matters as caste. Hanwant quietly insisted, saying, "I do not have a problem working with a Chamar, but if the Raika find out about it, then they will not cooperate with us; furthermore, nobody will rent a house to us – our landlord will not allow an untouchable on his premises."

After long discussions, we arrived at the compromise that we would hire the doctor, if he would refrain from telling anybody about his caste association – after all, his surname could also be interpreted as Rajput. But our doctor absolutely refused to agree to take the job under these conditions and I admired him for that. In the meantime, he had also been offered a post in the government which was infinitely more attractive than working for a project of limited duration.

While we were interviewing and dialoguing with other applicants, Ruparam was conveying increasingly urgent messages from his father, enquiring why we had not yet made good on our promise of applying the teeka. His herd was now near Rajpura and he was waiting for us. He was not only concerned about his own camels, but also about Mira who needed this treatment, he said.

Finally, we had assembled a veterinary doctor and all the necessary supplies, including the vials with the white powder, the sterile water, syringes and needles, the ear-tags, and a form that I had designed to record the details of individual camels. Everything was packed into the Ambassador and, at the crack of dawn, we headed along the narrow asphalt road that connects Sadri with Rajpura and seems to lead directly towards the silhouette of the famous fort of Kumbhalgarh.

The Raika were ready for us. After we had gone through the mandatory ritual of sitting on the bhakal, drinking tea and exchanging news and pleasantries, everything went entirely smoothly. The camels were caught and handled very efficiently. Hanwant put on the ear-tag, the doctor gave the teeka and I wrote down the name, age, status (pregnant/with calf/empty) and distinguishing features of each camel. It was exhausting work, but fulfilling – a major milestone achieved.

However, just when we had familiarised him with the project goals and introduced him to the Raika, our new veterinarian got a placement in government service and left us on the second day. It quickly became obvious that the Rajasthan government's

Department of Animal Husbandry had offered postings to all Rajasthani graduates of the veterinary college. Nobody was going to opt for a two-year job with an NGO project if he had the possibility of a permanent job with the government. Our only option was to hire somebody from outside Rajasthan, a situation we had wanted to avoid, because of expected language problems. A succession of doctors followed, but none of them managed to establish a rapport with the herders – this was not only their fault, but also that of the Raika who were "amused" at the ignorance of these young graduates vis-à-vis camels and often did not hesitate to make fun of them. After a while, we found that we had to resign ourselves to doing without a veterinary doctor. Meanwhile, Hanwant had also learnt to give injections and become pretty skilful at it; even I revived my dormant veterinary skills.

Ruparam documented pregnancies, abortions, live births, fate of the calves, etc. He also kept track of the movements of the test herd, noting down where the camels stayed overnight and on whose field they camped. Every time we visited our test herd, the herdsmen would bend over backwards to show respect, touch my feet and do their best to convey their gratitude.

However, these manifestations of deference also started to be coupled with niggling demands. Adoji hinted that Madam should also pay the grazing fees levied by the Forest Department, including the bribes. This would be only a few thousand rupees, not much for me. And it would "help us people so much, we are so poor." I was taken aback by this. After all, we had already spent a lot of money on medicines, why should we commit ourselves to suddenly take over all expenses? I was certainly sympathetic to their cause, but this problem would have to be solved at a different level, by interacting with the Forest Department, perhaps. A few days later, we got a phone call from the professor in Jodhpur, wanting to know what was going on. He had received a complaint from the Forest Department. Some Raika had stated that his camels had permission from the German government to graze in the forest for free... This was indicated by the ear-tags the camels were wearing. We quickly found out that Adoji was the culprit. When we addressed him, he was unrepentant.

In order to avoid being taken hostage to the demands of one group, we had to extend our project to other families. We also had to work with the Godwar Raika, Hanwant said. We had to try to involve them in our programme to keep a balance with the Anji-ki-dhani Raika who belonged to the Maru subgroup. It should actually be easier to work with them, since they were not as mobile as the Anji-ki-dhani people. Their villages were strung out along the base of the Aravalli Hills and they grazed their animals in the forest during most of the year, without having to venture far from their village. Whereas the Anji-ki-dhani people seemed to be continuously on the move, changing their camp sites almost daily, the Godwar camel herders tended to come back to their home village every night.

We picked up the thread in the village of Latada where I had had my introduction to the Godwar Raikas three years earlier. Savantiba, whose herd had been the first one that I visited back in 1991, remembered me and was willing to cooperate. After he had taken the lead, his brother, his nephew and two other camel owners from Latada also offered to have their animals tagged. On Christmas day 1994, Hanwant enlisted the five herds in Latada. We were pleased as punch about this; it increased our samples and afforded us the possibility to somehow make clear to Adoji that we were not entirely dependent on him.

But this sense of progress did not last long. I had been gone for Christmas and was eager to meet the new partners. We ear-tagged about forty camels here, Hanwant explained proudly while we were walking down a gully between the thornbrush-enclosed compounds. Suddenly, we were face to face with a Raika who looked at us angrily, extending towards us his fist in which he was holding a bunch of ear-tags with hairs and even some streaks of blood on them. I could not understand what he was saying, but there was no way of mistaking that he was in a belligerent mood. Hanwant tried to calm him down, slapped him on the shoulder, but the man was not to be appeased. We sat down somewhere and from all I could surmise, a stream of accusations poured out of him which Hanwant was steadfastly denying. Throwing the ear-tags at our feet, the man finally got up and walked away dejectedly.

Hanwant, usually a model of composure, was looking equally upset and almost on the verge of tears. Gradually, I wheedled out of him what had happened. Apparently, somebody had told the Latada camel herders, that the Anji-ki-dhani people had received Rs 4,000 in cash for each camel enrolled in the project. Naturally, the Latada people felt deprived and wanted to have the same deal. Unless they also received Rs 4,000 for each of the camels tagged, they would not cooperate with us, and therefore, they were giving back their ear-tags. Hanwant tried to convince him that all this was an evil rumour, that by no means were the Anji-ki-dhani people receiving preferential treatment. But to no avail, these Raika remained adamant that we had screwed them over.

Never before had I seen Hanwant so frustrated. Dejectedly, we drove off on our motorbike, discussing what we could and should do, whether the only sensible thing to do was to pack up. But that would have meant defeat and giving up, in some way also the end of a dream to help the Raika, the camel, and the relationship between them to survive and get the recognition it deserved. As would happen at regular intervals over the next five years, we just hung on despite seemingly unsurmountable obstacles and misgivings. For a few days, everything seemed touch and go, but then, as is always the case in India, things started looking up again. Savantiba and another herder in Latada, Rajaram, were still with us. Then a Raika from another village, Sewari, came to our makeshift office and also wanted to sign up. The draw of the teeka and the belief in its magical qualities – which from my perspective were far from proven – were irresistible. From then on, "rumours" also spread the other way – here was a source of the much-desired miracle medicines – and lured camel breeders from near and far to our seedy office, eagerly requesting their camels to be tagged.

Within a few months we had tagged twenty herds with a total of more than 300 female breeding camels. Activities settled into a routine. Hanwant and I would go on visits early every morning to the registered herds, record changes in the herd, such as births, death, sales, purchases and in return, provide owners with advice and treatment. The project motorbike that had replaced the Ambassador did its part in breaking down barriers with the local people. I had been unaware of the symbolism of the Ambassador – the extent to which it indicated power and wealth. Anybody who emerged from it was regarded as enormously privileged and moneyed, on a par with a politician running for election.

We perfected our method of registering herds and keeping track of individual animals, to the extent that we felt we could do away with the tags, which often fell off anyway. The method was quite simple. At the beginning, herds had seemed to us to be composed of similar-looking animals in various shades of brown between whom it was difficult to distinguish. After we had registered several herds, we realised that they could be broken down into matrilineages. The Raika customarily named female camels after their mothers. So in any herd there would be three to four animals with the same name and which would be mother, aunt, daughter, granddaughter or so. So when we registered a herd, we would first ask for the oldest camel, and then for the offspring. So now we ourselves could identify each animal by asking for its name and then its kinship with other animals of the same name.

Since all the ear-tags were imported from Germany at some expense, I suggested that we stop using them. But since the Raika had come to understand the tags as a ticket for free medicines, they strongly resisted this idea.

We also started amassing data. Earlier it had always been difficult to find out even the most ordinary things, but now people started to confide in us freely. Even more important than the medicines was the social part of our visits. People poured out their family problems, usually relating either to money (or lack of it) or to marriage arrangements.

Economically, the lives of the Raika revolved around camels or other livestock, but socially everything was dominated by marriage and weddings – making the match, the event and the ritual itself, and the many and far-reaching complications that arose when the arrangement somehow did not work out. The matrimonial process is probably central to the social life of all rural castes – but the way the Raika went about it was different from other Hindu castes in some important ways.

Like their Maru kin, the Godwar Raika also practise child marriages, in the sense that the liaison is fixed, although not consummated, when the bride and groom are still very young. Contrary to the general pattern among Hindus, it is the parents of the bridegroom that get burdened with most of the expense. The preferred type of arrangement is "*atta-satta*", meaning two families mutually exchange a boy and a girl. For instance, the daughter is married into a family which then reciprocates by providing a girl who can serve as a bride for her brother. Of course, this system works only for families that have a balanced number of sons and daughters. If families have no daughter to give in exchange for a bride for their son, then they either have to pay a substantial sum of money, or the son has to work in the family of his in-laws for seven years, as a so-called *ghar-jamai*. For this reason, the Raika often preferred the birth of a girl to that of a boy – a situation entirely opposite to that in the rest of Hindu society.

It is the parents of a boy that take the initiative and ask and look around for a suitable girl. If they hear of a promising candidate, they go and visit several times, inspecting the girl and asking details about her lineage. If both parties agree to an engagement, the girl's parents make this known by hosting a meal of *churma*, a sweetened dish made with wheat or millet in which gur and ghee is mixed. This stage of the process is called *gur galna* and signals that the parents of the girl have given their consent to the union.

The next step is to make the contract known to the rest of the society and all the relatives. This is done by holding an *amalgal*, an opium session which is announced by the *ṣargara*, the village drummer. This makes clear that the family has committed itself to the union. To seal the deal, the in-laws give one rupee to the girl in front of the assembled elders.

Next, the parents of the boy send four outfits for the girl, consisting of *ghagra* (the traditional nine-metre skirt) and *odhni* (the veil).

But before the actual ceremony, months or even years may pass because, in order to economise, it is usual to wait until several girls are in queue, sometimes as many as thirty or even thirty-five. Eventually, the date is set by a brahmin priest. Then a countdown of preparatory activities is set into motion, revolving around buying supplies, arranging the props, making the event known, and beautifying grooms and brides by rubbing their bodies with turmeric and ghee. Preparations, of course, take place in the villages of both the girl and the boy.

In the boy's village too, his departure, the *bandoli*, surrounded by all the villagers, is preceded by three days of partying, with both maternal and paternal relatives conducting predetermined rituals. For instance, the groom's sister will throw salt at him to protect him from the evil eye. And a very special role belongs to the maternal uncle who, upon his arrival on the scene, will honour his sister, the bridegroom's mother, with the gift of an odhni. Later, in the bride's village, he sits together with the bridegroom on the camel when his task is to hit the wedding arch, the *toran*, with his sword.

The decisive moment, at which the marriage is solemnised and bride and groom turn into husband and wife, is the *phera*, the circling of the fire seven times. After four circles, the officiating brahmin interrupts the procedure and requests the bride's parents to give her a gift – the *kanyadaan*. Usually this will be a camel or a cow.

After the phera, milk mixed with ghee is served. The best man cracks jokes, cotton is thrown, and then at the end of the night's festivities, the groom and his party depart for their village. The girls, of course, stay back with their parents. The last act for the time being is two days later when the girl's parents send ingredients for a meal to the groom's family.

So far so good. The real problems often begin at the time of *ana*, when the girl has to start living with her in-laws, usually at a fairly mature age of around twenty years. By that time, the girl has had plenty of time to develop her own ideas. It frequently occurs that the girl does not fancy her husband and then refuses to stay with his family. If this happens, then it is the father's duty to force his daughter to go. If he can't or won't do this, then the council of elders meets and determines a punishment. This is usually an outrageous sum of money and until this sum is paid, the family is given the "*olma*" (temporary outcast), which means that no other Raika can come to their house and eat food or drink tea, or engage in any kind of social interaction. Of course, marriage negotiations for the remaining children are also stalled. Nobody can marry into a family while it is under olma. In order to re-enter society, in addition to paying the fine, a big feast has to be paid for.

Savantiba, who had been such a pillar of support for us, had become a broken man due to a marriage dispute around his eldest daughter. After already having lived at her in-laws' place for several years, she came back home to her parents and stubbornly refused to return. It was not quite clear what her problem was. Her family was unable to persuade her to go. Savantiba was called by the *panches* who decided on a heavy fine. There was no way he could come up with the amount. At that time he owned only two camels and a small goat herd. For years his whole family remained excluded from the social system, with consequences for other children for whom marriages could not be arranged. Eventually, he managed to pay the fine and host the large dinner, but he had lost his spirit and joy of life and died shortly after.

There was very little we could do for Savantiba, although as a gesture of support we gave a job to one of his sons – as office assistant. But Hanwant was able to extend help to the Raikas in other matters. Child marriages, of course, were outlawed. If the police became aware of such a marriage in the offing, they would make threats of raids and arrests. But, it was not possible to call off such massive operations on short notice, when the perishable supplies had already been purchased, *lapsi* for thousands of guests was being stirred in the cauldrons, and the bridegrooms and their entourages were already on their way. The Raika banked on Hanwant's Rajput connections to ease interactions with the police. They sent him either to the *thana* (police station) to negotiate for lower bribes, or they asked him to be present during the wedding day as a kind of guard preventing the worst if the police really started arresting. Hanwant was very successful at this and several times sweet-talked the police from taking action. This was another matter that threw me into a bind. Child marriages were illegal and certainly the antithesis of social progress. How could we support such archaic customs, especially when there were so many cases where the arranged marriage had backfired and led to such social and financial hardships for families ? As an outsider, did I have the right, or was it prudent at all, to interfere in such matters? Whenever such incidents occurred and I mulled over the issues at hand, I eventually concluded that it was the society itself that had to decide to change and that any attempts to influence it would be futile, besides jeopardising the rest of our work. The Raika had requested my help for camels and not for social reconstruction.

With respect to camels, things were moving along nicely. Ruparam accompanied the test herd and conscientiously kept a diary with all significant and non-significant events. His data helped us to better understand the predicament these large herds were in. In their quest for grazing opportunities, they changed their night halts every two days on average, never staying for more than a maximum of five to six days in one place, unless it was in the rainy season. It was no problem for them to find a place to rest. In fact, as noted earlier, most landowners welcomed them because of the manure the herds left and recompensed them for this with flour, tea, sugar, and other items, sometimes even money. The herds changed places with the greatest frequency in April and May. When the first showers of the rainy season came, this time at the end of June, they had to leave the fields since these were to be cultivated.

In early 1994, Mira gave birth to a male calf. Ruparam came to Jodhpur to bring me the good news and, together with Hanwant, we travelled to Pali to inspect the second member of my nascent camel herd. Gautamji welcomed us and it was obvious that he and the other men in the herding group were pleased on my behalf. The baby was delightful, reddish-brown with a grey tint, sturdy joints and curly hair. While Mira's nature was more reserved, this one was a charmer that followed me around on tottering legs, pulling at my dupatta, exploring the texture of my hair, and nuzzling my face. I was enormously proud and distributed a box of sweets, as is the Hindu custom for celebrating a happy event. The new addition was baptised "Mahendra", taking the cue from "Moomal and Mahendra", the Sindhi love epic.

But my joy did not last long. Within a couple of weeks, another message was transferred, this time by phone. Mahendra had died, despite all efforts by Adoji to save him. It was not clear immediately from what – diarrhoea, pneumonia, or snakebite... now I was experiencing the ups and downs of a camel breeder's life, as well as the proverbial slow reproductive pace of the camel. It had been almost three years since I had bought Mira, and so far I had had only expenses and no income.

When we attended the Pushkar Fair this year, it was as insiders. We helped prepare the young camels by administering dewormers and even vitamins. Surprisingly, the Godwar Raika had never participated in the Pushkar sale, but always relied on traders to come a few weeks before and purchase their crop of young male camels. The traders had stopped coming during the last couple of years.

Adoji, however, sent off his youngsters with big fanfare for the fourteen-day march from Sadri to Pushkar. Sitting on a bhakal, he portioned off morsels of gur to his herdsmen, while mothers and youngsters were separated. An old female camel had been selected to accompany and guide the new crop on their hike to the market.

We drove to Pushkar on the motorbike, riding for the best part of a day. When we left Sadri early in the morning, it was

Sawaram Raika from Latada posing with a newborn camel just before leaving for work in Mumbai. Photo credit: Ilse Köhler-Rollefson.

Bhanwarlal Raika herding his camels during the monsoon. Photo credit: Ilse Köhler-Rollefson.

Hanwant Singh discussing camel health issues with a group of migratory camel herders. Photo credit: Xavier Lecoultre. Copyright: Rolex Awards for Enterprise.

Camel herd from Khabha going out for grazing.
Photo credit: Ilse Köhler-Rollefson.

The Raika camel herds depend on access to the Aravalli forests during the monsoon season. Photo credit: Ilse Köhler-Rollefson.

Start of the Camel Yatra. Photo credit and copyright: LPPS Archives.

The Camel Yatra in the midst of the Thar Desert near Rasla.
Photo credit: Ilse Köhler-Rollefson.

The Raika demonstrating for their forest rights in Sadri.
Photo credit and copyright: LPPS Archives.

Hanwant Singh explaining camel poo paper at our stall in Pushkar.
Photo credit: Ilse Köhler-Rollefson.

Dailibai Raika tasting camel milk ice cream at our stall in Pushkar.
Photo credit: Ilse Köhler-Rollefson.

The Raika delegation enjoying the Swiss Alps. (Left to right) Tolaram Bhopa, Rama Raika, Mangilal Raika, Dailibai Raika and Hanwant Singh. Photo credit and copyright: LPPS Archives.

The Raika and other pastoralists advocating for 'Livestock Keepers' Rights' in Interlaken. Photo credit and copyright: LPPS Archives.

so cold that we had to stop at every tea stand on the small road that snakes north along the Aravallis. By nine o'clock, we had gradually peeled off our blankets and coats, and by noon we were sweating under the hot sun and dodging the heavy truck traffic on the main highway from Jodhpur to Ajmer. By four o'clock in the afternoon, we reached the pass that separates Ajmer from our destination and offers a superb view of the wide sand bowl of Pushkar.

The Pushkar Fair may seem like chaos to visitors from outside, but it is actually an amazing feat of logistics – just ensuring water and food for the tens of thousands of animals that are brought there is no small deed. It may seem like an unstructured maze of people and animals to the uninitiated, but it is actually composed of long-standing *deras*. Every camel-breeding area has its own dera, a place where it ties up its camels, spreads out its luggage, and makes a fire. So the initiated easily know where to find the Raika from Mewar, the Raika from Anji-ki-dhani, from Sojat, and the Muslims from Jaisalmer or from Sanchore. The traders walk around in pairs, point their sticks at a camel and ask for the price. Once a deal is done, a red ribbon is tied around the tail of the animal. Before they can be removed, they have to be registered and issued a *chithi* from the Mela administration.

We also purchased a male breeding camel. Adoji had been begging for this. "Our bull is getting old apart from having served for four years, and I don't have money to buy a new one," was his frequent lament. "It is something the project should do," he averred. The idea appealed to me, not least because I wanted to know by what criteria the bull would be selected. I had many times tried to find out what the ideal camel looked like, but the answers had not been satisfying, partly because of the language problems, partly because – it seemed – the inability of the Raika to express this verbally. They always made some strange signs with their elbow that I could not interpret. This could be an opportunity to look at different animals, discuss their pros and cons – a real learning experience for me.

Of course, this was not the way it happened. Adoji was not making any moves to look at breeding camels. Maybe he was too busy selling his own. I kept asking him, but only received shrugs or unintelligible replies. Then, on the last day, when we were getting ready to depart, he came panting. "Madam, I found a very good camel; I already negotiated a price and made arrangements with the seller. We need the money," he said. Of course, I did not want to give the money without seeing the animal. "Where is it?" I asked. "I want to see it!" Hanwant was not around, unfortunately. "Somewhere over there," Adoji gestured towards another hill. "We need to be quick, otherwise the owner will be taking it back home."

Fortunately, Hanwant came along just at the right moment. Both of them took off while I trundled behind them, trying to comprehend Adoji's barrage of words extolling the attributes of the camel – "*nasalvala*" (of good breed), from Sanchore (in Rajasthan's Jalore district), of a good colour and height. It was also very good value – he had negotiated the price down to Rs 18,000. Rs 18,000! I could hardly believe my ears – this made it one of the most expensive male camels on sale at the entire mela. Good strong male camels fit for work cost about Rs 8,000–7,000, and for Rs 10,000–12,000 you could get something really special.

Hanwant was as sceptical as I was. The camel was nice all right, of a dark brownish colour (*telli*), without any blemish, perfectly turned out, with nice hair designs, and well behaved and the owner was really sad to part with him. But the price seemed pretty steep. Adoji did his best to prevent Hanwant from haggling, but he reduced it to Rs 14,000. That was still more than we had envisioned, but somehow, we also did not want to go back without a stud bull – our Godwar friends were keen to have the benefit of a superior bull that would, they maintained, significantly raise the prices of their young camels and contribute much to their economic returns. As the data Ruparam had been collecting indicated, the price of young camels varied quite markedly, from less than Rs 1,000 to as much as Rs 5,000.

We made the deal with the owner and Adoji proudly walked off with the new purchase. We never found out whether he had received a commission for this deal, but "Moti", as the camel was named, later proved his worth. People came from far and near to have their females covered by him and, as a consequence, Adoji's herd almost doubled in size. Moreover, Moti's offspring fetched more than double the price the Godwar Raikas had previously been able to achieve for their young camels.

Unfortunately, Moti was killed after only two years by electrocution from a high-voltage electricity line that had fallen down (or was purposely placed that way, according to some sources). But his legacy lived on, his genetic contribution was significant, and even now, all these years later, people refer to him and to the great quality of his offspring.

Chapter 8

THE MILK MIRACLE

"Water is soul, but camel milk is life."

– A Somali saying

"Camel milk is hazardous to human health."

– Rajasthan High Court judgement

Our research clearly indicated that the income of the Raika was directly linked to the number of female camels they owned and how efficiently these reproduced. Earlier, the Raika had had an infinite number of camels. "We used to have so many camels that we never even searched when some of them got lost," the Raika from Anji-ki-dhani claimed. Now, their herd sizes had decreased substantially, resulting in fewer calves being born and less money being made at Pushkar. In his diary, Ruparam had recorded the following statement by one of the elders: "At the beginning of the century, we had 10,000 camels belonging to our village; forty years ago there were 5,000. Now, there are about 1,000 camels and ten years from now, there will be none..."

Even though I did not take these figures literally, it was obvious that there was more than a grain of truth in the claim.

Hanwant and Ruparam were able to confirm the prevailing trend by conducting a survey of camel herds in the southern part of Pali district. Of the 174 families they interviewed, more than eighty per cent reported that they now had fewer camels than twenty years ago.

I was still trying to figure out whether camel herd sizes were decreasing because of a conscious decision to sell off camels, or involuntarily, due to losses caused by disease coupled with a lower reproductive rate. The Raikas insisted that the latter was the case, elaborating that, "When camels are kept on an empty stomach, diseases rise. When camels are hungry, many have abortions."

Ruparam had another interesting quote in his diary, according to which, "Earlier, female camels became pregnant by three years of age, but now they are at least four or five years old when they become pregnant for the first time."

All these shreds of information seemed to add up to a situation where the number of camels was too high in relation to the available grazing resources. Because of nutritional deficiencies, they were not able to live up to their reproductive potential, and, therefore, numbers were reducing. But how could one break this vicious cycle? It seemed to me the only solution was to keep a smaller number of camels and provide them with better inputs – be it feed or healthcare, so that the rate of loss – through abortions and calf mortality – was lowered. But smaller herd sizes would further depress the precarious economic status of the Raika...The answer to that would be to expand the range of camel products, taking the cue from camel pastoralist colleagues such as the Bedouin who made the most of every conceivable aspect of the camel – in contrast to the Raika who only sold male offspring.

But, in light of the many cultural restrictions that held for the Raika, this was a difficult proposal. Culling old and unproductive animals and making use of camel meat was certainly not an option because it went against the grain of everything the Raika believed. Even mentioning this would cast me in the role of a villain, not only in their eyes, but in those of Hanwant as well. The potential for making use of camel wool seemed virtually nil – the yields were small, the fibre very short, making it difficult to spin and process, and the wool itself quite scratchy.

But the milk... I longingly pondered the potential of camel milk as a source of income, recalling how camel pastoralists in East Africa manage their animals for milk, in fact, keep them for that very purpose. In the Horn of Africa's dry lands, camels are much better milk producers than any other domestic animals – not only in terms of daily yields, but, crucially, also with respect to the length of the lactation period. Whereas cows, sheep and goats give milk more or less only during the rainy season, camels can be milked all year round and continue to yield even during extreme droughts. The Somali, in particular, value camel milk beyond anything and associate it with strength and endurance. I had read about how camel milk was marketed in this country through a network of women. Then, in Mauritania, there was a famous camel dairy which had developed a range of camel milk products, including a delectable 'Camelbert' cheese and, in Israel, a scientist who had come up with several delicious recipes for camel-milk ice cream.

In addition, camel milk was also said to have certain extraordinary qualities and to be extremely good for health. Its exceptionally high Vitamin C content – three times higher than in cow's milk – was scientifically proven. In Kazakhstan, tuberculosis patients were systematically, and apparently successfully, treated with camels' milk. In Arabia, camel milk was regarded as an aphrodisiac. Researchers had not yet been able to prove any of these claims scientifically, but the empirical evidence appeared overwhelming.

In Rajasthan too, I heard comments that camel milk provided protection against typhoid and some other diseases. The Raikas themselves were a living testimony to its beneficial effects – with their scarce but strong physiques, their ability to march endlessly, their general good health. Camel milk was relished by herdsmen and their families as an excellent source of nutrition that invigorates and strengthens the body. When on migration, it formed the mainstay of their diet. Offering a guest a drink of camel milk was part of the hospitality ritual and anybody visiting a herd would be pressured to partake either in its fresh form or as tea.

But the taboo against selling camel milk, as explained to me by Dr Dewaram, was still very evident. Everywhere I had gone, we had heard it time and time again: one should not sell camel milk because certain deities, including Pabuji and Mahadev, had forbidden it. "Selling camel milk is like selling one's children" was one of the most popular proverbs. Instances were given of how the wrath of the gods had descended on the few people who had tried it: frequently, all their camels had died within a short time span. Selling of camel milk thus amounted to a forbidden subject. A report written by the scientists from the NRCC stated it explicitly: In India, camel milk is not marketed on any scale.

Should one try to educate the Raikas and enlighten them? Or would this be nothing but an act of interference from outside? Shouldn't they themselves decide? After all, there was something to be said for the refusal to commercialise this product and rather give it away for free when needed. From the outset, I had felt it culturally insensitive to tell people to sell their camels' milk so that they could pay for our camel medicines. I would not do it. Even if some Raika would consider selling camel milk, who would buy it? Hindus had no habit of drinking camel milk; the very idea was repulsive to communities who considered the milk of cows as a gift from God. I had noticed that many times when I had tried to tell villagers about the popularity of camel milk in certain Arab and Muslim countries.

By March 1994, however, we found that the tide was beginning to turn and opinions were changing quite radically. One hot and sultry evening, Ruparam returned from one of his fact-finding missions, bursting with excitement. "Madam, in Udaipur, Chittorgarh, and some other places, there is a camel milk market. Even some of my relatives in Mewar are selling milk and making very good profits. Please come and see for yourself!"

I could hardly believe my ears, but within a day Hanwant and I, with Ruparam in tow, mounted an expedition in our trusty Ambassador to Mewar to see with our own eyes. Our first stop was in Rebarion-ki-dhani, just outside Udaipur. One family here had actually hit upon the idea twenty-five years earlier, in a desperate attempt to escape from poverty. The father had started out with selling the milk of seven camels for Rs 1.5 per litre. His son had increased the herd size to eighty animals and now sold about 30–40 kg per day which made him quite a big earner by local standards.

Around Udaipur and Chittorgarh, a market had slowly developed and there were about twenty Raika camel milk vendors who each collected about 50–70 kg milk daily from herd owners. It was not a very spectacular procedure; they brought the milk in milk cans tied to their bicycles very early in the morning and sold it to tea-stalls. But for us, it was hugely exciting. Here, there was no talk of anything bad happening if one sold camel milk; it was just a means of squeezing out a little bit of additional profit every day. The milk was sold at a price slightly lower than cow's milk and quite a bit less than buffalo milk which was valued more because of its high fat content. It was significant that the milk was sold to tea-stands. It was mixed with the milk from other animals, thus the tea drinker would never know that his tea was made partially from camel milk. We hung around the town square, where many tea-stalls were located, and mingled with the crowd. Babutaram, a Raika with a yellow turban – which seemed to be the favourite colour here among the Mewar Rebari – was holding forth about the intricacies of camel milk marketing and the tricks of the trade, but annoyingly, I could understand very little of it. My partners in investigation were too engrossed in his tale to bother to translate to me, but I picked out the words Malwa and Malvi unt very often. Malwa, I knew, was an area outside Rajasthan, in the north of the adjoining state of Madhya Pradesh. "Malvi unt" would mean the camel from Malwa. Was there a special camel breed in Malwa? I wondered to myself, but decided that this was unlikely. Malwa really was outside the camel-breeding area – it was a fairly high-rainfall zone, not suitable for raising camels. The official list of Indian camel breeds did not include a Malvi breed and this region was not considered part of India's camel-breeding tract.

When Babutaram had finished his sermon and I eagerly looked at Hanwant for a translation, he summarised: "He is saying that the heart of the camel milk market really is south from here, in Madhya Pradesh, especially in the town of Jawra, although there are other towns in Malwa where camel milk is sold – Indore, Ratlam, Bhopal, and so on. Many of the Rebari from around Chittorgarh have actually migrated down there with their herds to sell camel milk. He says we must definitely go to Jawra and see the camel milk market there."

"And what is this about a Malvi camel – he was saying something about that, wasn't he?"

"Yes, he was. Apparently, there is a special kind of camel in that area that gives a lot of milk and many of the Rebari from Mewar have been buying it. I also don't understand completely."

Regrettably, we couldn't just continue driving to Malwa, because this would require at least a couple more days, and my family was waiting for me in Jodhpur. So we had to mount a separate expedition a few weeks later. Malwa was quite time-consuming to get to, being located in what Indian bureaucrats refer to as "the interior". The roads were hellish and there was little in the way of accommodation en route. While Rajasthan was equipped with tourist bungalows in most major places, northern Madhya Pradesh was a blank spot on the tourist map and bereft of any such facilities.

By the time we were able to leave for Malwa, it was mid-April and very, very hot. My family had already departed for the cooler climes of Europe, although they had left behind Snowy, a white, dwarf Pomeranian that Jon and Aisha had been given as a gift by the owner of a riding school. Snowy, named after the dog in Jon and Aisha's favourite literature, the comics about the adventures of Tintin, had been the runt of his litter and a bundle of tick-infested misery when he arrived, but had now developed into a fine and self-confident personality. I, on the other hand, had been ill with typhoid and was finding it difficult to regain my strength. My stomach could not cope with the regular spicy and ghee-laced Rajasthani cuisine, which presented problems on excursions since it was the only fare available. But this was the last opportunity to do this trip before autumn. In May and June, it would be even hotter and during the rainy season, in July and August, it would not even be feasible to travel – rural roads could sometimes be submerged for several days and one could easily get stuck for an unpredictable time period.

With several yards of a cotton dupatta wrapped around my head and fortified with water bottles, biscuits and fruit, I reclined languidly on the back seat as we finally set out for Malwa. Hanwant and Ruparam were in front, with Snowy self-importantly perched between them. We made it in good time to Chittorgarh where we spent the night in the comparative luxury of the tourist bungalow. Ruparam was the self-appointed "dog-walker", taking Snowy around on a leash for his evening and morning walk under the envious eyes of the hotel personnel. Early the next morning we were into unknown territory, soon crossing the border to Madhya Pradesh. This was very fertile agricultural land with black soil especially suitable for growing cotton but making for very monotonous scenery. I was draped over the back seat, wan and exhausted, whereas Hanwant and Ruparam were happily chatting to each other and apparently totally unaffected by the heat. Even Snowy, undoubtedly of German ancestry and handicapped by his luxuriant long coat, looked neat and fresh with his pink tongue providing both a cooling mechanism as well as a fetching splash of colour to set off his spotless white coat.

Hanwant and Ruparam – especially now that even Snowy had cosied up to them – were not my favourite group to travel with since I felt left out of their male companionship. They never integrated me into their conversations and only talked to me in a formal way, addressing me as "Madam". After all that we had been through together, a slightly more casual relationship would have seemed appropriate. But this was India, and Rajasthan in particular, where high-class women traditionally kept to the *zenana* and never ventured out at all, I reminded myself, wondering why I had to subject myself to this bone-rattling journey through potholes and blazing heat. I felt isolated, drained of energy and ready to quit at any opportune moment. It was only the lure of tracking something down that officially did not exist that kept me going.

But I had to give it to them – when it came to stalking informants, my crew was unbeatable. Once we made it to Jawra, a fairly substantial but unstructured town with a population of several hundred thousand, it was amazing how, by means of a few enquiries at selected tea-stands, they could find out the haunts of the camel milk sellers and their daily routines. Somehow, they saw things that eluded me but represented valuable clues about where to look and where not for them. We were soon heading for a particular sweet-shop at the other side of the town, and, sure enough, found hanging around there a middle-aged and corpulent Rebari who could unmistakably and, from far away, be identified as being from Mewar by the colour of his turban and the way it was tied. We gave the reference of our informants in Chittorgarh and he immediately invited us for a *lassi*, beckoning us to sit down on wooden benches in the back of the shop. Not only that, he looked at Snowy and asked, "And what does he take?" He proceeded to order a separate cup of tea which he poured into a saucer and which Snowy eagerly slurped up. An animated conversation ensued. It turned out that he knew about our project and its involvement in making medicines available, so he was very pleased to make our acquaintance. He would be happy to show us where the camels were milked and how the milk was marketed. But right now, the camels were out grazing somewhere and we could only see them in the evening. Maybe in the meantime, we would like to see the shrine that Jawra was famous for, which attracted great numbers of Muslim pilgrims from as far away as Pakistan and Iran.

Muslim pilgrims. Was this why there was such a big market for camel milk in Jawra? Because Muslims had less of a hang-up about drinking camel milk than non-Raika Hindus? Although I felt far too weak to engage in any cultural activities, my team insisted that I see the shrine. Because it was Muslim, they themselves had no interest in coming and would wait for me at a tea-stand, but they assured me that they would take good care of Snowy in the meantime, so I need not worry. Not having the energy to resist,

I secured the dupatta over my head and made my way into the confines of the shrine. I was dazed and tired, but could not help noticing that the shrine predominantly attracted people with mental and psychological problems, brought there by relatives who requested a divine cure by tying coloured ribbons around the pillars.

I joined the male part of the crew at the tea-stand, and Hanwant tried to relate something to me that our new friend had told him. "Madam, our Shankarji here says that about twenty per cent of the milk sold in Jawra is from camels. The sellers of buffalo and cow milk are upset about this and they recently even organised a strike against the sale of camel milk, saying it was dangerous for human health. Fortunately, the district collector, the chief of police and some doctors took a stand in favour of camel milk. The Udaipur dairy also produced a written testimony in favour of camel milk. So, you see, in this area, camel milk is really a big issue." It was especially interesting that information about such matters seemed to circulate only locally. Why had neither we, nor the Raika in Marwar, nor the Camel Research Centre, ever heard about this?

Now it was late afternoon, and Shankarji indicated that we could begin to make our way out of town to the field where the camels would be staying overnight and wait for their return. The temperature had cooled down a bit, but my weakness and nausea were not letting up. We arrived at an ordinary harvested field where the only indication of a milking operation was a pile of odds and ends that included milk cans, camel-hair rugs, and the usual implements Raika take on migration. The sun was getting very close to the horizon and there was no trace of the camels. Apart from that, where were we going to stay overnight? In Jawra, I had seen no hotels, only some hostels for pilgrims. Nobody else seemed bothered about these minor details. Snowy, visibly happy to be unleashed, was ferreting out rodent holes, whereas Hanwant,

Rupa and Shankarji had spread out a bhakal and were sitting on it with folded legs, presenting such a relaxed image that it reminded me of a Mughal miniature painting of emperors sitting on a rug and enjoying a cool evening – even if here the water pipes were replaced by cigarettes.

"So, when are the camels going to arrive?" I interrupted, as by now I was beginning to run out of patience.

"They will be coming after sunset," said Shankarji, continuing, "Actually, they are milked only at night – thrice. During the day, their calves are with them, and they have to be separated first for the milk to build up."

"They will be coming only at night?" I asked with a sinking feeling. "But how can we photograph them? My flash is not working." One of our main goals was to document the milking of the camels, so that we had proof and could refute the claims that camel milk was not marketed in India.

"Don't worry, everything will be okay. I think now you should take some rest," said Hanwant and instructed the other two to dive into the pile and retrieve materials that could be used for bedding. He must have realised that I was on the verge of collapse and, for once, I was grateful for being able to "take some rest". I sank onto the surprisingly soft and comfortable bed created on the edge of the field and immediately fell asleep. I woke up for brief moments a while later, awakened by vague dreams which seemed to involve moaning camels and the clanking of milk cans, but each time quickly drifted back to sleep, oblivious to all the crucial activities going on around me that I had wanted to record. Then, again, I woke up in the middle of the night when all noise had died down and there was a splendid moon crescent right above me. Snowy had snuggled up in the bend of my knees. A few metres away, I could make out some vaguely human shapes which I presumed to be Hanwant and Ruparam. But I had not woken up to relish the cool and quiet of the night – diarrhoea had me in its grip and I needed to get somewhere quick. The moonlight provided just about enough illumination to orient myself and I dragged myself into a corn field and sat there, asking myself why on earth I had been so crazy as to come here when I was distinctly unwell, and just as temperatures were reaching the yearly maximum. With what seemed like my last bit of energy, I crawled back to my bedstead where I collapsed in a dispirited heap. I awoke again in the early hours of the morning, just before dawn, feeling slightly more energetic. As I sat up, I could see the whole camel herd – maybe a hundred-head strong. Milking was already in process, but what was most amazing were the camels. In Godwar, the camels were generally of a brownish colour, while in Mewar, they had a somewhat lighter hue and were built more solidly and with shorter legs. But the majority of the camels here looked entirely different: they were almost pure-white and very small – the Malvi camel! The realisation that this was truly a different breed of camel suddenly made all the trials and tribulations worthwhile. Coming across a new breed is the equivalent, for an animal scientist, of finding a new species for the biologist, I thought to myself. This was something we could publish and which people would take note of. Quite apart from the fact that we now had proof that camel milk was already being successfully marketed in India on a significant scale!

Milking was already almost finished and Ruparam was busy talking to the camel herders and taking notes. Hanwant immediately ordered a bowl of tea to be brought to Madam and Snowy looked ready for the next adventure – what a good egg he had been on this trip, I thought gratefully. Just like Aisha and Jon, he added a human touch to our operation, and opened up doors. The Raika had never seen such a type of dog before and with their affinity for animals, they all doted on him.

While I sipped my tea, two milk cans were fastened to a waiting motorcycle and off it went. I was struck by the comparative affluence of these Raika. Not only did they have a motorcycle, but they also had a different air about them, totally unlike that of the humble and lanky, sparsely nourished Raika we worked with in Godwar. They gave the impression of being successful businessmen. The son of Shankarji, who seemed to be the driving force, had a notebook in which he carefully kept his daily accounts and in which he had also calculated his projected earnings for the month and the year.

In contrast to most other Raika, who always tried to appear as poor as possible, he was actually proud to divulge the amount of income he made. He said that his hundred-head-strong herd produced about 75 kg of milk a day. In addition, he collected 75 kg of milk from other Rebari. His daily income, therefore, amounted to about Rs 675 a day or Rs 20,000 per month – an enormous sum by local standards – maybe three times the salary of a government schoolteacher! However, he also had expenses – for petrol, salaries of the herdsmen who took care of the camels, medicines, as well as for the grazing taxes levied by the government of Madhya Pradesh.

Other young Raika from Mewar were now also getting into the business and starting to buy camels from Marwar in order to build up herds and sell milk. Shankarji cited the example of his nephew who had started a business five to six years ago with a single camel. In the meantime he had increased his herd size to thirty-five animals and was selling 20–25 litres per day at Rs 6.

These Raika from Mewar were fat cats compared with the Godwar Raikas and it was all due to a sense of enterprise and putting aside of old taboos about camel milk marketing.

But this was not the whole story. Local conditions were also on their side. There was also a special type of acacia, the mimmar tree, that grew only in Madhya Pradesh and not in Rajasthan, that had highly beneficial effects on milk yields. The whole management system seemed ingenious. All the milk was produced only by means of grazing on natural vegetation. The camels were never separated from their young and were only milked when the calves were asleep. Thus, the milk intake of the calves was not impacted and the Raika also made profit from selling young camels at Pushkar and other fairs. Another helpful aspect was that camels provided milk throughout the year and that their milk yields peaked during May and June, a time when cows and buffaloes hardly produced anything. Thus, camel milk filled a seasonal gap in the local milk supply. For this reason, some dairies were also accepting camel milk, although not officially. They would only issue a receipt in the name of cow's milk.

I had one more question, and this related to the Malvi camel. Was this a separate breed and what was so special about it? Yes, it was different, and it gave a lot of milk. It had been bred by the local Rebari from Madhya Pradesh who were once associated with the Maharajah of Sitamau. They, the Mewar Rebari, were actually trying to buy as many female camels as possible in order to increase the productivity of their herds. The only problem was that because of their small size, the young male camels did not generate good prices at Pushkar. For this reason, the male camels they were using for breeding were of the Marwar breed.

If they continued doing this – crossbreeding the Malvi females with Marwar males – then the Malvi breed would eventually disappear, I cautioned. But such long-term thinking was not a priority in the minds of the Mewar Rebari – like most businessmen throughout the world, they were interested in short-term profits. In any case, it was clear that the Malvi camel was a distinct breed.

We would have to come back later and document it properly, take measurements, and meet the Rebari from Madhya Pradesh who kept the breeding herds.

For now, it was time to head back to Jodhpur. The trip had been worthwhile enough, providing a wealth of information and new ideas, options, maybe solutions for the struggling Raika in Godwar. All the excitement had carried me to a temporary high, but once we were back in the car, exhaustion set in and the disordered state of my digestive system became a concern again. Periodically, I had to stop the car and make a desperate dive to escape from sight behind the nearest mound or bush. By the time we reached Jodhpur, I was almost comatose. Nobody was expecting me at our house in Paota, so Hanwant and Ruparam moved my bed directly under the ceiling fan, called a doctor, purchased medicines, doused me with weak, sugarless tea, and fed me with rice and curd. Ruparam and Snowy kept guard in case I needed anything, and Hanwant informed my professor, who immediately rushed over on his scooter. I tried to tell him of our thrilling discoveries between trips to the bathroom and he shared our excitement.

Once I had regained my strength, I wrote a proposal, "Poverty Alleviation for Raika Pastoralists through Camel Milk Marketing", and the professor contributed a budget. We submitted it to a funding agency in Delhi and they liked the idea. They sent a consultant to undertake a feasibility study, which confirmed the viability of our proposed strategy to introduce the concept of camel milk marketing to the Godwar Raika. This was to be achieved by motivating the Raika to sell milk, helping them to develop the appropriate management practices for milk marketing, arranging for the collection and the transport of milk, creating a local customer base, and by lobbying for the wider acceptance of camel milk. We were not so naïve as to assume that all this would proceed smoothly, so our proposal also listed the expected hurdles: overturning the prevailing taboos against the sale of camel milk, tackling the logistical difficulties of working with migratory herds, and overcoming the reluctance of consumers to accept camel milk.

By July 1995, the project was approved. The operation that had started under the Camel Husbandry Improvement Project (CHIP) was scaled up by several notches. We now had funds to rent an office; there would be a project director, a project manager, consultants, milk collectors on motorbikes, and so on. I was to be associated with the project by being responsible for monitoring and evaluation – this would provide me an opportunity to keep track of events once my scholarship was finished and I had to return to Germany, which was soon. It was all a bit overwhelming, especially the new headquarter, a relatively luxurious villa replete with marble floors, in a gully right off the Sadri bus stand. A gleaming white jeep with tinted windows and a driver had also arrived.

The challenge now was to engage and structure all the new personnel and assets into a meaningful operation. The project director had a background in veterinary medicine and was a local person – we had insisted on this to avoid language problems, since even people from other parts of Rajasthan were not able to understand the particular local Godwar dialect. The project manager was a fresh graduate in agricultural sciences who impressed us with good grades but had little exposure to rural life. His first field visit to a camel herd had been a shock for him. "Madam, see how they are keeping the animals in the open. They do not even provide a stable for them. I am sure they cannot even calculate a feed ration," he said, shaking his head in bewilderment. I tried to explain to him that the Raika kept their animals on natural graze and were very familiar with the various fodder trees and their effects on the health of the camels and, in fact, were making an effort to provide a balanced diet by moving around in search for different pastures. Therefore, they did not need a stable. I pointed at a field with small maize plants and asked him what plant was growing there. He failed this test of fundamental botanical knowledge and, rather uncharitably, I gave him up as a lost cause.

Among the other people who were hired was the youngest son of Savantiba, Chauga Lal, who was put in charge of making tea and running the kitchen. He was a sweet and helpful boy but had been through some traumatic experiences. While working in Bombay, he had come under the influence of a group of *hijras* (transvestites) who were involved in criminal activities and he had had a brush with the police. Although it was not immediately obvious, underneath the surface he was a deeply troubled boy looking for a direction to his life.

Then there was the old guard – Hanwant and Ruparam. In the course of the last few months, Hanwant had undergone a total metamorphosis. Earlier he had been shy and unassuming, usually hugging the background, only emerging at critical moments when he felt that I was in harm's way and needed protection. Along the way, he had developed a real knack of dealing with the Raika. He somehow had a talent of working with them – he humoured them, goaded them on, scolded them, listened to all their problems and then proceeded to give sound advice or to solve the problems himself. Wherever he appeared, faces would light up and groups of people crowded around him, like moths around a light. To my surprise, he displayed real feeling for camels and animals in general, somehow being able to fathom what was going on in their heads and, having closely observed the string of veterinary doctors, was now able to undertake many veterinary interventions like a pro. He had also been instrumental in raising my status among the Raika, impressing on them how hard I worked to make available medicines and other benefits. They had started addressing me as "Baiji", a local designation expressing both respect and familiarity, and usually meant for an elder sister. Their initial wonder at what this strange woman wanted had given way to reverence – which often made me uncomfortable because I felt I could not meet such high expectations – but which was also deeply rewarding. We were perceived as one unit and referred to as "Bhaba and Baiji".

Ruparam, on the other hand, had distanced himself a bit, spending more and more time on leave in his village. But once again, his father, Adoji, and the members of his herding group were the trailblazers and the first to be ready to sell their milk with the help of the project. They had pioneered the ear-tags and now they pioneered the sale of milk. Adoji stationed the camels at their usual haunt in Rajpura, and a boy, hired by the project, collected the milk by bicycle each morning. Finding buyers among the tea-stands in the vicinity of Sadri was a piece of cake, because there was a milk shortage in the area. The tea-makers were lured by free samples and when they had convinced themselves that the addition of camel milk did not change the taste of the tea, they were ready to become customers. None of them liked to advertise that they mixed camel milk with other milk, but at this stage this did not concern us. Within a short while, another herding group from Anji-ki-dhani that was grazing near Desuri, also wanted to join the enterprise, so we had nine families involved. Then progress stalled. Other Raika were simply not ready for this. They kept relating horror stories of two brothers who had once started selling milk and whose entire camel herd had subsequently died. The two brothers had also been moved to this step by a desire to step out of poverty. "First, one camel had strange symptoms and died a little later, then the next, and the next, and the next. Within less than six months, the last of their camels died!" one old Raika told me with a flourish.

Where we encountered such beliefs it was not wise to press it. For sure, the next death or disease of a camel in the herd of somebody who started selling milk would be blamed on this and we could kiss all our well-meaning efforts goodbye. But our nine Maru Raika families had been selling for almost two months now, and nothing untoward had happened. They were bagging a tidy bit of money. This slowly began to arouse curiosity and envy. Some of the camel herders had literate, educated sons whose minds were open. One member of this new generation was starting a private school to run it as a business, because the economic prospects of his father's camel herd could not satisfy him. He convinced his father to come on board, so now there were ten families. But after that, for several months, there was no progress.

Then Hanwant had an ingenious idea. He approached a Bhopa who was held in high esteem by the community and related the whole story to him. This was a different kind of Bhopa from the one who had acted as a priest of Pabuji and re-enacted the episodes of his life. This Bhopa was a medium in whom the spirit of a venerated Rajput hero, who had lived centuries earlier, manifested itself during states of trance. In this temporarily transformed state, the Bhopa exerted supernatural powers and was able to solve a plethora of problems. For this reason, the rural people trusted and respected him. In case of any crisis, be it alcoholism, daughters-in-law with a mental disorder (disconcertingly frequent), a massive disease outbreak in one's herd, a son bitten by a rabid dog, they would usually consult a Bhopa. Bhopas represented an important problem-solving institution in Godwar fulfilling the function of a human and animal doctor, family therapist, and even a general sounding board and confidant all in one. They usually had a normal job as farmer, shopkeeper or herder and held trance sessions once a week or at certain days in the lunar cycle. Many of them hailed from the Raika community – in fact, the caste is known for the large number of spiritual persons it has generated. Vinay Srivastava, in his book about pastoral renunciation, linked this to their solitary way of life and total immersion in nature, day in and day out. It is fascinating to witness how the spirit descends in a Bhopa – with the help of a fire and frenetic bell-ringing by attendants – leading to a total transformation in his demeanour from a humble Raika to a personage resembling the most regal of Rajputs, hyperventilating and wielding a sword, and even imperiously twirling his moustache.

Hanwant told the Bhopa, who officiated in a temple in the middle of the forest, about our observations in Mewar and Malwa and about our hope that camel milk marketing could really boost the Godwar Raika economically. The Bhopa agreed eagerly – he also felt that the times had changed and there was nothing wrong with selling camel milk. He supported the idea. As a token of his endorsement, he handed Hanwant a small bag with divined kernels of wheat and asked him to distribute this to the Raika together with his message that selling of camel milk was entirely acceptable in these modern days and not against the wishes of the gods.

It worked. The news spread like wildfire and wherever Hanwant went, people had already heard, and offered, even begged, to participate in the milk market. It was another case of the cyclical development so typical of everything in India, beginning with the weather pattern. First there is a long drought, then it pours torrentially. After the Bhopa had given his seal of approval, we now faced the opposite problem of accommodating all the demands for collecting milk and setting up connections with tea-stands.

While Hanwant was active in the field, talking to the Raika, arranging milk-circuits, ironing out small problems that were bound to occur, the rest of the project staff were busy with paper work and documenting the expansion of the project. Meticulous records about all events were kept, progress charts were made, and future milk turnover was estimated. The project was in business.

Fortuitiously, an old friend of mine from college days, Juliane Bräunig, a well-known expert on milk hygiene, was eager to undertake some experiments on camel milk. She was curious about two things: the feasibility of making yoghurt and, secondly, the hygienic qualities of camel milk – to what extent was it contaminated with bacteria, which germs were involved and how quickly did these multiply after the milk had been extracted from the udder? She was especially interested in verifying some widely publicised claims that camel milk did not go off as quickly as that of goats and other animals and had a much longer shelf-life. In particular, it had been asserted that camel milk could be bottled up for weeks and still remain palatable.

Because this was a scientific exercise, we first needed to assemble all the tools that a microbiologist requires for her trade – the tubes, the culture media, the petri dishes, the pipettes. Unfortunately, we could not get hold of an autoclave, so all this equipment had to be sterilised in one of the chemistry labs at the University of Jodhpur and then transported to Sadri. After this laborious exercise was successfully completed, we held a meeting with the staff to highlight the importance of following a set procedure when collecting the milk samples for Juliane's experiments over a period of seven days. Milk samples were to be collected from camels, together with samples from goats for comparison. They were to be taken from the vessel in which the milk output of the herd was collected before it was taken to the tea-stand, filled into pre-labelled test-tubes, and transported back to the office as speedily as possible.

One of the bedrooms in our project HQ was temporarily converted into a makeshift laboratory. Here, Juliane made serial dilutions of the milk samples and then carefully swiped a few drops on to the culture media. These were then left to incubate at room temperature and, every twenty-four hours, Juliane would look at them and check for bacterial growth as indicated by the emergence of white pimples. She would count the number of spots and record them in her notebook.

Chauga Lal was watching all this with great fascination. Helpful as ever, he was keen to make Juliane's life easy by handing her the plates and assisting with counting, but she strictly forbade him to touch them or even come near them. Chauga looked hurt and we tried to explain to him that this was just a normal precaution in case the milk happened to contain some dangerous bacteria that were proliferating in the culture media. But how do you explain the word bacteria in broken Hindi? I tried: "very very tiny animals are growing very very fast", but this was not very convincing since the pimples certainly did not correspond to the local concept of an "animal" – they did not have any mobility to show for it. And why should minute quantities of milk that normally would have been drunk fresh or been processed into tea suddenly become a dangerous substance? The disbelief was mirrored in Chauga Lal's face. When I tried to tell him that the reason why some samples developed more spots than others was because the camel breeders had not adopted clean milking practices, he looked as if he doubted my sanity.

But the worst was still to come. When the experiment had been successfully completed, Juliane decided that the cultures she had nursed and observed so carefully for the past days now, needed to be destroyed – after all, they represented potentially harmful infective material. Usually this would have been done in an autoclave, but without that, she resorted to direct combustion. She took all the plates into the little front garden of the bungalow and incinerated them one by one with the help of a cigarette lighter until they were reduced to smouldering piles of black ash. I could almost see Chauga Lal's brain ticking. For an entire week, the whole project had revolved around experiments – samples collected with great care and effort, then practically guarded by Juliane's life, each tiny pimple counted and recorded in a big book – and now the result was consecrated to fire. It must have seemed absolutely crazy to him.

I had many times been secretly amused about the importance of the supernatural to the Raika, and how often it was referred to as an explanation for sudden diseases, in the context of spirits that descended into Bhopas, or pertaining to the evil eye. But this incident somehow taught me a lesson and changed my perception. To anybody without a bit of scientific schooling, Juliane's activities must have seemed very much like black magic or some kind of fire cult.

The results of Juliane's tests showed that there was no difference between camel and goat milk in terms of spoiling time. But the curd that she tried to make from camel milk, with the help of freeze-dried cultures imported from Germany, was horrible, both in terms of taste and consistency – the milk clotted very slightly, but did not curdle at all. Adding rennet in order to turn the milk into cheese was equally futile. So this confirmed the claim of the camel herders we had talked to years ago in Jaisalmer: camel milk just was not suitable for making curd. Yet, it did not explain why the Raika had turned this into a virtual taboo, and were firmly convinced that some of their heroes had prohibited the very act of making curd from camel milk.

But, there was no opportunity to muse about this given the dynamics the project developed. In a short time, the participating

Raika earned more money from milk sales than from the sale of young camels. But their commitment often faltered once the project stopped providing the infrastructural support. When the project came to a close after about two years and no longer facilitated the transportation of the milk, some Raika felt it involved too much labour for them and stopped the sales. This was, undoubtedly, a factor for the herding group around Adoji because they were so much on the move and, therefore, needed to continuously re-establish connections with buyers. Others gave up because they made a connection between the sale of milk and certain events in their life (such as a death in the family). Still, a core of camel milk sellers remained, and the potential of camel dairy for generating additional income on a daily basis rather than producing income only once a year, as in the Raikas' traditional system, had been demonstrated.

It was evident that the logistics of camel milk marketing would be facilitated if the dairy cooperatives that existed in practically every village for the collection of cow and buffalo milk – that was then ferried to Delhi for processing – would also accept camel milk. But it seemed to be hopeless. The dairy cooperatives were not allowed to do this officially. At a pinch, when they had to fulfil certain targets, they might do it unofficially, but never openly. Early on, I had contacted and met somebody in the Rajasthan Dairy Federation to discuss the possibility of official support for camel milk marketing. The person I talked to showed interest and promised to look into it and sent a delegation of scientists to taste camel milk. As I found out much later, they had come to the conclusion that camel milk was distasteful and had no marketing potential.

There were more problems to come. In May 1999, Hanwant received an urgent message from Bagdiram, a Raika leader from Chittorgarh who was involved in camel milk marketing himself.

Shankarji, the very first camel milk seller we visited in Udaipur on our exploration five years ago, had been sentenced to six months in jail and a Rs 1,000 fine by the Rajasthan High Court in Jodhpur, for the act of selling camel milk. The judge had deemed that camel milk was "hazardous to human health" and selling it, therefore, represented a criminal act. The justification he had given was the absence of a reference to camel milk in the Rajasthan Dairy Act.

Hanwant immediately organised a series of meetings to alert all the Raika in Mewar and Godwar about this development, impressing upon them that this concerned all of them and needed a concerted response by the community. They collected Rs 20,000 to have their caste brother released on bail and also hired a lawyer who was willing to challenge the case in the Supreme Court in Delhi. We amassed evidence to support the case – scientific analyses about the composition of camel milk, reports on its therapeutic qualities, articles about its dietary value to East African camel pastoralists, the value the Somali people placed on it, and so on. Juliane also wrote a strong statement using her official letterhead. The strategy worked and the Supreme Court overrode the judgement of the High Court. Shankarji's family was overjoyed. It was a big success for Hanwant, and for the community as a whole.

But one problem remained with camel milk marketing. It can affect the health of young camels if they are deprived of an important part of their nutrition, especially if the camel milk producer is poor or greedy and tries to sell as much milk as possible without regard for the welfare of the camel babies, who are often tied up during the day to stop them from drinking. Keeping the camels in one place also makes them vulnerable to mange mites.

In retrospect, it has often occurred to me that these negative consequences for the young camels are almost certainly the explanation for the Raika social restrictions on processing and selling milk. For their traditional system was geared only towards producing male camels for use in warfare and for transportation. Keeping camels for milk represents a contradiction to this strategy and results in a greater rate of loss of young camels. So what seemed like an irrational "taboo" actually represents a nugget of wisdom.

Chapter 9

ETHNOVETERINARY MEDICINE

> *"...the Rebaris have a test of their own... for Surra in camels, and, in India, the knowledge of it is practically confined to them."*
>
> – *A Treatise on the One-Humped Camel in Health and Disease,* A.S. Leese *(1917), p 240*

My *magnum opus* on "Camel Culture and Camel Husbandry among the Raika" was almost completed. It concluded that the animal husbandry system of the Raika was exemplary in many aspects - ecologically, socially and from the perspective of animal welfare. After it had received the final touches, it would be circulated to the sixty members of the commission for their approval and comments. Now it was time to select a topic for the oral presentation in front of the whole veterinary faculty. I already knew very well which subject I wanted to talk about: ethnoveterinary medicine.

Ethnoveterinary medicine is the study of the veterinary practices of non-western cultures. It was a subject which had recently generated much interest in development circles, thanks to the efforts of a two-woman interdisciplinary team – Constance

McCorkle, an American anthropologist, and Evelyn Mathias, a German veterinarian. They had established this entirely new veterinary discipline by compiling a bibliography of the many references to traditional animal healing practices that can be found in ethnographies and the travelogues of early explorers. The bibliography had spurred further studies demonstrating convincingly that many cultures – notably those who have a long tradition of raising animals, such as the Raika – have developed their own indigenous systems and institutions for providing preventive and therapeutic healthcare to their animals. In remote settings of developing countries, where "modern" services did not reach, this was still the prevailing approach to animal healthcare. Ethnoveterinary knowledge had thus become recognised as an important local resource that needed to be integrated into development projects, serving as a foundation for improving veterinary care and enabling livestock keepers to obtain better returns from their animals.

Occupying far-flung spaces, camel nomads were likely to be even more dependent on their traditional healing knowledge than other groups living in not-quite-so remote places. I checked the pertinent literature which supported my hunch. The Somali recognised at least twenty different camel diseases, while the Tuareg differentiated more than thirty afflictions. A Belgian anthropologist working among Tunisian Bedouins had catalogued more than 1,100 terms relating to the camel, most of them pertaining to its health and disease. I also recalled that among the Rashaida pastoralists in Sudan, we had documented twenty-two known illnesses in a very short period of research.

Awareness about this gradually emerging body of traditional knowledge which could on some accounts hold its own against western veterinary medicine, had not yet filtered into the consciousness of conventional veterinarians, so I thought my lecture would be an ideal opportunity to introduce the professors to this topic. My supervisor was not entirely convinced of the wisdom of this. "The faculty is very conservative. They may not like it. Maybe you should choose a more conventional topic, to be on the safe side."

But I swayed her reservations and gradually managed to convince her by providing tidbits of Raika ethnoveterinary lore. "Even the British colonial veterinarians were impressed by the veterinary skills of the Raika. One British camel authority conceded that the Raika method of diagnosing trypanosomiasis from the smell of the urine is just as reliable as examining a blood smear under the microscope." Infected by my enthusiasm, my supervisor gave me the go-ahead.

I eagerly embarked on a new round of field research. During my first research forays in Bikaner, I had collected a slew of related information or rather it had amassed itself almost automatically. In response to any question on problems with sick camels, many Raika had readily reeled out lists of livestock diseases, complete with prescriptions for herbal and other local remedies. Later, Dr Dewaram had also introduced me, with some pride, to traditional healers; one of them was his great-uncle who treated camels with a hot iron and who, in Dewaram's words, "Knew more about treating camels than a veterinary doctor." And the ever-vocal Bhopalaram had always gone on about Asuji Raika, a camel healer who had once been of great help to the Maharajah of Jodhpur when all his camels needed for warfare fell prey to an epidemic. Asuji was able to cure this disease and the Maharajah rewarded him richly. Some said that it was Asuji who had first developed the concept of isolating camels that were afflicted by infectious diseases from the rest of the herd. Even now, several hundred years later, Asuji was a source of pride to the community and there were efforts, albeit until now unsuccessful, to have his statue erected in Jodhpur.

I had never really made much effort to collect this information systematically among the Raika, partly because it seemed so easily available as to present no challenge and partly because there seemed to be little congruence between the information collected from different individuals. Everybody seemed to have their own recipes. But two observations had gradually impelled both Hanwant and me to take this subdiscipline more seriously. First, there was the growing realisation that the vets we employed were not able to fulfil the expectations that we had from them. They were young fellows, fresh from university, who believed they knew it all, although they had hardly any practical experience and were often not able to cope with minor and routine cases. Even more disturbing was their sense of superiority over the Raika and their inability and unwillingness to develop any real rapport with them. While I was spellbound by the Raika and their innate skills in managing their camel herds, these fresh-faced college graduates viewed them more or less with contempt, having been alienated by their academic training from practical and down-to-earth knowledge and failing to see how it was an integral part of their culture. The Raika, of course, sensed this attitude immediately and reacted in turn by making fun of the "boys" we sent them and were not above deliberately making their life difficult. Some anthropological skills and perspective should have been instilled into them in college, I often thought in exasperation. While Raika ethnoveterinary medicine might have its limitations, it was often a better option than the non-functional delivery of modern medicine.

I was tied up in Germany for the moment, waiting for the comments of the professors on my dissertation. So I requested Hanwant over telephone to do a quick survey of the significance of traditional veterinary practices for the Raika. We devised a small questionnaire asking which type of veterinary services people usually availed themselves of when their animal was sick: veterinary doctors, traditional healers, self-treatment, or spiritual healers. Hanwant interviewed twenty informants and none of them expressed a preference for veterinary doctors. Which of the other types of delivery system was made use of, depended on the type of animal that was kept and on the nature of the disease. Sheep and camel owners usually resorted to self-treatment, whereas cattle and buffalo keepers approached traditional healers. If diseases hit violently or seemed to have no rational explanation, then people usually resorted to a spirit medium who was considered to be in a position to appease the gods.

The fact that livestock keepers made little use of modern resources, although almost every village in Rajasthan had a veterinary hospital where treatment was given for free, provided another pressing argument for studying ethnoveterinary practices.

I could hardly wait to be back in Rajasthan. Our first step was to identify the healers. But this proved more complicated than expected, for it was difficult to decide who was a healer and who was not. Practically every Raika we questioned turned out to be a bit of a barefoot doctor with a repertoire of practices and rituals up his sleeve. Some specialised in particular diseases. Others knew how to speak mantras, certain formulas inducing divine healing powers. All Raika, both men and women, were adept at preparing their own home remedies, using such ingredients as fenugreek seed, sesame oil, garlic, dried ginger, molasses, soda, and ghee. Occasionally, they also resorted to more exotic ingredients such as elephant or donkey dung. Sometimes, they treated not only animals, but also people. One example of such a multi-functional healer was a woman named Dailibai who lived in a leaf hut on the road between Sadri and Ranakpur. Daili was not only an astute ethnoveterinarian, but also acted as a midwife and knew how to relieve human muscle and bone pain with massage. When we first met her, she immediately impressed us with her outgoing but dignified personality. For some reason, she was not highly regarded by the community, despite her healing skills which she demonstrated to us. She was desperately poor and had picked up a cow and a goat that had been discarded by their previous owners because of broken limbs. Dailibai had managed to heal their fractures with traditional splints and although their legs had healed a bit crookedly, these animals roamed around during the day, but came back at night to provide much-needed milk for Dailibai's three sons and one daughter.

Just like Dailibai, virtually every camel herder could whip up, at the spur of a moment, a herbal poultice if his camel was injured or lame. He would search for a few minutes, invariably less than half an hour, among the plants in the vicinity and come back with a bundle of leaves, improvise a mortar and pestle by finding a slab of sandstone and a suitable rock, pound the leaves and then apply the green mass to the injured spot and bandage it with a strip of cloth from a discarded turban or odhni.

We decided that the criterion for being a healer was the number of patients he treated. There were some Raika whose reputation for their skills extended beyond their village and who attracted customers from sometimes very far away. They might treat up to ten cases a day and often their courtyards were filled with clients waiting to take them to their animals.

One locally famous healer was Motiram, a tall, white-bearded man with an angular face reminiscent of an Afghan warrior. His clientele included the Jat community and their buffaloes. Motiram was an intimidating and impatient man with a proud personality who did not like to reveal too much of his knowledge. "If you want to learn something, you have to learn it with your hands. What good is it to write this down?" he admonished us. However, he was not above titillating us with his knowledge, exposing us to small nuggets of his wisdom.

One day, he allowed us to accompany him to a buffalo that was having problems giving birth. The buffalo belonged to a Jat family and the men were out working the field. Two women, obviously the mother and daughter-in- law, nervously hovered around the animal whose birth process seemed to have come to a standstill, although the water had broken some time ago. Motiram removed his turban and rolled up his sleeve to examine the cow from inside. After feeling around, he took out his arm without any comment, and instructed the women as they stoked up the fireplace and assisted in preparing a mysterious concoction for the animal, sometimes clapping his hands and barking "*fatafat*" (hurry, hurry).

Once the buffalo had eaten the mixture, he withdrew into the neighbour's house where some men had gathered and were partaking in an opium ceremony. After twenty minutes, he reappeared in a more relaxed mood, saying something to me which I could not understand but which definitely sounded like a challenge. Once again he inserted his arm and after pulling a bit, a little black snout became visible. After moving and rotating a bit more to widen the birth canal, the tips of the front legs followed. Then he pulled the legs until the shoulder blades emerged. The rest of the body followed automatically and the women placed the newborn so that the mother could lick and shower it with maternal attention.

Motiram proudly walked back home, and when I asked him if he had received payment for his important service, he adamantly stated that his skills were a gift given by god, so he would never charge anything for treating cattle.

Another healer with a big reputation was K, who seemed the antithesis in character to Motiram – humble and even timid. He owned a herd of sheep, but was so busy with his patients that his two daughters, who looked to be around ten or twelve years old, were usually to be found taking expert care of them. Although K was friendly enough, he seemed unsure as to whether he could trust us, and was very reluctant to talk to us at first. We visited a few times in the evenings and sat with him in the small antechamber of his house, listening to the rustling of the neem trees and to the sounds exchanged between his ewes and their hungry lambs. Only after discussing all kinds of unrelated matters did he start to speak openly about some of his treatments and experiences. One of the more difficult veterinary interventions is opening up a twisted uterus and he gave us an account of several such cases and how he successfully dealt with them. One evening, when it had become dark, he confided that he was very afraid of the evil eye, saying that some tribal people have the ability to put a curse on people so that they bleed to death or die suddenly. He told us about another healer to whom this had happened. The curse was effected by a third healer from the Grassia community who reckoned the victim represented competition to him.

While the healers tackle a wide range of cases, there are others who specialise in "*daam*" which is treatment with a hot iron. Variations of daam actually exist in many cultures, including the Bedouins. In daam treatment, iron implements, such as a rod or a sickle blade, are put into a very hot fire made from cow or camel dung until they have become red and glowing. In the meantime, the camel is restrained with ropes which takes at least two people to do. The hot iron is then pressed on the respective body part for thirty to sixty seconds.

It sounds very cruel and is certainly painful. But even in the best of range racehorse practice, I had seen this used in certain otherwise incurable afflictions, such as chronic arthritis in the hock. It is an age-old treatment and there is some scientific basis to it: the resulting inflammation increases the blood circulation in the area, which can help to activate healing processes. I had also once witnessed a Bedouin father applying this treatment to the chest of his young daughter who had fallen ill with pneumonia. She lived to tell the tale of it and gradually her scars disappeared.

The Raika swore by this treatment to counter one particular disease that also perplexed veterinarians, the so-called wryneck syndrome. The camel suddenly seems to have a kink in its neck and problems in walking. This syndrome does not respond to conventional treatment but I have seen at least one case where daam seemed to be successful.

One thing is certain, daam leaves a permanent record of the disease an animal has gone through. In some herds, the majority of camels show traces of daam. Interestingly, the Raika do not necessarily apply the hot iron to the part of the body that is affected, but sometimes at diagonally opposite points. Once I had been initiated into this, I could wander through a herd and tell the Raika the disease history of their animals.

But this kind of rational treatment is used by the Raika only when they have an idea what is wrong with their animal and where the seat of the problem is. Sometimes, there are sudden outbreaks of diseases for which there is no apparent reason, so they conclude that the supernatural powers must be at work and the gods must be angry. In this case, they usually attend the session of a Bhopa spirit medium. Divine power descends on him and in this state he can solve quite a few human problems. I have seen little children bitten by a rabid dog being taken to the Bhopa for help. He ties a red holy thread around the wrists of dog-bitten children and advises them to go to the doctor. The Bhopas often give very good advice. They prescribe rigid regimens for getting rid of alcoholism and order depressed new wives to run around his temple and scream their hearts out to so they can let go of all their frustrations. For sick animals he speaks a mantra.

Within a few weeks, we had compiled quite a substantial dossier of Raika ethnoveterinary practices, although it was often difficult to decide what to make of them. Some seemed to make sense, others belonged more to the magico-religious realm. With the deadline for the lecture looming, there was little time to scrutinise them for efficiency, although it was apparent that many of the plants we catalogued also appeared in the Indian Materia Medica and had known medicinal effects. One of these was the locally produced oil of the karanji tree which the Raika used to rub on the camels as mange treatment. It was effective and a natural product, but could not be used on pregnant camels because it generated a lot of heat which could induce miscarriages. Also, it was considerably more expensive than a commercially available chemical preparation and there were only a few places where it could be obtained.

To me it seemed that ethnoveterinary practices were a mixed bag. One important factor was that the Raika trusted these remedies and knew how to apply them. And although they were keen to obtain and learn about commercial drugs, these could often cause more harm than good. Any amount of counterfeit drugs were on the market, and there was often no way to distinguish between fake products and the genuine article. Regardless of provenance, the Raika were nearly always overcharged and, finally, they had no idea about dosing them. They would both overdose – when the animal was very sick and seemed to need it – as well as underdose – when they had the urge to economise. Yet for some diseases, such as the dreaded trypanosomiasis, there were no traditional alternatives available.

Only a small part of the information we had collected could actually be used in my lecture. I decided to put ethnoveterinary medicine into a larger context by comparing it with other alternative medicinal systems, such as Ayurveda, homoeopathy, acupuncture, and Tibetan medicine. Then I planned to give an overview of the Raika practices. I had taken detailed photographs of many of their procedures, including the treatment with the red-hot iron, and (I hoped the unorthodox but sometimes effective ethnoveterinary practices would excite the interest of the professors). I did a dry run in the institute with my supervisor who gave me some suggestions on how to improve, not the content of my presentation, but the way it was delivered – I tended to speak too fast.

In my formal suit, I greeted the audience looking down on me from their benches and proceeded to give my talk. When the slide about the treatment with the red-hot iron came, a murmur went through the lecture hall and two professors – that much I could see in the darkened hall – got into a heated discussion, so loud that I could hear it. This disconcerted me and my last sentence, which should have been presented with a flourish, came out more like a timid squeak. "This is why ethnoveterinary medicine can make a significant contribution to livestock and rural welfare in developing countries and should, therefore, be integrated into the veterinary curriculum."

One could have heard a pin drop; finally there was some embarrassed shuffling of feet. No applause. The dean looked at me with a pained expression, but then caught himself to thank me for my talk and invited the audience to pose questions to me.

A few hands went up and the questions rained down on me, some posed in an aggressive tone. "How can you, as a veterinarian approve of such cruel measures as firing?" I retorted that it was used as the last resort and there are incidences where it seemed to work. But under the barrage of unfriendly questions, I started to falter – I had expected a less hostile and more measured discussion. I did not fight back.

Eventually, I was asked to leave the lecture hall and wait for the faculty to discuss their verdict. Inside, heated discussions went on. Finally, I was called in for the verdict. "The faculty has decided to accept your thesis, but you will have to present another lecture about a different topic after a minimum period of six months."

I had not been aware that this was, to some degree, an initiation rite for entry into the academic world. The professors – among the sixty, there were only two women – were shocked and challenged by the practices I had just invited them to reconsider. They might have accepted it, had I stood my ground and defended myself valiantly.

Now it was too late. And it was a severe setback, for the lecture component is usually just a formality once the written work has been accepted. This was an almost unheard-of precedent and seemed the end of my academic career, at least in Germany. My supervisor, too, turned against me. She had promoted me as her possible successor as head of the institute and my failure had proven a major embarrassment for her. She called me up to tell me how terrible my performance had been, repeatedly saying, "You are just not an academic."

The future suddenly seemed very bleak. Both Gary and I were effectively unemployed. Gary sometimes conducted tours to Jordan or took up short-term fellowships. For me, the situation looked even worse. There was a glut of unemployed veterinarians and, anyway, I had forgotten all my practical skills. My self-confidence had been undermined to the extent that I could hardly open my mouth to speak a coherent sentence.

A small chance lay in the fact that although ethnoveterinary medicine was not to the taste of the proponents of conventional medicine, there was quite a bit of interest in it in development circles. "Indigenous knowledge" had become a buzzword and, thanks to the untiring efforts of Evelyn Mathias and Constance

McCorkle in promoting the topic, research on ethnoveterinary medicine was expanding. Both of them were involved in organising the first world conference on ethnoveterinary medicine to be held at the end of the year in Pune in India. We had a meeting and out of that sprung the idea to put together a manual on traditional treatments of camel diseases, a book with real use for the practitioner, written in simple and easily understandable English and with illustrations.

I wrote a proposal for holding a workshop of camel experts in order to produce a camel manual and it was accepted very quickly. This restored my self-confidence to some extent. And the workshop was a great success. It was attended by Bakri Musa, my old friend from Sudan who was now working for the Department of Camel Affairs in the Sultanate of Oman, several experts from Africa, and a few colleagues from India. We sat together for two days, first prioritising camel diseases and then writing up traditional and modern treatments according to the best of our knowledge. Of course, two days was much too short a time and this was only the beginning of the process. It would take us another two years to edit and complete the material. But in the end, we produced what was probably the first-ever book on animal diseases that gave equal importance to traditional knowledge as scientific knowledge.

As for my Habilitation, it took me more than two years to get ready for it and once again face the faculty. This time, I had learnt my lesson and prepared a presentation that avoided anything controversial as well as any conclusions of practical relevance. Its esoteric title was "Indian Elephant Medicine Through the Ages" and it gave a historic overview of elephant treatment according to Ayurveda. Because of its significance for warfare and its enormous value, the elephant had been the first animal to become the subject of Indian veterinary research, more than 2,000 years ago. Most of the presentation was based on the analysis of ancient elephant treatises which placed a lot of emphasis on identifying the type and constitution of the individual animal in order to determine the appropriate treatment. My perusal of these scholarly volumes had been complemented with field research among the elephant keepers of Jaipur, Rajasthan's capital city, where about sixty elephants were kept by the traditional elephant-keeping community of mahouts, who used them for carrying tourists to Amber Fort. In case of sickness, these elephants were also treated according to old Ayurvedic recipes. The mahouts had old books with paintings of elephants displaying different symptoms.

I received my degree but my enthusiasm for an academic career in Germany had evaporated.

Chapter 10

"EMPOWERMENT"

"The Raika remained a simpleton. He ran into great loss. He never acquired the land. He confined his work to breeding the camel. We thought that those glorious days would always remain."

– Raika woman from Bikaner, quoted by V. K. Srivastava in *Some Characteristics of a 'Herding Caste' of Rajasthan*

"Raika men are straight like a cow; Raika women are cunning like a fox."

– A Raika proverb

The milk project had revealed the chasm in the thinking and culture between the Raika and rural life in Rajasthan on the one hand, and academically trained animal experts and urban India on the other. These two were worlds apart. Ideas that sounded good in a proposal and appealed to funding organisations were likely to turn into the ridiculous in the local context. Events in Sadri usually unfolded in a unique and entirely unpredictable way and these concepts often did not make sense to the Raika. It was difficult, and occasionally totally impracticable, to run projects in Sadri under the aegis of an organisation in Jodhpur.

After mulling this over, Hanwant and I concluded that a new organisation was needed, based in Sadri, and closer to the ground, one in which the Raika could be more immediately involved, and which could better convey and address their needs from their own perspective. So in the later stages of the milk project, we had started exploring the modalities of setting up a new voluntary society and looking for supporters. We needed to have seven members in order to be able to register the society and I, as a foreigner, could not be one. Obviously, we were keen that the Raika themselves be actively involved as members, but this was not as simple as it sounded. The earlier attempts by Dr Dewaram at setting up a society composed of Raika had failed due to fundamental contradictions inherent in the idea. The focus of the society was to be on livestock keeping but, paradoxically, this was not something any of the more educated Raika, who could grasp the concept of a voluntary society, were interested in or willing to support. In fact, when the educated Raika spoke at caste gatherings, they usually exhorted the herders "to stop running behind the animals" and drop livestock keeping altogether. On the other hand, the livestock keeping Raika whom we wanted to help, having had no education in the conventional sense or any exposure to the wider world, were completely unfamiliar with the idea of a voluntary society. The fact that they could not read documents and could sign only by means of their thumbprint was a minor aspect compared with their lack of understanding that a voluntary society would work with them selflessly, a proposition that was difficult to grasp if not totally alien. Unlike in other areas of Rajasthan, in Godwar there was no NGO working for social causes and upliftment, so the idea of outsiders coming to help local people and communities was a first and aroused suspicion. Rumours to the effect that I was scheming to take all their animals to Germany or hijack their children by plane kept surfacing periodically.

While the idea of social work and mobilisation was new, there was a strong tradition of charity in the form of handouts, such as free food or medical treatment. Mostly, such good works were practised by religious trusts and they were, more often than not, focused on animals. A favourite strategy of the affluent Jain community, who often acted as patrons of the Raika community, was to build and run *gaushalas*, homes for unproductive, ailing, and old cows that had been abandoned by their owners. Other wealthy people fed stray dogs, supported the construction of animal hospitals, or financed veterinary treatment camps. For any kind of activity carried out in the guise of religious salvation, there was abundant money around as was evidenced by the large number of temples that sprouted everywhere.

There was also a tradition, continuing from the feudal days, for the Raika to ask the Rajputs, with whom they had close relations, for help and support and, very often, for money. There was a definite obligation for these patrons to do their best to grant such requests – and gain status and followers in the process. Because I was likewise perceived as rich and powerful, I initially also received a flood of pleas for loans of money or for outright financial support. Almost as soon as I had a friendly word with anybody, they would turn around and ask me for money, often substantial sums of it. To begin with, this upset me greatly because I felt that people were friendly to me only because they thought I was a walking money bag, rather than because they appreciated me in my own right as a person. Gradually, I came to realise that these requests did not only happen to me as a foreigner, but to Indian people as well, including Hanwant. By giving loans one established respect, power and obligation for reciprocal support that could be mobilised in times of need.

The established approaches for giving or receiving help, thus, were either through religion-motivated charity or due to historic patron–client relationships. For outsiders, such as us, to help people by making them stronger and enabling them to shoulder responsibility was a new experience. We had determined that it was precisely this kind of social mobilisation that was needed. The Raika should once again take pride in their occupation. I was tired of hearing the Raika described as backward. True, socially, they were extremely conservative. They practised child marriage, but since couples did not start living together until they were mature, the situation was not that different from arranged marriages standard throughout India. But the animal husbandry practices of the Raika were sound under the given circumstances, whether they related to camels, sheep, goats, or cattle. In a situation of unpredictable rainfall patterns and water scarcity – evident from the wells that had run dry around Sadri, from which farmers had drawn water for irrigation with diesel pumps, leaving the land fallow – grazing livestock was the best and most sustainable way of making use of the land.

Maintaining mobile livestock required experience and skill – who else but the Raika would be able to control large herds of animals just by means of their voice or steer them through traffic or along the side of highways with just a bamboo stick? Who else had knowledge of where grazing was likely to be available in a particular season and what were the likely effects of the grazed vegetation on the animals – on the taste of their milk, their fertility, on their health in general? Who else knew the name and life-history of each animal and that of its forefathers and mothers, or could identify each one of them, or have such a close bond with them that they responded to being called by name?

Besides the advantages of the Raika animal husbandry from the perspective of ecology and animal welfare, there was also its significance for the economy of Rajasthan. The camels they bred and sold at Pushkar provided a livelihood for many poor families who used them to transport goods, both in cities as well as in rural areas. But this was only a relatively minor aspect compared to the importance of sheep-breeding in which the majority of the Raika were involved. The mutton they produced was a key export item that generated substantial amounts of foreign currency. Others raised goats which satisfied the growing liking for goat meat among middle-class Indians. In some areas, the Raika were breeding cattle which were famous for disease resistance, character and productivity, yet these were yet to be formally recognised as a breed.

It seemed to me the Raika were animal breeders par excellence and not only should they be proud of it, but all the other communities of Rajasthan should too. Rajasthan prided itself on its heritage, but by heritage it usually meant the forts and other architectural remains of the maharajahs. To me it seemed that the Raikas' relationship with their animals was equally worthy of conservation as a uniquely human heritage.

These were lofty thoughts compared to the reality on ground. The Raika received neither acknowledgement, nor credit, nor any subsidies for their economic activities. Being such prominent livestock breeders, one would have expected that the services of the government's Animal Husbandry Department would have been geared primarily towards them. But this was emphatically not the case. As we had found out during our ethnoveterinary research, there was hardly any interaction between the Raika and government veterinarians. The government vets looked down on the Raika because of their "backward ways", their own vision of animal husbandry being a row of black-and-white crossbred cows tied up in a neat stall and fed with concentrates made from grain and green fodder. The Raika on their part did not trust the government vets, hardly ever approached them for help, and even refused to have their animals vaccinated by them. It was, hence, not surprising that animal epidemics, including foot and mouth disease, were rampant.

So when we finally set up the new society, its goals were specified as "assistance to livestock-dependent people by measures that included documentation and promotion of traditional knowledge; the control of animal diseases; improvement of income from animals; social and educational support as well as pasture development." After a long and thorough search for an appropriate name, we baptised it "Lokhit Pashu-Palak Sansthan", or LPPS in short. This meant "Welfare Organisation for Livestock Keepers".

Our first field project was entitled "Empowerment for Raika Camel Breeders". Its purpose was to continue and consolidate the activities we had started under the Camel Husbandry Improvement project and the Milk Marketing project. Eventually, we also hoped to expand these activities to new areas and envisioned setting up satellite centres in other camel-breeding areas, such as Barmer district that borders on Pakistan and has an especially high camel density.

This time around, we encountered many of the same problems that had been there two and a half years earlier – finding an office, hiring staff, and so on. But the big difference was that, by now, we had the confidence of the Raika and could act according to our own judgement rather than being dependent on guidance from a distant head office. Our first office was a tiny room on the second floor of a building overlooking the bustling Sadri bus stand. There was barely enough room for a desk, a chair, and a small medicine chest, but there was a balcony on which we could seat guests. We had hardly moved in when, one morning, Harjiram, the old and dignified camel herder from Khooni Bavri, climbed up the stairs with his big herding stick. His white beard had grown even more impressive, but his nose seemed thinner and his face rather wan. His eyes were as bottomless as ever, a curious mixture of dreaminess and alertness. Catching his breath, he folded our hands between his, and mumbled countless greetings. "So glad to catch a glimpse of you, Bhaba and Baiji..." he said. After being seated on our only chair on the balcony, having unnestled his tobacco pouch and sipped the first mouthful of tea, he was ready to come out with the purpose of his visit. "My son, Ghisulal, who is working in Bombay – I have told you about him many times – is coming home in a few days," he said. "It is now time that he starts his married life and his in-laws will send his wife to start living in our household. I am not strong any more and sometimes need help with the camels. Therefore, it would be good if Ghisulal could get a job here in the area, so that he does not have to go back to Bombay. Is there any chance that you can give him a job in your project?"

This was a long speech for Harjiram. Since Ruparam had left us for a better-paying job in Surat and we actually needed to employ a field assistant, I was eager to say yes, yes, but Hanwant was more careful.

"What kind of job is Ghisulal doing? And for how many years did he go to school?"

"I don't know exactly what he is doing. I think he is working in a sweetshop. And he studied till Class 8. His handwriting is good."

"Send him to us when he comes. We will see what we can do... and whether we can give him a job. Is there anything else we can help you with?"

"No, that's it. And I wanted to see you. By God's grace, you look really good." He gave a beatific smile and then pulled out his opium bag. "Take opium, Hare Ram, Hare Ram," he murmured, trying to force generous bits of the sticky mass on us.

Ghisulal came to introduce himself within a week. He was a lad in his early twenties, quite well nourished, and with a happy, round face that reminded me of a Renaissance angel and presented a stark contrast to the haughty features of his emaciated father. We arranged a one-month trial period during which his wacky nature became apparent, but he also endeared himself to us. Because he had learnt to speak Hindi during his sojourn in the city, he and I could communicate quite well on a verbal level, although we remained separated by huge gaps in worldview. He made it his self-assigned task to teach me about the ways and mores of the Raika in particular, and India in general. Despite his many years in an urban environment, he was familiar with all aspects of camel rearing from childhood. He was also an expert in interpreting camel voices. One evening we were listening from a distance to a camel herd that was coming home from its daily round, making the usual concert of indescribable bleating and moaning sounds. While I did not pay much attention to the details and just filed away the cacophony as "noises of a camel herd coming home", Ghisu was able to interpret each individual sound. "This uthni has a baby camel and is eager to feed him, this one is pregnant, and this one has lost her baby." He seemed totally proficient in camel language and I recalled what I had heard about the ability of Raika in the desert areas to interpret pugmarks. Just from the foot impressions, they were able to determine whether a camel was pregnant, what sex it was, and even its kinship with other camels.

But, sometimes, I was not so sure of the accuracy of Ghisu's assessments. On another evening just after sunset, we were driving by motorcycle on the asphalt road from Sadri to Mundara when we suddenly hit a couple of boulders that catapulted our vehicle high into the air. By sheer good luck we bounced down straight and did not go over, but my behind was burning and my heart racing. I wanted Ghisu to stop and get the boulders out of the way to prevent any further accidents, but he just accelerated, leaning forward as if competing in a race, deaf to all my interjections. "These boulders were put there by dacoits trying to loot us. If we stop, they will beat us. This is India, Baiji! Things are different here than in your village!"

I was not sure whether I should believe him. This was a fairly densely inhabited area. In fact, right next to the boulders stood a small farmhouse where buffaloes were tied up. Would a dacoity take place so openly? It seemed to me more likely that these boulders had been left there in the wake of somebody repairing a puncture or something else that had gone wrong with a car or truck.

His understanding of geography was also intriguing and probably quite representative of the concepts of the Raika and the rural people in general. I had already realised that "Bombay" was a generic term. When people said their son was working in Bombay, it did not mean that he was actually employed in that city. He could be working in Surat, Madras, Delhi or any other place and "Bombay" just referred to outside the immediate area.

According to Ghisu, the world was flat, as was evident from a story he related to me in great earnestness about some people who set out to catch the sun. They walked and walked towards where they had seen it disappearing until they came to an ocean and then realised that the sun lived behind the ocean. He also seemed to be firmly convinced that the "world" was composed of India plus one additional village outside its borders from where all the white people hailed. One day, he excitedly burst into the office, exclaiming, "The people from your village have come! Why haven't you gone to meet them? Quick, quick!" He urged me along, guiding me to the town square where a bus of French tourists had stopped and was visibly disappointed when I did not embrace them.

But it was the ups and downs of his social life that really enthralled me.

I had visited his betrothed and met his in-laws before the *ana* had taken place. She was young – I judged her to be less than twenty – sweet, and very shy. Because Ghisulal was such an egregious and jolly fellow I felt that it would be quite a good match, but a few weeks after she had come, Ghisulal started to get more and more worried about her. "She is behaving strangely. A *bhoot* has taken hold of her," he kept saying. "We must do something to get rid of the bhoot."

"How do you know that it is a bhoot that is the problem?" I retorted. "What kind of symptoms does she have?"

"Oh, she does not talk anymore and often cries. The bhoot also stops her from working. She just sits and does nothing. It is very difficult to get her to do anything. It's a clear case of a bhoot affecting her mind." Then he continued with a hopeful tone in his voice, "Don't you have any medicine for controlling the bhoot? Maybe something from Germany? You must have the same problem there!"

"Actually, we don't have such bhoot cases in Germany very often, if at all. I want to see her for myself and talk to her."

Ghisulal was happy about this, so the next morning we left shortly after dawn by motorbike to Jhoopa where his father customarily stayed at this time of the year when there was no grazing around Khooni Bavri. Despite the early hour, the heat was oppressive and turned the slightest exertion into an ordeal, at least for me, but Harjiram was already up and about, sitting on a charpai on a small platform in front of his very small one-room hut taking puffs from his chillum. According to local etiquette,

I could not just walk into the hut and look at the "patient", but would first have to take tea and exchange pleasantries with Harjiram. While Ghisulal dived inside to arrange for the tea, Harjiram also expressed his concerns about his daughter-in-law as he prepared his morning opium fix. He referred to her as "Beravali", the woman from Bera. "Please get her some medicine and cure her quickly," he said.

Once I had finished my tea, I stepped through the open door, taking a few moments to adjust my eyes to the smoky darkness inside. A few rays of daylight filtered in through a hole in the roof, and a glow came from the corner where the *chulha*, the earthen stove, was located. Otherwise, Raika huts are usually bare of any furniture, with the exception of a few cooking utensils – the *kagti*, a flat bowl made from clay for making bread dough, the *oriyo*, a round plate on which the dough is rolled out, the *velam* or roller pin, the *kelri*, a concave iron pan for making roti, and the *phookniya* – an iron blow pipe for fanning the fire. That is it, apart from a couple of mattresses stacked in the corner.

Crouched on the floor next to the chulha was a shapeless and motionless figure. I greeted her and sat down beside her, but there was no visible reaction. Not knowing what else to do, I put my arm around her shoulder for a bit and just sat there, quietly. After a while, she briefly lifted her dupatta aside and I caught a glimpse of her face, which seemed totally bereft of any emotion. She said something I could not understand, but it was not difficult to imagine what had happened. The poor girl had been sitting alone in the hut, next to the chulha, for several weeks. With Ghisulal gone most of the time, her only company was her father-in-law who was out herding during the day and with whom she was not supposed to interact directly in any case. Since Ghisulal was the only son and his sisters had been married and lived elsewhere, she had nobody to talk to, and as it was not considered proper to venture outside the hut, she had been sitting in the darkness for days on end. Unsurprisingly, she was in despair, and being uncooperative probably was the only means available of conveying that she could not put up with this situation indefinitely.

I suggested that the best thing would be to send her home to her parents for a while so that she had somebody to talk to, aware that recommending Ghisulal to spend more time with her and take an interest in her would be considered highly improper. When Harjiram heard my recommendation, his comment was, "But if she goes back to Bera, who is going to cook food for me? We need her here!"

I insisted. "If you don't send her home, she will get worse and eventually you will have to take her to the hospital which will mean a lot of expenditure. I strongly recommend you take her to her pir as soon as possible. In fact, it is your duty to do so!"

Ghisulal seemed to understand. But he still could not let go of the idea of a bhoot and asked again. "Are you sure this will suffice? Maybe I should take her to a Bhopa to expurgate the bhoot."

"Why don't you? I would give it a try," I said, having witnessed several times how the advice of Bhopas helped and made good sense.

Later, Ghisu reported back. "Baiji, this was a good idea. I took her to the Bhopa and there was another newly married woman whom a bhoot had taken hold of. The Bhopa ordered both of them to run around the temple seven times and to scream as loudly as they could. Afterwards, she was normal and when we got to her pir, she seemed almost happy."

The story had a happy ending – at least for a while – because the Beravali had already become pregnant which necessitated more stays at her parental home. When she came back with her young son to Harjiram's house, she had gained in standing and also now had an emotional outlet as well as something to keep her busy.

Back to "empowerment". I was determined – and this was also the stipulation of the funding organisation – that this was not going to be a charitable project in the sense of providing free hand-outs, but should enable the Raika to chart their own future and to make responsible decisions, a yet unheard-of approach in the local context. The last thing we wanted was to make them dependent on us. But we already had done considerable damage to this effect. The herders we had registered several years earlier now expected us to supply them with free medicines – forever; they had begun to perceive this as *their right* and *our obligation*. This could not continue and it anyway went way beyond our resources. Besides, it was grossly unfair towards all the other camel herders from further away who wanted to sign up with us. The only solution was to start charging for the medicines.

After long and heated discussions, we decided that in future the registered herders would have to pay fifty per cent of the costs, while new herders would have to pay the full price. Obviously, the old herders were not pleased about this; some were even angry, and gave us short shrift for a while. But it was heartening to realise that the newly joined herders felt privileged having access to medicines at all. Even if they paid us the full cost, our medicines were still cheaper than those available to them elsewhere, plus they had the guarantee that they got authentic "*asli*" medicines and not fakes. As we had gradually become aware, the local market was flooded with counterfeit or duplicate medicines which looked very similar to the real thing, but contained substances without pharmacological effect. Moreover, many of the medical shops overcharged the Raika or sold them medicines whose expiry date had long passed. Because of their illiteracy, the Raika were easily duped. While they performed their traditional treatment interventions adroitly, they had no concept of the great diversity of modern medicines on the market, nor of the need to adhere to particular dosages. When it came to injections (teeka), they knew only two types which they distinguished on the basis of colour – the white one and the yellow one. The white teeka was the good one, whereas the yellow teeka was actually contraindicated in camels, although many veterinarians used it, not being aware of its often lethal effect. Further, in order to economise, the Raika would often distribute one dosage among two animals or, in case they felt that the animal was severely sick, they would double or triple the dose.

Sometimes, a Raika would come into the office and proudly display medicines he had obtained very cheaply, in the belief that he had made a very good deal and maybe also as a subtle hint for us that the medicines we supplied were too costly. One day, Kanaram traipsed in, leaving his heavy, beaky, inlaid shoes on the steps, and lowered himself on our crooked metal chair. After exchanging the usual pleasantries, he started searching around in his dhoti. Shouting for tea, I assumed him to be hunting for his opium, but instead he produced, carefully tied in a white handkerchief, two vials containing a white powder. He held them out to me and commented, "Look, Baiji, I bought these two *dabbas* for only Rs 40, whereas you charge Rs 40 for only one teeka!" He said all this with a look on his face that reminded me of a dog who has been beaten by his owner for a misdeed he had not committed. I took one of the vials from him and read the label. "But this is not the teeka for tibursa, this is an antibiotic, totally useless if you want to prevent tibursa!"

I had had enough and one of our first empowering strategies was to hold training camps where the camel breeders were taught about modern medicines – what they were used for, how to dose them, when and how often to apply them, and how and where to inject them. Since camels are susceptible to only a couple or so infectious diseases – mainly trypanosomiasis and mange – familiarity with only a very limited number of medicines was required.

These training programmes were very popular and we also invited people from rural development organisations in other parts of Rajasthan so that they could use this knowledge in areas where we could not reach. At the same time, worried that we were placing too much emphasis on modern knowledge, we did our best to reinforce and maintain the traditional treatments. In retrospect, this may not have been necessary, since whenever traditional treatment worked, the Raika would naturally give it preference – it was not always cheaper, but in these cases they were confident in what they were doing and could act autonomously on the spot without having to contact us and wait for us to come.

As we had accumulated plenty of photographs of the various diseases and of traditional as well as modern treatment methods, I arranged these into a slide show. It was not only the Raika who loved these shows and broke out in discussions among themselves about what they were seeing. These presentations were also useful for convincing others that the Raika and traditional healers were not just quacks, but had accumulated a vast body of knowledge which was not always congruent with modern wisdom, but an important resource in its own right.

It was clear that we needed partners in other parts of Rajasthan if we wanted to have more than a strictly local impact, for we had limited resources and, with just one motorbike for transportation, our sphere of action was limited. There were plenty of NGOs around working for the welfare of rural people, and we wondered whether they could become our allies and help us reach a larger number of Raikas. In order to know what these organisations were doing, what we could learn from them, and whether they might be able to help the camel breeders, we undertook a study of the ways in which other NGOs conducted livestock projects. In the hot April of 1998, Hanwant and I crisscrossed all of Rajasthan by motorbike to look at projects that also focused on livestock. To my dismay, we found that the NGOs often worked on exactly the same lines as the government. They supported artificial insemination and crossbreeding of the local cows with exotic cattle, and they arranged veterinary treatment camps. Their efforts were often geared to replacing the rich traditional knowledge of the rural people – which I had come to understand as their biggest asset – with technical information gleaned from the western world. Some of the methods being used seemed designed to disempower local communities by making them dependent on outside inputs and putting no value on their own resources. None of them worked with the Raika or with camels.

Based on these observations, we developed our second strategy for "empowerment" and set out to showcase and promote ethnoveterinary medicine and other aspects of indigenous knowledge. We received help with this task from students, although unfortunately, these were invariably from European rather than Indian universities. One of them was Ellen Geerlings from Holland, who intensively researched the sheep husbandry practices of the Raika and uncovered the intricacies of their breeding system. Since sheep are prone to many more illnesses and ailments than camels, the Raika had developed a highly complex disease classification system and their epidemiological knowledge easily surpassed that of most veterinarians. We disseminated the information we accumulated to other NGOs by hosting workshops to which we also invited representatives from the government's Department of Animal Husbandry. At these occasions, the traditional healers were given the opportunity to demonstrate their knowledge and thereby refute their reputation as "quacks".

Thanks to Hanwant's organisational talents and the special touch of Rajput hospitality and etiquette he added to everything, we pulled off these encounters between the traditional and the modern with panache. Sometimes, however, even the best-laid plans could go awry. The rainy season regularly produced organisational nightmares, with the electricity sometimes staying off for days, and telephone connections interrupted for indefinite time periods. When it started pouring, roads could quickly become submerged and it became impossible to reach or leave Sadri. Visitors could easily get stranded and often had no opportunity of informing us of their changed travel schedule.

On one occasion, we felt extremely honoured that Professor T. K. Gahlot, a professor from the Bikaner Veterinary College and a world-famous authority who had recently published the definitive volume on camel surgery, had deemed us important enough to visit, bringing along half a dozen of his best students. We indulged in the luxury of a hired jeep to take him to the field in style. At dawn of a beautiful morning, the professor and his students were ready for a hands-on adventure. Their suits, ties and polished boots provided a favourable contrast to my rather faded salwar-kameez and the plastic flip-flops that I had identified as the most practical footwear in the rainy season when one always had to be prepared for wading through puddles. The professor very tolerantly ignored my unprofessional outfit and graciously invited me to share the front seat of the jeep with him. When we arrived at the camel herd, the professor was absolutely delighted to find a couple of specimens afflicted by intriguing surgical problems – one camel had a congenital deformity, the other an eye abnormality. He willingly accepted the invitation by the Raika family for a round of camel milk tea and, sitting on charpais in the small hut, held forth to his students about possible therapies and surgical interventions. The visit was going well. But in the meantime, it started drizzling and it seemed inconvenient to him to walk back to the jeep, parked about fifty metres away. Why had nobody thought about bringing an umbrella, he admonished me gently. Let's wait until it stops, he said, and continued lecturing to his rapt audience about some of the exciting surgical cases he had operated upon during his distinguished career. Instead of abating, the drizzle intensified into a torrential downpour, until no sane person would have stepped out. The rain had turned into such a dense curtain that one could hardly see a few metres from the door. The roof of the hut was anything but watertight and water was dripping through it at many places, making it difficult to find a safe place for the professor in his impeccably tailored clothes.

After an hour or so, there was a bit of a let-up in the deluge and the curtain of rain lightened momentarily. Taking our chances, we raced to the jeep, stuffed ourselves into its interior as fast as we could, and then we were off slithering and splashing through the mud. But what we had hardly registered while coming was a dried riverbed which had meanwhile turned into a whirling stream. The driver brought the jeep to a halt. "I don't think we can cross this. We will probably get stuck," was his sober prediction. The professor, however, was in a hurry to get home and be done with this wet and soaking experience. "It is already almost ten o'clock and you have not arranged breakfast," he reproved me, pointing at his watch. "Tell the driver to get going. Why is the fellow so reluctant? Are you paying him by the hour?"

There was no escaping his authority. The driver gave me a resigned look, started the engine, and took the jeep down the gently sloping embankment. After only a few metres down, the engine stalled and water started flowing into the cabin, up to our ankles and rising further. Scrambling out and half-wading, half-swimming through the waist-high water to the bank, we saw the jeep, having shed its weighty passengers, starting to float and drift away with the current. Fortunately, it was snagged by a rock which prevented it from being washed out of sight, but with the jeep decisively out of action and no shelter within view, there was little alternative but to head towards Sadri on foot. Miraculously, the adverse situation had somehow changed the dynamics in the group, generating an unlikely *esprit de corps*. We traipsed along to the tune of "Singing in the Rain" until we hit the asphalt road to Sadri, where we were picked up by a jeep taxi. Back in our headquarters, we stripped off our drenched clothes and wrapped ourselves in bedsheets and blankets, and the professor instructed his students to make paranthas, and the whole episode (which later came to be known as "drowning Dr G") ended in good spirits.

And so our efforts of changing deeply ingrained beliefs and attitudes and trying to get outsiders to understand the perspective of the Raika and appreciate their knowledge, went on, always taking unexpected twists and turns. Often, we felt discouraged about the lack of progress, and the continued ups and downs made for a rollercoaster of emotions. Between Hanwant and myself there were tensions, too. I wanted things to move quicker and suggested he should share more of the responsibilities with the Raika, for instance, with respect to allotment of resources. Why was it us who should decide at what price to make available medicines? Couldn't the Raikas themselves decide who was poor and should qualify for reduced rates? "You can't change them overnight. It will take time," he said.

One day, the postman handed us an official-looking large letter with a colourful logo and a German stamp. "Congratulations!" it read. "We are pleased to tell you that your project has been selected as the 'project around the world' for the EXPO 2000 that will take place in Hannover, Germany, next year." It was in response to one of the numerous applications I had made it my habit to fill out. I had almost forgotten about it. As it turned out, selection did not only mean that we were invited to Hannover, but that our project was to be depicted in a big book with many others from around the whole world. This gave us a much-needed boost of self-confidence. Another came after Hanwant was invited to a reception hosted by the German Embassy in New Delhi; he met one of the attachés, Gunnar Denecke who proceeded to take great interest in our work and was to become a pillar of support on another project we were pursuing.

It was no exaggeration to say that ours was truly a bottom-up project. However, it came with the drawback that we had very little to show in terms of infrastructure – to the extent that it was sometimes difficult to explain or provide evidence to visitors of what we were actually doing and what our work was about. From our visits to other NGOs we knew that they all had offices, vehicles, meeting rooms, and photographic displays of their achievements and activities. Ours, by contrast, was a shoestring effort – we had only one motorbike and our office did not even have enough wall space to put up more than a single poster. Whenever we organised a function, we had to rent a meeting-room in the Mukti Dham temple, while our training programmes were arranged quite literally in the field, wherever one of our camel herder associates happened to be camping! When visitors came to see our work, we would often have to send out Ghisulal the evening before to locate and track down camel herds, so that we could be sure to find one the next morning.

The idea of a "centre" that could serve as a focal point for our activities and function as a meeting point between traditional and modern veterinary knowledge, germinated in my mind. We could put up posters and exhibitions and it would be much easier to explain our work as well as provide evidence of Raika knowledge. Some time ago, we had bought a piece of agricultural land in a beautiful spot right at the edge of the Kumbhalgarh Sanctuary. Although its location was a bit remote – about 7 km from Sadri – it was otherwise ideal for putting up a building and had enough space to provide treatment to entire camel herds. An exploration of possible funding opportunities revealed that partial financial support might be available from the German Ministry of Economic Cooperation if the League for Pastoral Peoples could contribute a substantial sum. Christiane Herweg, the president of the League, immediately agreed to undertake a special fundraising drive and this was successful.

At the end of 1999, we were informed by the ministry in Germany that our application had been granted, but that the money would have to be spent within one month or so, since the financial year of the ministry was coming to a close. It seemed impossible to construct a whole building in such a short time span, but Hanwant's organisational talents in mobilising support and sourcing building materials came to the fore, coupled with the amazing industry and proficiency of an almost all-women construction team from the Meghwal community. The Meghwals, who are leather workers by tradition and regarded as untouchable, impressed me no end.

Undeterred by their veils, long skirts, chunky silver jewellery on their ankles and plastic bangles covering their arms, the ladies toiled away day in, day out, from nine in the morning until six in the evening with about an hour's break at midday, seven days a week, taking a break only every two weeks, on full moon and new moon days. Lila, Anchi and Gulabji kept moving stones and dirt and mixing cement the whole day, and always in a good mood – their labour took on the semblance of a musical, for they sang and laughed almost continuously. In under a month, they managed to put up a building consisting of a large hall and two smaller rooms.

The only thing that was not achieved by the deadline was the wiring and the electricity connection. When I mentioned this in the report to the ministry, they sent a stern rebuke, saying they could not see how a building could be of use if it had no electricity. They felt that this undermined the whole effort and I got the impression that they wanted their money back. I felt like pointing out that in this part of India there was no power available most of the time anyway, so that this was only a minor detail for people who so often had to cope without it, but thought better of it and just replied that the wiring had been carried out since.

Thinking like a public relations pro, Hanwant was keen to make a memorable and creative event out of the inauguration of the building. This was exactly what happened, although not quite in the manner that we had envisioned.

His friend from the German Embassy, Gunnar Denecke, was happy to accept the invitation as chief guest and to officially declare the building open. We invited the director of the Animal Husbandry Department from Jaipur, whose support of our work was vital as we were dispensing medicines to camels. Delightfully, the Rani-Sahiba from Ghanerao, a historically important fiefdom near Sadri, had accepted our invitation. She had spent most of her life in purdah but recently come out and entered local politics. Also included in this cast of illustrious personalities was the Raika priest, the most respected person in the Raika community, from the famous Mataji temple in Mundara. My sophisticated friends from Delhi, Purnima Singh and her mother Premaliya, were on the guest list and, of course, the entire Raika community was also expected. Hanwant arranged for a big wedding *shamiana* or tent that could host 2,000 people, a speaker system, food, and even musicians. It was going to be a spectacle worthy to behold, on much the same scale as a royal Rajput wedding. About the only requisite missing was a bridegroom mounted on an elephant. But there would be a string of colourfully decorated camels to carry the honoured guests to the tent.

When I arrived in Sadri ten days before the big event, preparations were in full swing. It was a busy time for LPPS anyway and as was happening more and more frequently, there were also visitors who wanted to see our work. In this case it was a famous Anglo-Indian photographer and his wife, who wanted to do a full-scale spread about the Raika. I talked to them briefly and they rattled off a list of the important people in the government and the publishing industry that they were connected to. They had enthralled our staff, taking them out for dinner in the fanciest eating joint Sadri had to offer and giving them a whiff of the big, wide world of VIPs and celebrities. There were also broad hints at a generous donation to LPPS. I thought this was fine and concentrated on my own work. But when Hanwant realised that our field assistants were no longer performing their assigned tasks and had been neglecting their regular duties in order to escort the journalists to Raika households for photography sessions, he had a serious talk with the boys, explaining priorities and that they could do this only outside their working hours. Without our staff as intermediaries, however, the Raika did not cooperate as camera-objects, and the photographer apparently became pretty angry. He departed to Delhi in a huff, but not before spreading some malicious rumours about me and about Hanwant and the intentions behind our work.

It left a very unpleasant taste, but there was no time to ponder about it, as the countdown for the inauguration day had begun. Our guests from Delhi were arriving the next day and needed to be picked up from the station, brought to the hotel and shown around our projects, including a visit to the sewing-centre that LPPS had established as a means of income generation for women from all castes. At the same time, the tent still had to be put up and equipped with flooring, chairs and a podium. Two frilly entrance gates, similar to those used for weddings, had to be erected, one at the entrance to the LPPS campus and one about a kilometre away. The speaker system needed to be checked, water, tea and snacks organised, as well as lunch arranged for the expected 2,000–3,000 guests.

The grand ceremony was planned for eleven o'clock, although I should have known that meant noon, at the earliest. The Raika from further away started trickling in the evening before and throughout the night, accommodating themselves in the tent. The food was also prepared in the night – it was typical Raika wedding fare: *lapsi* – sweetened wheat gruel with lots of ghee. Further support staff to serve water and food streamed in from dawn onwards and had to be shown their duties. Fortunately, our embassy friend and my Delhi pals got on really well and could be left to themselves. Then we received the phone call that the director of Animal Husbandry was about to arrive. He and Gunnar as well as the priest were received and garlanded about a kilometre away from the training centre and made the final stretch on beautifully decorated camels. While they dismounted and were garlanded with strings of marigold, an Ambassador inched its way through the throngs of people. It came to a slow halt and the Rani-Sahiba, a famous Rajput beauty in her younger years, and even now a breathtakingly gorgeous apparition, emerged in a glorious light-pink Rajput ensemble, lending glamour to the occasion. Like a queen – or maybe more a rockstar – she was immediately engulfed by a crowd of admiring subjects.

Everything was going to plan and even almost on time. The tent was filled to the hilt with men in red turbans sitting in neat rows, while the Raika women in their wide skirts and surrounded by small children had huddled together in a separate group. I was sitting together with some local officials – the police constable, the bank manager, the bus-company owner, and others – in the first row thinking nervously that we were a little bit behind schedule, if only by German standards. The honoured guests had been led and seated on the dais and the traditional puja to Saraswati, the goddess of wisdom and learning, that is the custom at such occasions, was about to start by lighting the lamp. The Rani-Sahiba had just been handed a burning candle to ignite the first wick, when I became aware of a commotion at the back of the tent. I could see a tall Raika with a long herding cane trying to push through the seated crowds and make his way to the dais. Others were trying to stop him, but he kept everybody at a distance by beating around with his herding stick and yelling something in a high-pitched voice. I could not understand his expletives, but when he came closer, I realised it was actually the photographer who had put on the traditional Raika attire. The people in the front row got up to restrain him, but he hissed, "Don't touch me, don't touch me," in a hysterical way. Evading their attempts to subdue him, he leapt onto the podium, and grabbed the microphone. While he started to make a speech, his wife or girlfriend handed out some sheets of paper to the honoured guests seated on the dais and threw a pile of them into the audience. Then she started snapping photos of the photographer making his speech accompanied by wild waving of his stick. Somebody had turned off the speaker system, so what he was saying was not comprehensible. Some sturdy young men not discouraged by his cane finally managed to bring him under control. I got hold of one of the photocopied sheets and had a glance at the text. It was a slew of charges against LPPS, Hanwant and me, accusing me of being a missionary, of being a bogus veterinary doctor, of taking advantage of the Raika, of letting them die of AIDS, and many other things.

The unforeseen interlude was over very quick – the fake Raika was led away by the police to the police station in Sadri. The ceremony continued, with the Rani-Sahiba making a moving speech, the German attaché lauding our efforts, the priest giving us his blessings and the director of Animal Husbandry unveiling a plaque commemorating the inauguration of the training centre. I found the whole event harrowing, worried that somebody might take the accusations about me being a missionary seriously, as this would have jeopardised all our efforts and could lead to the closure of LPPS. Fortunately, the guests seemed to be rather amused and had even enjoyed the thrill added by the photographer's performance. At least it wasn't your average formal function with long boring speeches and nobody fell asleep.

The photographer was eventually arrested in connection with drug charges, so that problem was solved. But his visit had fuelled the local rumour mill, and the grapevine was soon reporting that the big ceremony had actually been to celebrate German government control over the forest around our campus. Why otherwise would the German attaché have played such a prominent role? Satellite photos in our office showing the change in vegetation around the Kumbhalgarh Sanctuary over a period of seven years were cited as further evidence. Donated to us by a friendly geography professor, these photos had been displayed together with the documentation of our ongoing work. The opinion was that an innocent grassroots NGO could not be in possession of such material.

By now I knew that it was best to ignore such rumours and that it was more important to focus on work. One of the most important strategic commitments in our project proposal had been to help the Raika set up their own society, so that they would eventually become independent of us. But how would this body relate to their already existing traditional structures? The Raika had their own governance structure – the caste panchayat, basically an assembly of elders that was composed only of men, the *panches*. This panchayat would meet regularly to discuss the goings-on of the community, especially marital problems, and then dole out punishments as it saw fit. There was no election procedure for becoming a panch – any man who felt so inclined and had the time could start participating in the meetings and thereby become a panch. So, it was usually older men who no longer herded animals that composed the panchayats. There were panchayats at several levels – at the village level, then for 22 villages (the *samafle),* 44 villages (the *chatala),* 88 villages (the *parsotala),* and the whole Godwar region (the *nav-pragna).* If a decision could not be reached at one level then the case was referred to the next level. The top level was very rarely called, since it was an expensive undertaking in which 3,000 to 5,000 panches would participate and would have to be fed and provided with tea.

Both Hanwant and I had always been keen to get the approval of the panchayat for the project, but most of the panches were initially very unapproachable. It took several years for them to open up and start inviting Hanwant and me to attend their meetings. These gatherings initially filled me with awe, although I rarely could understand what was being discussed. You could always tell that the panches were meeting by the assemblage of heavy, beaked and embroidered shoes outside a Raika house.

But we also could not ignore the fact that the panches and their decisions were not always highly regarded by the community. There were allegations about corruption and suggestions that their decisions could be influenced by bribes and favours. Their opinion could be swayed by one cup of tea, was a lament I heard frequently.

It gradually became apparent that the majority of their decisions related to social issues – problems pertaining to child marriages, or matters to do with upholding traditions, prescribing the type of dress that women should wear, including the length of the ghagra and the wearing of a full set of plastic bangles on upper and lower arms. Several of the women I knew resented these decrees and confided how they yearned to sometimes wear a sari or to try out the comfortable salwar-kameez type of clothes that I had adopted. At regular intervals, the panches also made rules to curb excessive tea drinking and specified the amount of money to be spent on various ceremonies. For a long time, the panchayats even forbade the building of *pukka* houses. An old Raika from Sirohi district once told me that, in earlier times, the panchayat had excommunicated people who had bought property and built pukka houses because this meant that it reduced the land for grazing for the rest of the community.

On the other hand, matters related to their pastoral livelihoods, such as grazing issues or how to improve animal healthcare, were rarely discussed. An Italian anthropology student, Tommaso Sbriccoli, eventually put his finger on what the problem was: the panchayat was mostly composed of people who no longer owned any livestock and for that reason took little interest in pursuing matters relating to animals and to the grazing question. By contrast, the Raika who owned animals had no time to attend meetings since they had to tend to their livestock. Earlier, when practically the whole society was still dependent on animals, and everybody had shared the same interests, this had been different.

Working with the panchayat, thus, seemed unlikely to resolve our dilemma, although we were keen to maintain good relations with them, in order to not be excommunicated ourselves.

We were still perplexed about how we would build a Raika society that could gradually take over the role of LPPS in the face of what seemed insurmountable hurdles. The logical conclusion was to work with women instead of men. It is well known among development organisations that women usually respond much better to new opportunities.

Raika women are certainly strong and this is well recognised by their men. They are often referred to as the finance ministers of the family and make many of the household decisions about how to spend the family income. They sell dung, and if the family breeds sheep, they also make the deals with the livestock traders. For some reason, they have a better understanding of money, are good at keeping accounts and make sure that they have not been cheated. We have seen cases of men who have sold camels at Pushkar and then were unable to tell the difference between a hundred and a twenty-rupee note.

Unfortunately, breeding camels is perceived as solely a man's activity. I know only one woman, Geribai, who herself herds camels – because her husband, an able-bodied man prefers to involve himself in caste politics as a panch. Geribai is strong, but kind, dotes on her children, but is also strict with them. After she has cooked, supervised the milking of the camels, and taken care of their minor ailments, she goes out and herds the family's twenty or so camels, while her husband joins the panches in meetings at somebody's house and drinks tea and opium water.

Yet, when her husband or any other family elder is present, she will sit at a distance on the floor with her face covered. Only if she feels she has something urgent to contribute to the discussion will she part her veil slightly to the side and then whisper her opinion.

Raika etiquette decreed that women do not sit on chairs and it was regarded as extremely disrespectful and practically unthinkable that they speak up or unveil in the presence of their husbands, his peers or elders. Once the husband had left the room, however, they would talk more freely and uncover their faces, but no force in the world could even then get them to sit on a chair. There are incredibly strong women in Raika society – for instance, my friend Dailibai – who chart the course of their family's future, including economic affairs and marriage arrangements, because their husbands are for some reason incapable of it...but they would never sit on a chair.

Recognising that the Raika men were highly resistant to change, we made many attempts at addressing and involving women in our activities, but somehow these were almost invariably undermined. Once, when our project was awarded an international prize and we had reason for celebrations, we planned to hold a big party. Since we could not invite everybody, we wanted to leave the decision over the guestlist to the community. We had a meeting with the panches, asking them to decide how many people from each village should attend and I made a special plea that it was very important for me that women and children were among the guests. So the panches sat down on their haunches in a tight circle and debated for a while, finally trundling over to communicate their decision. "We have decided that from every village in the samafle, six men will attend," they declared. "What about women and children?" I asked. "We don't want to cause too much of a financial burden to you, so we have decided it is better for women and children not to come," was their response.

Another time, we organised an exposure tour specifically for young animal breeders, so they would get a chance to get out of their villages and learn about some of the relevant institutions in Rajasthan, including the capital from where decisions were made, the wool market, the camel research centre, the sheep breeding farm, among others. But who signed up for it? The majority was old men. "The young people can't come – who will look after the animals?" and "We have been working so hard all our life, we also deserve to enjoy ourselves", were some of their explanations. So only a small number of young people participated, although, thankfully, also a number of women, including Matra, who is one of our neighbours and another strong and independent woman. What happened, when the group visited the various places? It was the women who asked all the questions and took an interest, while the men remained mute and detached. One major victory, however, was achieved on this tour: removed from their usual environment and being taken to restaurants for food, the women actually sat on chairs! This caused quite a bit of grumbling among the men, with some enquiring from Hanwant why women were given equal standing.

Much of the deferential behaviour of women that so aggravates me is, of course, just there to keep up appearances towards the outside world and because it conforms to accepted standards of conduct. Kaki was another Raika woman who was also quiet in front of her husband but left no doubt that she was running the show in his absence, ordering around younger men and eagerly giving demonstrations of her knowledge about sheep diseases and how to treat them. She eventually became a board member of LPPS because of her analytical skills, being able to identify problems as well as solutions.

The same women to whom we owed the construction of our training centre showed their mettle when they were working on one of the famine-relief works that the government initiates for income-generation during droughts. They are paid by the government to construct earthen dams and reservoirs and do road work. In 2002, one of the worst drought years on record, they felt the man who was supervising the work and keeping record of their working hours was cheating them. When he refused to pay them what they thought he owed them, they ripped off his shirt and put the fear of god in him. They then hired a tractor and went to the administrative office in Ghanerao, successfully complaining about the man. Yet, the same women will not reply when you ask them for their husband's name. It would be a sign of disrespect to utter it, so they will ask another woman to answer this question for them.

So empowerment is our most difficult challenge. We can teach the Raika technical skills, we can tell the world about their indigenous knowledge, their love of animals, their skills in making use of an arid environment, the general desirability for humanity at large for this lifestyle to continue, but we cannot "develop" them. This is something they have to do for themselves.

I have to admit that, quite frequently, I get very frustrated about our work and even angry with the Raika. What good is it all for? Would it not be better to withdraw? I might like the way they treat their animals, but I can't agree with their social practices. Do I have the right to meddle? Should I not just remain a neutral bystander? Have I wasted quite a few years of my life trying to change them? Just when I am ready to give everything up, I am once again charmed by the way one of these recalcitrant, opium-befuddled, bearded old men lavishes love on his grandchild. Or the old scoundrel Adoji, with whom we have had so many fights over the years, reports to me how well one of our new camel babies is doing: "This is really a '*naslvala torda*' (a young camel true to breed) – you should keep it for breeding." Or the most stubborn of our old diehards will suddenly observe that, "Baiji is not at all looking good," and order a glass of *chhaach* (buttermilk) for me. To which Hanwant will respond, "Baiji is not looking good because she is so worried about you Raika. What will become of you in the future?" And they take this completely seriously.

And even at the height of a drought, when they do not know where to find food for their family or their animals, they never lose their dignity, nor their vanity.

Love means accepting people how they are, despite or maybe

even because of their faults. So while I often wonder why and how on earth I got myself into this quandary, even curse myself for having done so, there is no way back. Besides, it is partly that conservatism, that adherence to the old values and refusal to become like the rest of the world, that marks the special nature of the Raika.

Chapter 11

THE FOREST

"Camels do not degrade the desert vegetation; in fact they conserve it. It has been shown that in an area where camels have grazed on grass, the vegetation has fared better than in a similar area protected from camels."

– *The Camel. Its Ecology, Behaviour and Relationship to Man*, H. Gauthier-Pilters and A. Dagg (1981)

"Kumbhalgarh Wildlife Sanctuary is one of the last strongholds of the rich floral and faunal diversity of the Aravallian ecosystem and the species are to be conserved as gene pool for the coming generations. As such the grazing should not be permitted within the Sanctuary area."

– Response of the CEC in IA No. 1536 in IA No 548, filed by the Raika Sangharsh Samiti, village Latada, Pali district, Rajasthan, dated 13.7.2006

From the beginning, it had been clear that the Raika considered the lack of grazing areas for their camels as the root of their distress. It was the poor nutritional status, the chronic hunger of the camels, which troubled them. When they had to watch this day by day, powerless to do anything about it, it made their life a misery. The

Raika felt like mothers unable to feed their children on one hand, but also realised that it impacted their own economic fortunes. Ruparam expressed this succinctly in the diary that he kept as part of his assignment:

> When the camels are kept on an empty stomach, then the diseases also rise. When the camels are hungry, then many have abortions. Earlier, the camels often became pregnant every 3 or 4 years but today the situation is so that females only give birth in 7 years, so their numbers are getting less. The diseases have become more. In the last 6-7 years about 200 male and female camels died of mange. Earlier the camels were of good breed and some females gave up to 19 kg of milk. And there were not so many diseases.
>
> The jungle has become limited and there are less trees and shrubs and the situation is that even in the *chaumasa* (rainy season) the camels are hungry. At some places there are game sanctuaries and in the winter more fields are cultivated and the people can't go there anymore with their camels and the camels are hungry in the winter and in the summer...In the chaumasa, if the camels are to graze in the forest, then Rs 150 have to be paid for each one and the poor Dewasis don't have the money for that so the camels are starving in the chaumasa.

We knew that unless we attacked this problem, everything else was just cosmetic. But the grazing and fodder question was such a complex and intractable conundrum that it often seemed more sensible to stay away from it.

We had once, during the milk-marketing project, experimented with feeding green fodder to camels. To my surprise, the herd camels had not shown any appetite for the nutritious and green *rijka* (alfalfa) that the project provided. Habituated to dry fodder, they were just not willing to change their tastes and food habits. The types of dry fodder which were used to feed the draft camels plying in the towns, such as the leaves of the khejri tree and the bordi shrub, were not available in our area.

Even when we broke off this trial and focused our efforts on camel health, the nagging feeling remained that we were treating only the symptoms rather than the underlying cause, i.e. nutritional deficiencies of the camel herds and their negative impact on reproduction, milk yield, and the growth rate of the young ones. Although our healthcare was popular, there would be no success without solving the problem of providing camels with adequate nutrition.

It took us years to grasp and disentangle the factors contributing to the starvation status of the camels. They included the feeding habits of camels, changes in land ownership and land-use patterns, population pressure, conservation attitudes, and long-established deeply ingrained social relationships and dependencies.

Zoologists classify camels as "browsers", since they prefer to eat trees and shrubs. They do graze on the ground, for instance, on thistle, but they favour tree branches, which they pull down until they snap, to then strip off the leaves with an almost vacuum-cleaner-like suction. They can access branches as high as 3.5 metres, so only giraffes and climbing goats have a longer reach. And they have no qualms about extremely thorny and spiny plants and in fact, seem to prefer them. They grasp even the sharpest and most vicious spikes with their long, prehensile lips and then somehow ingest them, leaving one to wonder about the walls of their mouth and why these do not become perforated in the process.

Rajasthan has many excellent fodder trees with highly nutritious foliage, many of them belonging to the leguminose family and high in protein. Camels are especially fond of the various acacia species, such as the famous khejri tree and the desi babul, the local acacia species. Based on information from the Raika, we have recorded at least fifty-two plant species that the camels eat even in our own, local area, almost all of which are trees.

Before 1947, all land was owned by the maharajahs. But each village had a community pasture, the gauchar, for which livestock owners had to pay a small grazing fee. In addition, the maharajahs, being well aware of the importance of livestock for the rural economy, accorded them grazing privileges even in parts of their hunting reserves. These areas were known as *gudara*. And when a European type of management system was installed in the Aravalli forests during the colonial period, the Maharajah of Jodhpur made sure that the animals of the pastoralists retained grazing rights.

The big change came after 1947. When India gained Independence, land began to be privatised on a large scale. A land-ceiling act came into force that obliged the maharajahs and other noblemen to reduce their land holdings. People from the farming castes, as well as the so-called "scheduled tribes" and "scheduled castes", were given some of this land for free. The Raika were slow to recognise the implications of the privatisation of land that had once been a commons for them and, for a very long time, ignored the option of investing in land ownership. In fact, their caste panchayats continued to prohibit private land ownership, arguing that it would reduce the grazing land available to the community as a whole. They even outlawed construction of pukka houses with the intention of supporting maximum mobility. In an environment where rainfall is unreliable, this made sense in many ways. Animals have to remain on the move in order to go wherever rain falls and vegetation is available; mobility also prevents overuse. In Rajasthan and other drought-prone lands, mobile livestock keeping is superior to sedentary farming as a livelihood strategy and, in good years, herds grow automatically, practically like a fixed deposit.

For a while, the Raika did not have too many problems, because even though land was now increasingly privatised, crops were grown only during the three months of the rainy season. During the rest of the year, when the fields were fallow, farmers were happy when herds grazed on them as they provided manure that enhanced soil fertility. But the situation transformed further. More and more farmers began to dig wells on their properties; the availability of diesel-driven pumps enabled them to grow two or even three crops a year by means of irrigation. The amount of land that was lying fallow and accessible for grazing thus steadily decreased. This development was dramatically visible on some satellite photos of Sadri and its vicinity, made available to us by Paul Robbins, an American geographer.

Besides cultivable land, there is another category of land that can be utilised for grazing in theory, the "wastelands" – defined as land not suitable for cultivation. But this land also changed for the worse since nobody seemed to take responsibility for its management. Especially in Pali District, most wasteland has become overgrown by angrezi babul (*Prosopsis juliflora*). As shown by the eminent Rajasthani scholar N. S. Jodha, when the feudal system dissolved, the village gauchars began deteriorating. The user fees were eliminated and the village panchayats failed to enforce the rules. People began to see the gauchar as a free-for-all, which they used but no longer cared for. Not only did they neglect to punish people who cut the trees, but also did not protest when the more powerful parties of a village appropriated the land and built houses there. There are some exceptions to this general rule of gauchar neglect and, interestingly, these often occur in villages where the Raika are strongly represented and have a majority over other castes for whom livestock is not crucial.

Concurrently, access to the Aravalli forests also tightened. Already in British times, timber extraction from these old hunting reserves of the maharajahs had started. In 1953, the Rajasthan Forest Act was passed. It enshrined the traditional rights of the local people to collect dry wood and grass without any charges. Grazing remained legal, although a fee had to be paid for each animal, depending on its size, but hunting, tree cutting and coppicing were prohibited. Only the Forest Department could manage the forest commercially for timber and for gum.

Then, in 1971, a wildlife sanctuary named Kumbhalgarh Reserve was established in parts of Pali, Udaipur and Rajsamand districts with the intention of conserving the habitat of wild animals such as leopard, sloth bear, wolf, hyena, sambhar, and the grey jungle fowl. To this end, 582 square km along 85 km of the western face of the Aravalli Hills were designated as a protected area. The sanctuary was managed by the Rajasthan Forest Department with the help of fifty full-time foresters. Unfortunately, it was smack in the middle of the hereditary monsoon grazing grounds of the Godwar and Jojawar camel breeders, as well as other local livestock keepers.

While grazing was still allowed in parts of the reserve against a grazing fee, it was now prohibited during the rainy season, just when it was needed most. The forest establishment holds that grazing during the rainy season is especially damaging to the vegetation. The Raikas deny this, stating that grazing instead stimulates tree growth, and some ecologists support this view. The zoologist, Hilde Gauthier-Pilters, who studied camels in the Sahara, observed that the camels' grazing behaviour is wholly attuned to the low-carrying capacity of the area. Camels never take more than one or very few bites from a plant and then wander on for a few hundred metres before they take the next one. She also emphasised that camel herds spread out widely which dissipates their impact on the vegetation and contrasted this with the grazing behaviour of sheep that huddle together and eat grass down to the root. The padded feet of camels are also supposed to be gentle on the soil, not churning it up like the sharp hooves of goats and sheep.

But Gauthier-Pilters conducted her studies in the Sahara where the ecology is quite different from the Aravalli Hills. And although she concluded that, "unlike slow-moving cattle and intensely grazing goats, camels are economical feeders which never overgraze the vegetation," she also conceded that, "trees from which camels obtain a significant amount of nourishment may grow better if they are periodically protected from browsing."

The impact of livestock grazing on the vegetation and on biodiversity is a highly contentious and emotive issue. In the classic conservation view, livestock grazing is the root of all evil that automatically damages the vegetation and sets in a vicious cycle of desertification. Livestock is thought to be incompatible with wildlife conservation. When protected areas are set up in India, whether it's a national park or a sanctuary, one of the first steps is to evict the livestock. People living inside or at the outskirts of the protected area are encouraged to switch over to keeping crossbred cows and to stall-feed them rather than to let them graze. In Rajasthan's Ranthambore National Park, famous for its tiger population, crossbred cattle and stall-feeding was supported through the setting up of a dairy and an animal health programme. But such projects have no record of success. In the Gir Sanctuary for the Asiatic Lion situated in Gujarat, eviction of cattle encouraged the lions – for whom cattle was a favourite prey – to leave the sanctuary in order to hunt.

An entirely different view is held by another group of

conservationists who are more sympathetic to the pastoralists. They believe that livestock, vegetation, and wildlife have co-evolved over a long period and contend that biodiversity actually increases under managed grazing pressure. They point out that many plants require grazing to thrive. And some wildlife depends on the presence of livestock. For instance, in Rajasthan's Bharatpur Bird Sanctuary, the Siberian cranes stopped coming when buffalo grazing was banned: buffaloes had kept the growth of water weeds under control; without them these plants proliferated and prevented the cranes from digging up the tubers that were one of the main ingredients of their diets. Similar cases of such symbiosis between wildlife and livestock have been reported from other parts of India. For instance, domesticated buffaloes are integral to the ecology of the Chilika Lake in Odisha, India's largest wintering ground for migratory birds. As documented by Dr Balaram Sahu of the state's Department of Animal Husbandry, the buffaloes swim in the lake at night to feed, and their manure sustains the fish population. Furthermore, their footprints create little puddles in which insects that feed the migratory birds breed.

Globally, awareness about the ecological relationships between pastoralists and wildlife is growing and, in 2003, in the run-up to the World Parks Conference (a major gathering of conservationists which is held every ten years), international conservationists organised a workshop for the mobile indigenous peoples from around the globe. Bagdiram, accompanied by Hanwant Singh as translator, represented the Raika community. He and other delegates from nomadic societies emphasised that pastoralists and indigenous societies have developed many traditional practices, such as rotational grazing, grazing reserves, splitting up of herds in small groups, and re-seeding to protect the vegetation. After all, vegetation is the foundation of their livelihoods, so it is in their own best interest to nurture and protect it! The deliberations of the pastoralists were taken note of and the meeting resulted in a formal declaration about the benefits of the mobile people to the rest of society. This declaration was approved by the delegates of the World Parks Conference.

Inspired by this movement for recognition of pastoralists as guardians of the environment, we attempted several times to initiate a research on the impact of camel grazing on the forest vegetation of the Aravalli Hills. We hoped that, with scientific facts, we might be able to induce a policy change in the sanctuary management and legitimise controlled camel grazing in suitable areas. But such research is time-consuming and requires an extended period of investigation to take into account annually fluctuating amounts of rainfall. And, given the contentiousness of the issue, even scientific facts are probably not sufficient to change the perspective of forest officials. In addition, there is that blight that mars interaction with many government departments in India and is likely to throw a spanner in an otherwise balanced solution: corruption. Foresters may be sincere in their wish for a pristine forest that provides a safe haven for the native wildlife unblemished by grazing livestock, but some have not been above lining their pockets with bribes or fines charged illegally from various parties for allowing access to the resources they are charged with protecting.

Almost all rural people residing in the vicinity depend on the forest or find it convenient to make use of it. It is like a supermarket that satisfies one's daily needs. The customers include the tribal women who collect dry wood and carry it as head loads from the forest to the Sadri market, farmers who cut branches of the plaas (*Butea monsperma*) tree as buffalo fodder and transport them home on the backs of their bicycles, anybody who plans a bit of domestic remodelling and needs some construction materials, and the huge number of people who do not own a gas stove and need to stock up on their personal firewood supplies. Apart from the Raika, who have to find food for their animals on a daily basis, it is the tribal women who depend most on the forest for filling their stomachs. By selling a head-load of dry wood, they make just enough money to be able to afford a meal, and if they are unable to do this, they will go hungry.

But these subsistence users are probably small fry compared to the people who mine the forest for big profits – by logging the valuable hardwood trees and by poaching the wildlife and selling its body parts as ingredients to the Chinese medicine market.

There is plenty of scope for generating extra income by turning a blind eye towards illegal activities. If one is to believe the Raika, the hierarchy of forest officials has perfected their method of maximising returns by fudging a bit with the system. It works like this: According to sanctuary rules, some forty per cent or so of the protected area is to be kept open for grazing, while the remainder is to be enclosed for regeneration. The enclosures in which the vegetation is given an opportunity to regenerate are scheduled to be reopened after seven years. But this does not happen and, apparently, many of them have been kept closed for ten to twenty years, or even longer. They are overgrown with lush and nutritious greenery while the patches that are officially open have been grazed down to the bare brown soil. Of course, this creates the desire for camel owners and other livestock keepers – in fact, any self-respecting herder with a heart – to willingly shell out whatever money he has for the satisfaction of seeing his animals eat good food.

Dirk Flöter, a German master's student, who conducted his field research with us, explored the intricacies of the system in one particular village. The only grazing areas that are declared legal and available against the official grazing fee are located deep in the forest and it takes two to three hours just to get there. So each day the herds spend four to six hours walking to and from their grazing areas. As a small lake in the forest is the only watering place in the area, it must be included in the daily round. But the foresters have made access to this lake virtually impossible by blocking all approaches. The only remaining entry to the watering point is a steep slope which gets very slippery during the rainy season. Camels, whose flat, frictionless feet are adapted for desert sands, regularly fall down on this slope and break their legs. I had always puzzled about the high incidence of fractures among camels in our area and this was the explanation.

Gradually, over the years, as their trust increased, the Raika revealed to us the extent to which they had become clients to the forest officials. For decades, they had routinely been paying much more than the legally sanctioned grazing fees – huge sums of tens of thousands of rupees – in order to remain in the good graces of the foresters and make sure that their animals would not starve. On top of the cake of cash, was the icing of at least one goat per village per year that the foresters had become habituated to and regarded as their inalienable right.

Hanwant, who feels as deeply about the Raika as he does about conserving the forest, became incensed. He took note of all bribery incidents and compiled a list of culprits including the amounts they had pocketed. When it became known one day that the forest minister was going to visit Sadri, Hanwant mobilised the Raika, letting them know that now was the time to get even. On the day in question, the streets of Sadri were thronged with the Raika and its thoroughfare had turned into a sea of red turbans and nothing else. When the minister and his entourage visited with one of their local party friends, a delegation of white-bearded Raika deputised by the crowd requested a word with the minister. He waved them in and, after introductions, they handed him a rolled up piece of paper.

Within a couple of days, all the officials on the list had received their marching orders to new postings at the other end of Rajasthan.

But the legal situation is continuously in flux, far from transparent and can change one day to the next. In mid-March 2000, Hanwant and I were snaking on the motorbike through Sadri's cluttered main thoroughfare, dodging vendors with their rickety pushcarts, cows, a litter of piglets, and the usual assemblage of street dogs, when a worn-out jeep that we recognised as belonging to the local forest ranger came towards us. He leaned out waving a smallish piece of paper which he pressed on us with a big smile. "This has just come – a new order. Please take note of it!"

It was a shabby piece of paper, badly photocopied on grainy greyish paper and hardly legible; no easy read, it had to be painstakingly deciphered letter by letter. After we had pored over it for some time, it became apparent that the note chronicled the attempt to disseminate an order by the Supreme Court through the various tiers of the Forest Department. The original order had been issued in English, way back in 1996, and prohibited the removal of any types of forest products, including dried and green wood as well as grass and leaves from wildlife sanctuaries. In the process of being passed down through the various levels of the forest administration, it had been translated into Hindi. Amazingly, the Hindi version included "grazing" as a strictly prohibited activity, although this had not even been mentioned in the original version in English.

If this order was for real, its effects would be dramatic and even devastating for the two forest-user groups that depended on it the most. When the news spread among the Raika, the immediate reaction of many sheep breeders was that they would have to sell their animals. Sheep prices plummeted by more than fifty per cent. Even foresters were uneasy about the wisdom of this order, it was rumoured. Neglecting to cut grass would make the range more prone to wildfires. And what about the undesirable and invasive species which almost everybody wanted to get rid of – the foreign acacia? Its removal was also illegal under the order.

What could we do? Our first action was to write a letter to the chief wildlife warden in Jaipur enquiring about the status of "grazing". If this had not been mentioned in the Supreme Court order, how could some of the forest administrators just add it to the list of prohibited activities? Of course, we never received a reply.

Nothing dramatic happened either and, over the months, everything went back to normal. Undoubtedly, the Raika offered the foresters a higher bribe than usual and, after some hesitations, this was accepted. The same applied to the tribal women who could afford it least. It seemed as if every attempt to "save the forest" by stricter regulations only created additional opportunities for bribes.

For the Raika, the situation always becomes acute at the beginning of the rainy season when they know they will have no place to graze their camels in other than the forest. At this time of year, they hound and beleaguer Hanwant, believing that he will be able to help them. The only possibility he saw for tackling the issue was repeating the feat he had achieved with regard to camel milk: making a public interest litigation suit at the High Court in Jodhpur in the name of the Raika from Jojawar, stating that the forest regulations were responsible for the decline of the camel population in Rajasthan.

We compiled extensive documentation for an advocate in Jodhpur who agreed to take on our case. The comprehensive dossier included scientific articles about the effects of camel grazing on vegetation, population statistics, data on the economic significance and potential of camels, as well as information about the extent and process of animal genetic resource loss. Our lawyer prepared an impressive case, waited for a favourable constellation among the sitting judges, which, in March 2003, decided in the favour of the camels. The Chief Justice of Rajasthan agreed that camels were important and that they needed a place to graze. He stated that camels were a crucial part of Rajasthan's biodiversity that needed to be protected and ordered the village forest committees to grant the customary pasture rights to the camels from Jojawar.

The delight over this development did not last long. In 2004, the Central Empowered Committee (CEC), a special body set up by the Supreme Court in 2002 to save India's forests and wildlife, again circulated a letter to all state governments admonishing them to implement the Supreme Court order of 2000. In this communication, grazing was enumerated as one of the activities strictly prohibited in all protected areas – although, as we had noted before, the original order referred to had not actually mentioned it.

Thus, in the summer of 2004, the Rajasthan Forest Department refused to issue the usual grazing permits, going against the recent decision by Rajasthan's High Court that "rightsholders" were allowed to graze. In essence, this meant the total abolishment of the long-standing customary rights of the Raika.

Decisive action was called for. At Hanwant's suggestion, the Raika formed a "struggle committee" (Raika Sangharsh Samiti) and with the help of our old friend, Purnima Singh, this committee hired Vinoo Bhagat, a Delhi-based advocate. He wrote a letter to the CEC asking to detail which activities were permitted and which ones were prohibited. He also requested the CEC to clarify to the Rajasthan government that it did not prohibit the Raikas' grazing. The Rajasthan High Court itself was approached to spell out whether its earlier order was still valid, but this referred the case to the Supreme Court.

By February 2006, our advocate filed an application on behalf of the Raika to the Supreme Court requesting a clarification whether it meant a ban on the traditional grazing rights of the Raika in Kumbhalgarh Sanctuary that had previously been confirmed by the Rajasthan High Court in its order dated 26 March 2003. He made the case that if the ban was implemented, "the Raika as a cultural and ethnic group and the camels they breed will cease to exist in the near future."

In response, the Supreme Court in April 2006 ordered the CEC as well as the state government to file their responses by the second week of July. We were holding our breath about the expected replies. Then, out of the blue, Bagdiramji, Hanwant and I were invited to a global gathering of pastoralists in a remote corner of Ethiopia. It was a unique opportunity we did not want to miss and decided to go. Nervously, Hanwant was trying to make use of the organisers' satellite phone to monitor from Ethiopia what was going on in our absence, but could not get through to the LPPS office.

As soon as we landed in Delhi, Hanwant's mobile started to ring non-stop, with cries for help from Sadri. "We can't graze our animals in the forest any more. Please do something to open the forest!" "Where are you? We have heard that you lost the case and therefore are hiding out in Jaisalmer!" "Thank God you are back. We've heard rumours that you died! Come to Sadri fast!"

Before taking a flight to Udaipur in the early afternoon, Hanwant and Bagdiram rushed to meet our advocate and picked up the reply of the CEC to the enquiry of the Raika Sangharsh Samiti. They reached Sadri after dark and the only person who could provide the low-down was Mangilal, a sheep breeder and board member of LPPS. He confirmed the confused messages we had received over the mobile. "Yes, the herds are no longer allowed to enter the forest – since about four days. A few days ago, a member of the Central Empowered Committee came to Sadri on a fact-finding mission in a convoy of jeeps. He had a meeting with some Raika and asked them all kinds of questions. And yes, there is the rumour that Bhaba fled to Jaisalmer. Other people said he was killed in an accident."

Next morning, we got more information from two researchers, Paul Robbins and Anil Chhangani, who were running a project on the ecology of the Kumbhalgarh Sanctuary. They vividly described the visit by the CEC and how all animals were now grazing along the roads instead of in the forest.

When Hanwant talked to a few more people, it gradually became clear that some powerful personages – who will remain unnamed here – had ganged up against him. They were jealous of the trust that the Raika placed in him and resented how he was able to gather them in big meetings, fearing that he might use this for his own political advancement. In his absence, they had spread the message that the forest would not be opened as long as the Raika continued to meet and liaise with him. On the other hand, if they stopped seeing him, the jungle would be opened within a day or a couple of days at the most.

This intelligence was confirmed at dawn next day when a delegation of Raika surreptitiously knocked at our door to beg Hanwant to remain quiet and lie low until the forest was reopened. Hanwant happily agreed.

But one day passed, then another, and another – three days went by without anything happening and it became more and more difficult for the Raika to keep their herds away from the forest.

The mood changed again.

The Raika started losing faith in their other patrons, held

meetings and begged Hanwant to come. To these messages, he replied, saying, "I can't do anything, you have to do something yourself. Do a demonstration or something to show your strength!"

Yet, as more and more Raika started petitioning him, growing desperate, he instructed them to refute the data compiled by the CEC about their land holdings and livestock numbers. LPPS staff went out with forms to collect the correct information from the Raika panches and had it certified by the sarpanch and patwari. Gradually, the replies trickled in and it was confirmed that the CEC had produced inaccurate data, and not broken down the livestock numbers by caste but attributed all of them to the Raika, including buffaloes and cows, which are kept almost exclusively by other castes. The land holdings had also been misrepresented by a factor of almost ten. Not all villages sent back the data; some of them refused.

It was a tense time and our mood was low, because we felt everything was stacked against us. The rumours about white people being behind the trouble had surfaced again. It was even said that I had bought the forest and put in place the grazing ban! Nevertheless, we continued collecting information and translating evidence from Hindi into English, including many newspaper clippings about the situation in Kumbhalgarh.

When the case was heard at the Supreme Court on 4 August, Hanwant, Heeraram Raika, the secretary of the Raika Sangharsh Samiti, and I went to Delhi to observe the proceedings.

Our lawyer presented the facts, mentioning that social unrest could be expected unless the grazing issue was resolved in the favour of the Raika; he even made a cross-reference to the Maoist movement being fuelled by landlessness and predicted a similar situation could evolve in Rajasthan. However, he was no match for the star lawyer of the CEC, Mr Harish Salve, who argued for regulated grazing and called for an assessment of the carrying capacity by the chief wildlife warden.

By September, the principal chief conservator of forests and the chief wildlife warden of Rajasthan came out with a report in which they concluded: "...in order to protect one of the last remains of Aravalli biodiversity, it is recommended that grazing should not be permitted in the Kumbhalgarh Wildlife Sanctuary area."

At this stage, there was not much we could do. Fearing that the Raika case could have implications for other pastoralist groups throughout India, our advocate even recommended that we withdraw the case. While we were weighing our options, another law, highly relevant for the Raika was approved by parliament: The Scheduled Tribes and Other Traditional Forest Dwellers (Recognition of Forest Rights) Act, 2006, which provides rights to communities that can prove they have used the forest for three generations or seventy-five years.

This development again totally changed the scenario, as would some five years later the announcement in February 2012 by the Rajasthan government to convert the Kumbhalgarh Sanctuary into a National Park.

We foresee further legal tussles for the years ahead unless some enlightened leadership in the forest establishment reconsiders its customary aversion against livestock grazing and takes note of how nature conservation can go hand in hand with livelihood support to rural people. In some European countries, such as my native Germany, grazing by livestock is the most frequently employed nature conservation measure, and shepherds (there are no camel herds in Europe) are often paid by the government for the environmental services they provide!

Chapter 12

CRISIS

"BDR, BSF IN SHOOT OUT OVER CAMEL SMUGGLERS
Bangladeshi and Indian border troops exchanged heavy fire for about five hours yesterday morning after smugglers tried to bring in camels at Shibganj in Chapainawabganj..."

– *The Daily Star*, Dhaka, 28 February 2003

By the end of 2001, things were not going too badly for LPPS. Our small organisation had become established, in a minor way. It employed about half a dozen full-time and part-time staff. With the opening of the training centre, we had shifted our office to Butibagh, a piece of land that I had purchased in 1997. Originally a wheat-field and located about 5 km outside Sadri, adjacent to the Kumbhalgarh Sanctuary, Butibagh had by now become the hub of all our activities. Raika, and other animal owners, would drop in at any time of day or night if they had a sick camel or any other problem, or just to pay a friendly visit. Sometimes they would bring their families to show them the facilities which included a computer, a display of ingredients for ethnoveterinary medicine in plastic jars, a small library, a growing row of files, and albums of photographs from our activities. The steady stream of visitors also included people from the government and non-government organisations, as well as foreigners. We were able to host students who came to undertake field research and they often did very useful work. One of them, Dirk Flöter, had conducted a meticulous camel herd survey that suggested that in our immediate project area, among the eighty families which had registered with us, the camel population had remained stable.

Our work had veered from its exclusive focus on camels to encompass livestock in general. In fact, at the suggestion of the Raika, we were planning a sheep project. The rationale was that many more Raikas had sheep than camels and so a much larger part of the community would benefit. It was clear that the sheep breeders were also under enormous pressure. Wool prices had dropped to an almost unprecedented low because of a worldwide glut – people nowadays wear less woollen clothing, as synthetics are used instead. And, of course, the sheep breeders also had a grazing problem. They were just as badly affected by the restrictions in the Kumbhalgarh Sanctuary as the camel breeders.

I had written extensively about the Raika and their indigenous knowledge and they had become quite well known in some circles. Due to the continuing efforts of people like Evelyn Mathias and organisations such as ANTHRA, ethnoveterinary medicine had become more widely accepted, and although it would be an exaggeration to say that it had been absorbed into the mainstream, it had become a recognised component of livestock development projects.

LPPS was also involved in the LIFE (Local Livestock for Empowerment of Rural People) project, an initiative started by LPP to promote livestock development that built on local knowledge and resources rather than adopting western-style intensive production, and is socially and ecologically sustainable. Improving economic returns from livestock is an important avenue of rural development and poverty alleviation in developing countries. This premise is sound where livestock is one of the most important assets in poor rural communities. The approach historically adopted by most aid agencies, as well as governments, has been to promote high-yielding animals from Europe, notably the black and white Friesian cattle. This tactic has very often resulted in failure, since the intended beneficiaries are not able to provide the expensive inputs – for instance, feed and veterinary care – that are necessary to maintain these demanding animals. One of the unintended side effects has been loss of biodiversity – caused by the extinction of many local types and breeds of livestock that are better adapted to the local climate and environment. This loss of domestic animal diversity had been recognised as a major concern for future food security by the Food and Agriculture Organisation of the United Nations which was trying to alert governments to the problem and motivate them to protect their indigenous breeds. The LIFE initiative was a push to also inform non-government organisations about the need to consider questions such as the conservation of animal genetic resources in their work.

A new approach to livestock development was urgently needed: one that was not just oriented towards maximum productivity but also considered its wider social and ecological implications.

I was coordinating this LIFE project and it necessitated a lot of travel to visit other organisations working with livestock keepers. I was continuously on the go, and now had far less time to spend in Sadri.

Although camels were no longer our exclusive concern, we, of course, continued our work in that area. The trypanosomiasis prophylaxis was made available at a slightly subsidised rate, as was mange treatment, and whenever a camel was reported sick, LPPS staff tried to help.

In November, the Pushkar Mela was on again; if I had counted correctly, it was the tenth time in a row that I attended it. As had become a routine over the years, Hanwant and I drove the 200 km on the project's motorbike, and I was by now well familiar with the temperature regime this exposed us to, ranging from biting cold to relentless heat. During the first 50 km, the cold was so intense that, despite having wrapped ourselves in blankets we had to stop at every tea-stall just to keep the blood circulation in the extremities going. This was followed by a brief transitional period when our bodies were at equilibrium with the outside temperature. But for the remainder of the day, the sun scorched down, combined with a dessicating wind to put us at risk of mummification. By late afternoon, when we sailed down the pass that separates Ajmer from Pushkar, life on the motorcycle was again bearable, although by then my posterior felt like a glutinous mass. We checked into our usual address, a modest residence temporarily converted into a guesthouse close to the mela ground.

Our first order of business was to wander up to the dera where the Anji-ki-dhani Raika and the Godwar Raika had set up their camp. Adoji was there, Gautamji, Harjiram, and the entire usual crowd. With them was Mastersahib ("Ma'sahib"), a retired Rajput schoolteacher who owned a large herd of camels and was a great supporter of LPPS. They spread out the bhakal, arranged two burlap sacks as cushions, urged us to make ourselves comfortable, and passed round the chillum. They milked one of the female camels that acted as nanny to the youngsters that were to be sold, made tea, and handed me a freshly made maize roti to which they knew I was particularly partial. We spread out our tired bodies amidst the Raika and a few camels. Most of the animals had been taken out for grazing for the night and would return in the morning. Hanwant asked how the mela was going – so-so, neither particularly busy, nor really slow. Everything seemed to be as usual and my mind drifted off contentedly. Strange how this has become part of my life now, I thought. As I looked up at the star-studded sky, trying to find a shooting star, I picked up a piece of conversation about a Raika meeting that was to be held the next day. "By the way," somebody was saying to me, "Bagdiram was here looking for you; he wants to see you." Bagdiram was a Raika leader from Chittorgarh. He owned camels which were herded by his sons. He was very literate and had often participated in our workshops and other functions. When in Pushkar, he usually stayed in the Raika temple somewhere in the maze of small streets and alleys surrounding the holy lake.

It was time to go back to the hotel anyway so we decided to drop by the temple to see if we could find Bagdiram. The temple, which belongs to the Maru Raika and does not entertain the Godwar Raika, is close to the Brahma temple and is adorned with red sandstone reliefs of camel riders. Access to a non-Raika and especially white people is prohibited, so we were refused entry by the guards posted at the door. Bagdiram was in, however, and, after a small boy conveyed a message to him, we were granted admission. A tall and portly man in his fifties, Bagdiram is immediately identifiable as a Raika from Mewar from his greenish turban, a beige kurta and dhoti. He carries with him a small bag in which he keeps important documents relating to the community, such as our report on camel milk marketing. We sat on a foam mattress in his small room and after an exchange of pleasantries, he came out with his news. "I am deeply concerned because, even as we speak, hundreds of camels are being assembled in Old Pushkar. They have been bought by butchers and by middlemen who will take them to slaughter houses in Uttar Pradesh and West Bengal."

Hanwant and I looked at each other. In the previous year, we had already heard vague rumours that not all camels at Pushkar were being sold as work-animals, and that some were destined for the meat market. But it had been impossible to substantiate this and when we had tried to make enquiries, nobody actually seemed very sure. I had mentally filed the information as one of the many rumours that were floating around. I had never forgotten the strong reactions I had encountered at the beginning of my research when I asked about the use of camels for meat. If a few camels that were unfit to work were slaughtered, I did not see too much wrong with that. But this intelligence coming from Bagdiram, a respected community leader, was different. And he was talking about "hundreds" of camels.

"What kind of camels?" I asked. "Old and sick ones?"

"No, not old and sick ones. Big strong ones that have a lot of meat on them. In fact, many female camels also," Bagdiram explained and then added, more emphatically, "This can't be allowed to happen. It goes against our Raika culture. I need your help to stop this!"

Camel herds were already in decline. If young female camels were being sent for slaughter, the implications were catastrophic. Breeding herds would dwindle and native bloodlines could disappear. One drought or epidemic could bring about a decisive population collapse.

"This is really very bad," Hanwant said, adding, "Yes, of course we will help. What do you want us to do?"

Bagdiram pulled out some papers from his briefcase and putting on his reading glasses, he explained. "I am writing to the district collector of Ajmer so that he prohibits taking camels for slaughter from Pushkar. Pushkar is a holy city and this should not be allowed to happen. After all, there is already a ban on taking cattle out of the state. Why can there not be the same rule for camels?"

After a brief pause, he continued, "You must help me write to the district collector and to other concerned agencies. You must get this out to the press and inform all authorities. First of all, you have to come to the big meeting that we have called tomorrow and where we will discuss the issue."

The meeting the next evening followed the same pattern as the many other Raika meetings we had participated in. It was called for at 7 pm in the big hall on the ground floor that represents the precinct to the inner sanctuary where the image of the goddess is placed. People started arriving in batches by about 7.30 pm and by 8 pm large parts of the hall had filled up with many hundreds of Raika men sitting on their haunches. The colour patterns of their turbans indicated the part of Rajasthan they came from. Hanwant and I were seated in the front among some of the educated Raika with social ambitions or a political agenda and who wanted to make speeches. The only non-Raika, except Hanwant and me, were two representatives of veterinary pharmaceutical companies who wanted to promote their medicines for sheep and raise awareness about the counterfeit medicines that swamped the market.

The meeting was opened with a blessing by the temple priest, and then people started giving speeches. The oratory and rhetorical talent in the Raika community is considerable, although speaking styles vary. But the pattern and content of the speeches are relatively consistent. The educated Raika, recognisable by their attire of a leisure suit and the absence of turbans, generally exhort the traditional Raika to give up keeping animals and instead concentrate on sending their children to school and pursuing urban livelihoods. *Sammelan, shiksa, samaj* is their battle cry, meaning organise ourselves, get educated, and project our interests as a caste community. As abandoning animal husbandry does not go down well with the silent majority of listeners, most of the audience usually drop off to sleep to drown out the admonishments. Then there is a minority of speakers, among them Bagdiram and Bhopalaram, whose strategy is to present estimates of the contribution the Raika make to the national economy, which is considerable given that they breed practically all the camels, most of the sheep, and large numbers of goats and cattle. They use these figures to argue for support and subsidies from the government for supporting livestock development that will enable them to get better returns from keeping animals.

This evening too, there were a number of fervent speeches in this vein which went on and on and which I only understood partially. Then it was Bagdiram's turn and he talked about several general issues before touching on the topic of camel slaughter, rather gingerly. I sensed it was something that was deeply embarrassing to the community and that they would rather skirt the subject than openly admit that some of them in their midst were bending their age-old rules and god-given duty. Rather than castigating anybody, Bagdiram requested the community to officially distance itself from selling camels for meat and to sign his letter to the district collector. Stopping short of pressing for reprimanding or excommunicating those Raikas who did sell female camels, he passed around the letter for signatures and thumbprints.

After his presentation, it was Hanwant's turn and he spoke about the need for unity among the Raika and the urgency to preserve the camel. By the time his impassioned presentation was finished, it was way past midnight and, with no end to the line of speakers in sight, we retired.

The next morning, Bagdiram gave us a photocopy of the letter to the district collector with all the signatures.

> Today on Saturday, 25 November 2001 (Kartik Sudhi Num V.S. 2058), in the Ram Raika Temple in Pushkar, at a meeting of the All-India Raika Animal Herders' Association, our community (samaj) decided the following:

1. Our main livelihood is from the keeping of animals, therefore, we have to save the female animals; if we sell them, our life will be finished. Therefore, the society decrees that the females are not to be sold to slaughterers *(kasai log)*, only to other animal-keeping communities who also understand animals as their children.
2. In this Pushkar Mela, female camels are being bought by slaughterers and taken to foreign slaughter houses. Therefore, the number of female camels has decreased very much.
3. A letter is to be written to the district collector in which we request him to take action against the slaughterers who have set up tents, are buying up the female camels and taking them away during the night.
4. If no action is taken, our community will make a demonstration.

This is written on the basis of what the people of the Raika community have said and at their request.

The letter provided evidence and underscored once again, in their own words, that the Raika kept animals not only to make a living, but because it was their identity without which they would be somebody else, not Raika. Nothing could express it better than by the phrase "animals are like our children". Reading the letter reminded me once again what had attracted me to the Raika more than ten years earlier. In one sense it made me almost happy, for it gave proof that it was possible to depend on animals economically, without relegating them to the status of machines and a means of production, and still feel responsible for them and their welfare. In the rough and tumble of daily routine, this was not always evident, especially as these days I rarely had an opportunity to go to the field, talk to camel herders, and enjoy the serene atmosphere.

But what could we do now? Both of us were on a hectic schedule. Hanwant had urgent commitments in Sadri and I was to leave for Germany within a couple of days. We quickly dashed off letters to all the authorities that could conceivably be concerned about the issue. With these we enclosed copies of the Raika letter as well as a report, "The Camel - A Threatened Livestock Species," which we had prepared some time ago and which summarised most of the salient points, although not these latest developments.

When I came back to India in January about two months later, we had not received a single reply. The only response we ever got reached us about six months later.

24 May 2002

Rajasthan Government, Directorate of Animal Husbandry, Jaipur

Letter no. FV 2030
To
Hanwant Singh Rathore
LPPS
Ambedkar Nagar
Sadri

Reference: Letter to the Minister of Animal Husbandry, LPPS 278/2001, 28 November 2001

Subject: Action against slaughter of female camels

Dear Sir,

We collected information about the above subject. According to the Deputy Director of the Animal Husbandry Department in Ajmer, 5381 camels were sold during the Pushkar Mela in 2001. According to the white departure slips, no animals were taken to West Bengal. Apart from that no animal herder complained about this matter to the mela officials. Nevertheless, if anything like this is the case, then the Government of Rajasthan can give an order against it.

The government has programmes for the control of the main camel diseases such as trypanosomiasis, mange and hemorrhagic septicaemia. If there is an epidemic, then the district disease control centres provide service. The department also arranges camps for the control of diseases.

We agree that it is a good idea to reserve the traditional camel breeding areas.

Your suggestion to cooperate with the government regarding training and camel milk marketing is welcome. The state covers an area of 3,42,000 square km of which 25% is desert. In this area, the Jaisalmeri, Bikaneri and Marwari camel breeds are at home. In the rural and remote areas camels play a big role for transportation and agriculture.

Your organisation can arrange a district level training camp. If you have such a proposal, you can send it to the Department.

Director, Animal Husbandry

The gist of the letter seemed to be that the director of Animal Husbandry doubted that camels were sold for slaughter. How could we get proof for our statements? How could we convince people that here was a big cause for concern that needed urgent action?

It was ironic – and embarrassing – that just at this juncture, we were getting international recognition for our efforts to help the Raika. In fact, a prestigious award was bestowed upon us for saving the camel culture of Rajasthan which came with a Rolex watch and a handsome amount of cash for furthering the cause. We were fêted at a party in the Anglo-Indian Club in Hamburg that was attended by top journalists from selected media, leading to lots of publicity and an appearance in German TV. Moreover, the conservation of "animal genetic resources" was starting to develop into a hot issue. In June 2002, the World Food Summit took place at the Food and Agriculture Organisation (FAO) in Rome and, at its Civil Society Forum, Hanwant gave a presentation to a huge audience on the role and practices of the Raika as stewards of domestic livestock breeds. Many other NGOs, thinking on similar lines, were present and one of the official decisions made was that an international treaty on animal genetic resources should be negotiated.

While matters were thus moving rapidly ahead internationally, as soon as we came back to Rajasthan, we were faced by apathy. It was hard to find an explanation, but probably the existing structures were just not designed to take up a matter of this sort. The National Research Centre on Camel is responsible only for research and not for policies. The Department of Animal Husbandry focuses most of its efforts on cattle and crossbreeding. Neither of these institutions is people-focused and, while they might start or expand efforts to keep camels on government farms in order to save them, they would never adopt the perspective of the Raika. Since the camel is undoubtedly a part of Rajasthan biodiversity, one might expect conservationists to care. But alas, they are concerned only with wildlife and not with domestic animals. Although this large animal does not pass through the eye of the needle, it manages to fall through all the gaps.

Finally, the proof that camels were taken even beyond West Bengal for slaughter, came from an unexpected source a year later. In February 2003, I went to Bangladesh on an assignment to train NGOs about the need to conserve indigenous animal breeds. One of the NGOs that I worked with, Integrated Action Research and Development (IARD, specialised in documenting indigenous knowledge and had heard about my interest in camels. The director, Sukanta Sen, had compiled a fat dossier of newspaper clippings with photos of camels from Rajasthan that were sold in Bangladesh at the occasion of Bakr-Eid – the Muslim festival at which it is customary to sacrifice a goat or other animal. Because camels were new to Bangladesh, they had obviously created quite a stir.

On my flight back from Dhaka to Kolkata on Biman Airways on 28 February 2003, I was leafing through this dossier when the stewardess handed me a copy of Dhaka's main English newspaper, the *Daily Star*. Immediately, a headline on the left side of the first page jumped out at me: "Border incident with camel smugglers."

> *BDR, BSF IN SHOOT OUT OVER CAMEL SMUGGLERS*
>
> Bangladeshi and Indian border troops exchanged heavy fire for about five hours yesterday morning after smugglers tried to bring in camels at Shibganj in Chapainawabganj...

So here it was, in black and white: smuggling of camels across the border between India and Bangladesh was even leading to shoot-outs. Now we had solid proof!

Again, under enormous time pressure, since I was only stopping over briefly in India, we photocopied the new evidence and mailed it out to more than half a dozen magazines and newspapers.

No response.

The rest of 2003 was so frenzied with other activities that neither Hanwant nor I were able to attend the Pushkar Fair that year. At the international level, lots of momentum was developing around the issues that were driving our work. Notably, there was a move to get pastoralists organised globally. Mongolian camel breeders, Iranian shepherds, Peruvian llama herders, Maasai from Tanzania and Kenya, Jordanian Bedouin and many other representatives of ancient herding cultures met at the sidelines of the World Parks Conference in Durban in South Africa. The problems they reported were very similar to those of the Raika – encroachment on their customary grazing grounds, absence of veterinary care, lack of respect and support by the government. Bagdiram, Hanwant and I attended this event, and discussed with the others how to overcome the myths about pastoralism as being inefficient and environmentally destructive when they were anything but that. This was when the foundation for the World Association of Mobile Indigenous People (WAMIP), was laid.

LPPS itself organised an Asian level conference on community-based management of animal-genetic resources in Sadri in which government officials and researchers from countries including China, Nepal, Bangladesh, Pakistan, Sri Lanka, Vietnam, Laos, and the Philippines participated, never mind that there was no government representative from India. We took them to the field and they got first-hand exposure to the Raika and their precarious existence. In view of our limited infrastructure, hosting such a big gathering of government officials who are accustomed to a lot of pampering and rarely go to "the interior", was quite a challenge, but it went off brilliantly and many perceptions were changed. The goodwill we had created with government representatives would be very helpful for our cause in the future.

This meeting was followed by an even bigger one that LPP hosted in Kenya together with another NGO, Intermediate Technology Development Group (ITDG), to bring together pastoralists and make them aware of, and project their important role on, conserving livestock biodiversity. While Hanwant and Bagdiramji were representing the Raika cause at this global forum in Nairobi, Ramesh, our long-standing field assistant, accompanied the Raika to the Pushkar Fair. Their report was alarming. In previous years, the purchase of camels for slaughter had been a hush-hush affair to which nobody admitted openly. Now the whole climate had changed. The dealers, who earlier operated clandestinely, had now put up a number of huge tents from which they openly conducted their business. The animals that they purchased were not marked with the customary ribbon around the tail, but by clipping buyer-specific patterns into their hair.

According to Ramesh's report, this included 2,000–3,000 camels. The heightened demand had evidently been good for business at large. The prices had gone up significantly which was good for the Raika. But it was, of course, not good for the mostly very poor customers who needed a working camel. The traders from West Bengal were taunting the camel breeders that within five years they would finish off the entire camel population of Rajasthan. At the fair, the trade was so brisk that all camels were sold within the first couple of days. As a consequence, the camels were gone quickly and the event had fallen flat for the thousands of international visitors that the fair attracts during its final days, promoted as it is as a major event by the Rajasthan Department of Tourism.

It took until the beginning of 2004, for life to turn less frantic and for us to be able to sit down and plan the next steps. We had made a New Year's resolution to turn 2004 into the "Year of the Camel" by organising a number of activities which would hopefully generate attention around the issue. One of them would be to organise an international camel conference in Sadri, with experts from all over the world. Secondly, we would re-survey the camel-holdings in our part of Rajasthan for which we had reliable data – rather than government figures – from our initial work in 1995. These could serve as a baseline against which to compare the current camel population. When the results came in from the household survey painstakingly performed by LPPS field workers, we were shocked. They revealed an astonishing fifty per cent decline in numbers during the last nine years. The interviewed families attributed this fairly drastic reduction to three main factors: disappearance of grazing land, diseases and lack of income.

This trend obviously signified a distinct change in livelihoods for the Raika families who had previously obtained their income from livestock keeping. From being independent rural producers, they had turned into wage labourers in cities. The conditions they worked under, very often in sweetshops, dhabas or in construction, were often horrendous, as reported by the parents of children working there: long working hours, from five o'clock in the morning until midnight; no place to sleep; lack of hygiene and contaminated drinking water, making for frequent illnesses.

But the trend also had profound implications from a national perspective. Thirteen years earlier, when I had first come to India, the country had been proud of having the third largest camel population in the world. By now it trailed far behind Pakistan – somewhere on rank eight or nine in the world.

To us, this indicated a lost opportunity for economic development in the rural areas that could prevent young people from having to migrate into cities and ending up in slums. It was at this time that exciting stories from various parts of the world came to light where camels were being promoted with strong support from governments. Most tantalising was the work done in Dubai where camel milk was advertised as the "white gold of the desert" and new and startling facts about its health-enhancing qualities were being investigated. In the Emirates, camels were being milked with automatic milking machines and highlighted as energy-efficient dairy animals suitable for hot climates as, contrary to dairy cows, they did not require air-conditioning. This work under the aegis of a German scientist, Dr Wernery, had the special support – and financial backing – of the country's ruler. This was no exception. The Sultanate of Oman had established a Department of Camel Affairs which was headed by my old friend from Sudan, Professor Bakri Musa. In Central Asia too, there were efforts to develop camel dairies, and a conference on "Using the Camel in Combating Desertification" took place in Ashkabad in Turkmenistan. During a field trip, we were shown how female camels were kept by eateries along the highways to be milked whenever guests stopped. At this conference I met the energetic Nancy Abeiderrahmane who had actually pioneered camel dairies and had set up a successful company in her adopted home country of Mauritania. Her Tiviski dairy was doing exceptionally well and she had created a whole line of camel dairy products, including a culinary delicacy called Camelbert.

Later in the year, Hanwant and I travelled together to Mongolia for a conference on "The Present State and Perspectives of Nomadism in a Globalising World," held at the Mongolian National University in Ulaanbaatar. My friend, Sabine Schmid, who had been working with camel nomads in the Gobi Desert for many years, invited us to meet them. In the tiny machine of Mongolian Airways we landed on a forlorn airstrip in the middle of the desert, drove through a red and craggy desertscape and then dropped in on a number of camel-breeding nomad families. The contrast to India could not have been more pronounced. Here it was clearly the women who were in charge, while their husbands were hardly to be seen. The women milked the shaggy two-humped Bactrian camels that were tied up in long lines outside the yurts and processed the milk into an endless variety of products, including a type of hard and salty cheese that was routinely offered as a snack. They fermented the milk and then distilled it into "camel vodka" which they offered to us with great glee and which went down very smoothly. Another product these enterprising women had developed was toffee made from camel milk. They also used the long and lustrous hairs of the Bactrian camels to knit gloves, caps and mufflers which they marketed through an eco-tourism project they were involved in. Even schoolgirls were making toy camels from felt and wool and offered them to us. Not to be forgotten, camel dung was highly appreciated as a source of energy that provided a strong and smokeless fire. Back in Ulaanbaatar, we learnt that a local company had a cosmetic series based on camel milk in the pipeline. On the dark side of the coin, we learnt from Sabine that Mongolia's camel population had drastically reduced after the country became independent. While there had been over 800,000 heads in 1955, the number was now reduced to 220,000. This was due to the political developments and the transition from a communist regime to a market economy. Previously, camels had been communally owned but, in 1992, animal holdings were privatised. Many of the camels were subsequently sold for meat, in order to generate income for the cash-strapped population in the economic crisis that followed the dissolution of the socialist system. The absence of transport camels had undermined the mobility of nomads and initiated a cycle of overgrazing around their settlements.

Experiences from other countries made it clear that the historically evolved Indian notion of the camel as merely a means of transportation was very restricted and that it needed to be broadened. For the camel to survive, diverse economic incentives had to be created. We needed some cultural cross-fertilisation – to make Indian, especially Rajasthani, policy-makers aware of the tremendous potential that was waiting to be awakened in the local camel population. We hoped that the international conference that we were planning with experts from other countries would play an important role here.

Chadar	Covering sheet
Muri	Reins
Mura	Halter
Pathiya	Necklace
Gorbandh	Chest decoration
Tokriyo	Bell
Gunghro	Kneebells
Nevri	Footbells
Bakanyia	Head covering
Daman	Foot ropes
Nakl	Nose-peg
Chamrak	Nose-leather

By the time of the camel conference at the end of November, not much had changed in the status quo. Basically the same scenario prevailed at New Year. But, at least one minor detail had been fixed: the brahmin astrologer whom Hanwant routinely consulted in such matters had recommended 15 January as the departure date for the yatra. If the stars were on our side, then everything would go well, he was convinced.

Five days before the auspicious date, we had amassed a pile of camel jewellery, including gorbandhs, necklaces, ankle-chains, some silly-looking ear covers, and under-saddle covers. We had also purchased new mattresses with which to cover the metal-framed Indian saddles for a smooth ride. We had acquired tents and sleeping bags, printed stacks of propaganda leaflets appealing to people to save the camel and describing the rationale of the yatra, as well as colourful camel calendars to give away as gifts.

But not a single camel had materialised in flesh and blood.

Hanwant did his best to soothe me, saying that he had lined up a very good camel from Barmer, and that it would reach here shortly. But I could tell that he was beginning to be a bit concerned himself. Over the last fifteen years, I had frequently experienced how, in Rajasthan, huge problems sorted themselves out in the last minute. I prided myself of having become quite stoic by now and that I had left behind any Germanic tendencies of micro-management. But this situation put me on edge, as failure to execute the camel yatra at this late stage would be hugely embarrassing. We had made a very public commitment in interviews that had been published by Rajasthan's major daily newspaper, the *Rajasthan Patrika*. The impending yatra had also been announced with some fanfare on the website of LPP, and a blog was to record our forthcoming adventures. We had even offered the opportunity to others to join us on the yatra, for a day or a week – fortunately nobody had responded.

The doubts about whether we could make it happen were coupled with continuing worrries and fears about my own physical fitness. Would I be able to endure an 800 km trek and all its associated discomforts? Would there ever be an opportunity for a shower? Would Hanwant be up to it – after all he was exercising even less than I was?

By 12 January, things were looking a tad more hopeful. Ma'sahib had managed to get hold of a male camel owned by an Adivasi gur trader to transport his wares from Mewar to the Godwar area. Suddenly it was there in Butibagh, tied up to a neem tree. It was brown, small, and sturdy – not the world's greatest looker, but at least functional, if not as friendly as the kissing female camels that I had gotten used to.

On the morning of 14 January, the camel from Barmer arrived, together with a harrowed-looking man who had walked it from there. It was a fine and healthy specimen, very tall and it held its noble head high. But it was very jumpy and nervous. In fact, the caretaker reported that the animal had the habit of scraping along trees or running under low-hanging branches – in an apparent stab at getting rid of his rider. Archie, a PhD student from Germany who was researching "the camel as a dairy animal," gave the new arrrival a close look. He was at least as camel crazy as we were and had regaled us with many stories about his experiences with camels in Dubai and how he had taught them to be machine-milked. Wearing a wide-brimmed cowboy hat, he stood close to the huge animal and looked him probingly in the eyes. "This camel is not trustworthy," he pronounced with the air of a true camel whisperer.

I was fervently hoping he would be wrong.

When I reported this to Hanwant, he just waved my doubts away. "Two of the team members are on their way. They are bringing their own camels, and they are camel experts. So they can handle any camel," he said reassuringly.

"And what about the cart?" I asked, adding, "I thought we were going to have a camel cart for transporting the luggage."

"Oh, that problem is also solved," beamed Hanwant. "My brother-in-law has found a cart, plus a camel, plus a boy from his village. He has boarded them onto a truck and they will be here in the evening."

From then on, people and things started arriving. Most of them on their own initiative, donated by the community. The tent company, which usually put up our tents at conferences, set up a huge shamiana, including white chairs and a red carpet. The microphone man drove up in an autorickshaw to contribute his speaker system. The Meghwal women brought homemade namkeen for our trip. A rented bus from Jodhpur spilled out Hanwant's family and extended kin. Bhopalaram Raika and Bagdiram Raika called from the Sadri bus stand announcing their arrival asking to be picked up by the LPPS motorbike. The local TV channel called to find out details, the video guys who normally film weddings investigated the set, the neighbours' kids were everywhere. One special surprise organised by Hanwant was the arrival of a family of Bhopa musicians with their Pabuji Parh and their musical instruments.

By evening, the place was teeming with people – the LPPS campus had turned into an autonomous organism functioning according to its own rules. The musicians were tuning their instruments and putting on their finery for the night's performance. Outside the kitchen, two huge cauldrons were bubbling with dal and vegetables, under the supervision of a volunteer cook from Rajpura. A contingent of women from the LPPS self-help groups were making *batti* – round balls of chapati dough, while one of our Jat neighbours was stoking the ashes in which they were to be baked, and yet another helper had taken charge of making and serving tea.

LPPS staff was frenziedly scurrying around, trying to collect the things that they wanted to take on the yatra. Hanwant was busy working his two mobiles while keeping an eye on everything. Indeed, the two "team members" had turned up, each with a camel in tow, although I hadn't had a chance to meet them. Then a big truck drove up with some difficulty, as the access road to Butibagh was rather rudimentary. The back door was lowered and out peeked a very friendly looking dark-brown camel. His handler, a boy about fourteen years old, just gave it a low vocal command and up it stood and calmly stepped down the ramp. Utterly composed despite the crowds around him, the new arrival immediately spotted the nearest neem tree and marched towards it. Seeing this amiable camel, plus the sturdy and top-condition cart that was rolled down from the truck, immediately made me feel more relaxed. Hanwant had been right in insisting on the cart.

In the midst of packing our stuff and supplies for the next four weeks, which was nowhere completed, we had to make arrangements to feed and provide a sleeping place for all our unexpected guests. Dinner was in process and some of the vistors were rolling out bedding they had brought along. A hive of Rajput ladies had invaded my room and was blocking access to the bathroom; my rucksack for the trip had disappeared under a pile of their belongings and finery. Irritated, I was pondering what to do when the sounds of the Bhopa's fiddle, the ravanhatta, floated through the night. That's when I knew that it was time to live for the moment and worry about tomorrow, not now, but when it came. We were going to experience the Sadri edition of Woodstock and enjoy the night's entertainment. Nothing could be more fitting and auspicious than listening to the exploits of Pabuji and how he brought the red-and-brown she-camels to Rajasthan six centuries ago, before setting out on our own journey to save Pabuji's heritage.

The Bhopa ensemble had unrolled their colourful padh and tied it between the branches of two neem trees. They provided a striking scene, straight out of *One Thousand and One Nights*, the father wearing a swinging ankle-length gown in bright red and two rows of ankle bells, the elder daughter in a beautiful dress in orange, the younger daughter in the black outfit typical of Kalbelia dancers and the boy in a white suit and multicoloured turban. Hanwant started to introduce them to me, but the musician preferred to do this himself. "I am Tolaram Bhopa from Jodhpur, this is my son Narayan, my daughter Sarda and my child Laxmi," he said with a bow, a little jump to activate his ankle bells, and twanged the strings of his ravanhatta. From then on, it was the typical mix of recitation, song and dance, with Sarda holding the lamp and Laxmi giving little samples of her dance skills. The entire audience was captivated, even the Rajput ladies came out of the seclusion of my room. Endless rounds of tea and harder drinks were served throughout the night into the early hours of the morning. Somehow, everybody found a place to sleep.

At dawn, throngs of local people poured onto the campus, bringing baskets of garlands. The famous Raika priest from Mundara drove up in his Ambassador and gave us his blessings, the banners were unfurled, and dozens of garlands placed around our neck. Bhopalaram Raika and our local painter had mounted two of the camels, I was lifted onto Moti and then our caravan was off. There was no going back now – we were on the move, only to be stopped and blessed and garlanded again and again on the short stretch to Sadri where the flower ladies generously donated more garlands and our fruit vendors supplied us with bananas and guavas.

The crowds only thinned out after we had passed Mundara and were on the stretch to Bali where we were going to have our first night halt. We walked and rode about 20 km on the first day and received a royal reception by Ma'sahib and his extended family, but I fell asleep before dinner was served.

Only on the next morning was it possible to take stock of who was with us on the yatra. The Raika camel experts were Jotaram Raika, an old camel hand, who had come with his own, very young-looking camel; Punaram, the owner of Moti, the oldest camel, who was deputed to pull the cart; and Kumaram, the boy who had come with the camel and the cart from Hanwant's brother-in-law's village. A last-minute addition was Gheverji who had heard about the yatra only yesterday morning and had immediately decided to join. LPPS staff included Ganesh Ram Raika, an expert camel healer, Punaram Raika, our cook, and amazingly, our womens' worker, Archana Mathur. Unexpectedly, the whole Bhopa family had come and seemed determined to stay on board.

But how could the entire Bhopa family come with us? They were hardly equipped in their dainty costumes and dance outfits and had probably not even brought a change of clothing. I discussed this with Hanwant and he fancied that Tolaram, the father, accompany us. He would be a good source of information and could teach us the whole Pabuji epic while we were on the road. He could play a tune every time we entered a village and get everybody's attention. But the rest of the family needed to go back to Jodhpur. When we suggested this to the Bhopa, he agreed and said it would be good if Narayan and Sarda would go to Jodhpur, as his wife was expecting her eighteenth child and she needed help with the younger kids. His younger daughter, Laxmi, however, tearfully clung to her father and insisted that she come with her dad. I had my misgivings, but there was nothing to be done, as Laxmi had already made herself comfortable on the cart among all the luggage. All of about seven years old, she cheerfully accompanied us for the whole trip – never once complaining.

Taking Tolaram Bhopa along on the trip turned out to be possibly the most important decision we made, as he lightened up the physical toil with his jokes and consistent good humour. His tunes were a lifeline. Whenever we were tired or fed up, he would play a song and it would immediately lift our spirits. Not just of the human team members but also of our camel colleagues who wore their typical stoic depressions throughout, but always turned their ears to absorb the sounds coming from the ravanhatta. Maybe they also enjoyed hearing the story of Pabuji and how he brought their ancestral red and brown she-camels to Rajasthan!

In the first week, we covered close to 200 km, distributed thousands of pamphlets and calendars and settled into a routine. Not only the human participants, but also the camels: Moti, Chikal, Toffee, Coffee, and Kalu. I had adopted Toffee, the friendly camel that had arrived together with the cart, as my riding mount and he made an excellent, gentle but alert, companion. As an all-male group, they formed a strict hierarchy.

It was the height of the breeding season, but when a female camel was in the vicinity, only Moti, the highest ranked of them, started to prance and make gurgling love-sounds. But this happened only rarely – showing how rare camels had become, even in Rajasthan's arid west.

Excerpts from my diary

19 January

100 km from Sadri on the way towards Bikaner, and my feet are full of blisters! Sitting on the camel doesn't help – I have blisters on my behind too. Just another 5 km to go today before we stop.

We had a lot of people to see us off when we left Sadri. Television coverage too. Some people came with us for the first few days, but now there's just the hard-core left.

We have a musician with us who strikes up a tune when we arrive in a village. That brings lots of people out to see us. A good way to get to know the villagers and start conversations about their lives, their livelihoods and their livestock.

21 January, evening

BALOTRA, ABOUT 200 KM FROM SADRI

Tomorrow is a rest day – thank goodness! It's been hard-going: 20 km a day is OK, but 35 km a day is hard, especially in the dark.

But it's very rewarding. We started off with a huge sendoff from Sadri – more than a thousand people. I was garlanded hundreds of times – I could scarcely see because of all the flowers around my neck! We had 10 camels and 20 people travelling with us to begin with. Now there are 5 camels and 11 people, plus a couple of support people riding in a jeep.

There has been a magnificent response from the local people on the way. People invite us in for meals, for tea. They write comments in a book we're carrying. They all say they see so few camels nowadays, and that the lack of grazing is the problem. We've had TV coverage and several calls from national newspapers like *The Hindustan Times* and *India Today*.

We've been in the cultivated area so far – all irrigated. From now on we'll be going through desert. We're heading towards Jaisalmer. We will assemble a lot of camels together to make a big impression when we enter the city.

27 January

YATRA PLANS ENTRY INTO JAISALMER

We're now in Achla, a Raika village near Devikot, about two days from Jaisalmer.

There are lots of camels here – the people need them to fetch water and carry things. All castes use camels, not just the Raika. They gave us a huge welcome when we arrived in the village.

It's been easier going for the last few days: we've been off the all-weather roads, and there have been fewer villages to slow us down. But the main reason is that we're now a lot fitter!

We're planning a big entry into Jaisalmer when we get there on 30 January. A camel rally and a ride through the city. Should be fun!

31 January

CAMEL PROCESSION THROUGH JAISALMER

We had a big entrance into Jaisalmer yesterday. Twenty-five camels – all beautifully decorated – and their keepers joined us, and we made a big impression when we rode into the city and around the fort. The media were there: newspapers, magazines, TV.

But it was cold! Eight degrees celsius today. I must admit I stayed in a hotel last night so I could keep warm.

Today, we're heading towards Bikaner. We hope to be there in about ten days.

4 February

CAMEL YATRA IN POKHARAN

We're now in Pokharan, famous because it's where the Indian government tests its nuclear bombs. 450 km since we left Sadri, and another 250 km to Bikaner. We start off in the morning, and keep walking or riding until after dark. It's tough going in the sand, and we're not sure which way to go now, as there aren't any towns between here and Bikaner. There are eleven of us still on the yatra: nine on camels and two in the jeep.

We plan to arrive in Bikaner on 13 February – unless we get lost in the desert!

9 February

LOST IN THE DESERT?

It's been tough crossing the desert. Sometimes the track forked, and we didn't know which way to go. Some of the time we were crossing dunes, without any tracks to follow at all. We thought we were lost several times, but we managed to find our way again.

Yesterday we found that another 2000 camels had been sold for slaughter at a market near here. Selling camels for meat used to be unknown in Rajasthan: the animals were far too valuable. The males were used to haul carts, and the females for breeding. But the decline in the amount of grazing land – lots of new crop fields irrigated by tubewells around here – means that it's no longer possible to keep big herds of females. The problem is that irrigated cropping isn't sustainable: the groundwater level falls, and the fields are left dry and barren. As the original drought-adapted vegetation has been uprooted, the land is no longer useful for camels or any other type of livestock.

The government is now looking into this issue, partly as a result of the workshop and conference we held in Sadri before we left on the yatra.

We've now arrived in Jhajhu, just 60 km from Bikaner. It should be easier from now on: we're on asphalt roads for the rest of the way. Plus, we're cheating a bit: we've either walked or ridden the camels all the way so far, but now Hanwant and I have succumbed to the temptation of sitting on the camel cart we are pulling with us. Comfort and bliss!

We hope to arrive in Bikaner in the afternoon of 11 February or the morning of 12th. We're planning a rally through the city on the 13th. We'll be staying at the National Research Centre on Camel in Bikaner.

12 February 2005

YATRA ARRIVES IN BIKANER

We have arrived in Bikaner, and I am happy to report that all twelve members of our expedition and the five camels (as well as a dog who joined us about 180 km ago) are all in fine fettle. We received a very warm welcome

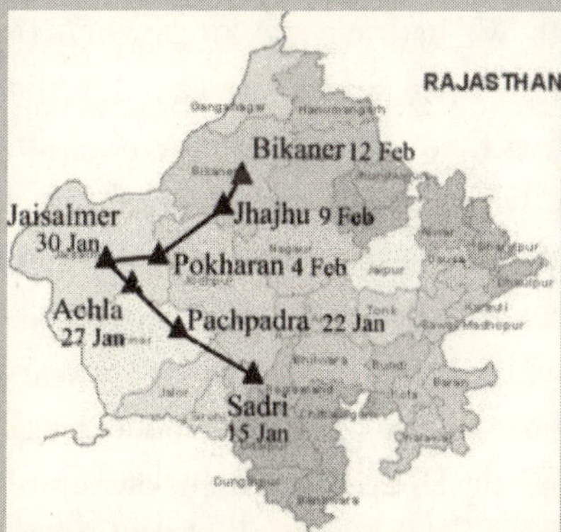

by the National Research Centre on Camel and had the first hot showers since the start of the yatra.

India TV covered most of our last day, which was very exhausting because of the extremely heavy traffic that we had to wade through for about 12 km in order to reach the NRCC. However, our camels did not blink an eyelid among throngs of trucks, military vehicles with tanks, and the ugly urban jungle.

It will take some time to get used to normal life again, and we already miss the silence of the desert and the hospitality of its people. We have seen how far tubewells, tractors and high-yielding crop cultivation have made inroads into the desert, and it is not a pretty picture. Of course, I will be accused of romanticising, but in the remote areas people seem to be the happiest and most hospitable ones. The famous Thari culture is still alive in many places. It has been a fantastically fulfilling experience, and Hanwant has already said we should do a yatra every year.

The yatra transformed us, made us stronger. We became lean and habituated, almost addicted, to walking long distances. We realised how little one really requires in terms of amenities to live well. We had felt like kings when riding on our camels through the big open spaces, but also diminished and anachronistic when riding them through the dense traffic of the few cities en route. We became very close to our camels, and deeply impressed by their steadfastness and reliability, never ever complaining, even if the cart had to be pulled strenuously across sand dunes. They just kept going. I had relished becoming friendly with Toffee who behaved more like a pet than a camel. For Mira and her offspring, I had always been an absent owner; often there were many months between my visits and while I was always happy to see her, the bond was by far not as strong as with Toffee with whom I had gone through thick and thin. After the yatra, Toffee, Coffee and Chikal stayed with us in Butibagh and enjoyed being pampered and without strenuous work.

For a long time after the yatra, Hanwant and I were nostalgic for the desert and now found Sadri rather too civilised. Having become accustomed to the largely clean and pristine landscape of the Thar, we noticed the plastic bags and the rubbish around the local villages all the more, so we started a local clean-up drive, picking up trash and loading it onto our camel cart. When the Pushkar Fair came up in November, we decided to go there on camelback rather than by motorised transport. We saddled up Toffee and Chikal and rode to Anji-ki-dhani to join the Raika taking the young camels to Pushkar. Separating the offspring from their mothers was an emotional event, and all night we listened to the heart-rending wailing of the youngsters. It ebbed out over the next few nights and, by the time we reached Pushkar six days later, they seemed to have forgotten about their mothers.

Back in Butibagh, after the fair had been concluded, both Chikal and Toffee indicated that they had had enough of their quiet, peaceful life as pets – they became more difficult to handle and started to fight with each other. It was now the height of the breeding season and their hormones told them that they wanted to be with female camels. Sadly, we gave them one more hug and waved goodbye to them as two Raikas gladly led them away to their future careers as breeding camels.

Chapter 14

JAISALMER

"Marry me into a village with many she-camels."

– A saying in Jaisalmer

2006

During the yatra, we had been confronted with the disturbing developments that were rapidly transforming the Thar Desert. We had seen the almost irreversible damage that was done to the soil, to the native trees and plants, and to the whole ecology wherever water had become available through tubewells. The government was subsidising all the inputs required for this so-called "greening the desert": electricity and diesel to pump out water, in addition to the chemicals – fertilisers and pesticides – which high-yielding crop varieties require to thrive. The irrigation of huge tracts of land by means of exploiting groundwater had become "profitable", at least in the short run: in many places water was being pumped out around the clock, and the pastoralist landscape with its bounty of trees and shrubs had been replaced by huge fields of monocultures, usually mustard or wheat. This development pleased many people, especially technocrats in the ministries who measure progress by short-term output, as well as by the amount of fertiliser and pesticides that farmers apply to their fields.

Thanks to this short-term mentality, the groundwater resources in one place were generally finished for good after about six or seven years, and the farmers – or "tubewell nomads" as we called them – shifted to new areas and drilled another well. Each time they moved, they left behind them bare stretches of land without the trees and shrubs that had earlier protected the soil from erosion and provided forage for livestock throughout the year. It was a dustbowl in the making.

While the Indira Gandhi Canal had not been part of our itinerary during the yatra, we had been told many times that it had eliminated prime camel-breeding areas, confirming the observations made during our earlier trips in 1991 and 1992. In villages, close to the canal, that had once been famous for providing the best camels in Rajasthan, such as Nachna and Mohangarh, not a single camel could now be found. Many of the farmers that had been allotted land were not local, but came from Punjab and had no relationship with camels. Out of fear for their crops, they had invented a range of cruel practices to keep free-ranging camels from damaging them. They shot them with guns or subjected them to a slow and painful death by tying their mouths shut or attaching thorny shrubs with wires to their tails, causing constant pain and preventing the camel from resting.

The area around Bikaner especially, had become unrecognisable due to the extent of irrigation and construction. I remembered how, just fifteen years earlier, a horse-drawn tonga had been the only conveyance available to ferry me from the railway station to my hotel; at that time most of the traffic had been composed of camel carts quietly and unobtrusively transporting their loads. Now the city's thoroughfares were clogged with heavy traffic, fumes, and noise and I pitied the occasional camel that was pulling a cart among heavy trucks.

Yet, during the yatra, we had also experienced the "old" desert where progress had not reached and people needed to live in tune with the resources that the desert provided. They harvested run-off rainwater with age-old techniques and made it last throughout the year. They cultivated crops only during the rainy season and depended on livestock – camels, cattle, sheep, and goats – to transform the hardy vegetation into an array of delicious food, without resorting to irrigation. We had been received with impeccable courtesy by many families to whom we had been total strangers. They had plied us with cool glasses of cumin-flavoured buttermilk, certainly the best remedy against thirst. They had served us delicious meals of freshly baked *sogra* (unleavened millet bread) with ghee from free-ranging cows and a vegetable dish made from the pods of the khejri tree. They had shown me (because I was a woman) the interior of their lovingly embellished houses made from mud bricks, painstakingly maintained by the women with regular coats of *gobar* (cow dung). They had entertained us with a bounty of stories, with jokes, and sometimes music. The life of these people was certainly hard, but they did not show it. They were hospitable, humorous and generous. In fact, in non-material terms, I would call them immensely rich.

During our workshop in November 2004, the camel breeders from Jaisalmer had made a lasting impression with their carefully groomed moustaches, their multicoloured turbans and sheer power of their personality. They were mostly Rajputs and seemed to have a totally different outlook on life compared to the Raika. While the Raika were often subservient and always leaned on us to sort out their troubles, these guys were used to solving all problems on their own. One of their leaders was Bhom Singh, a mountain of a man, barely literate, but with a mind that was

But it was necessary to not only work from the top, but also from the bottom and to mobilise and raise awareness of the camel breeders themselves – not just in our small universe in Sadri, but throughout Rajasthan. With the help of our dedicated Raika leaders, Bagdiram and Bhopalaram, we contacted and invited camel breeders from all over the state. We identified them through word of mouth, by asking in which villages were there large camel holdings, or which were famous for the good quality of their camels. From one village, we were referred to the next. Through my earlier research, I was aware that Achla near Devikot in Jaisalmer was famous for camels, so we used that as an entry-point into the camel breeders' network. They referred us to other villages with large camel herds. A week before the meeting, we drove around to personally invite as many people as possible. Although we offered travel money, many of the camel breeders were reluctant to accept our invitation, saying that they were illiterate and would not be able to read the signs on the buses – they were afraid of getting lost. We insisted that they come. We kept talking to them over the phone, but the feedback was doubtful. Until the day we had set for their arrival, we were not sure whether anybody, except our old stalwarts, would turn up.

In the end, practically all the camel breeders we had invited came. It made for a new and composite picture, as it included not only our traditional Raika constituency, but members from a range of castes spanning the whole social spectrum – Rajputs from Jaisalmer, Bishnois from Barmer, Jats from Bikaner, Gujjars from Nagaur, and Sindhi Muslims from deep in the Thar. The most endearing participant was a boy from the Van Vagri community in Hanwant's native village. The Van Vagris make their living by hunting and by protecting farmers' fields from wildlife; they are shunned by other rural communities and are completely isolated from the mainstream. As they are not registered as voters, no politician has taken on the concerns of this totally illiterate community that nevertheless has a highly intricate culture in which women have a strong position. The Van Vagri boy attended because his group owned a few camels for pulling their carts and because Hanwant had insisted that he come. But he had experienced tremendous problems travelling by bus, as the conductor and some other passengers did not want him to board. Fortunately, he had persisted and managed to reach Sadri.

While the interest of the camel breeders exceeded our expectations, the response from the decision-makers and technical-support organisations was extremely disappointing. Although we had personally invited many, and they had assured us they would participate or at least delegate a colleague, none actually showed up.

So the meeting was essentially one of grassroots people. This had its advantages as we could get quickly to the core of the matter. After a round of introductions, the participants broke into three different working groups based on geography – arid zone (Bikaner, Jaisalmer, and Barmer), Aravallis (Udaipur, Chittor), and intermediate zone (Pali, Jalore and Jaipur). A facilitator guided the discussion in each along the following questions:

- What are the reasons for camel population decline?
- Why have grazing opportunities been lost?
- What are the consequences?
- What are the ten most important plants that camel feeds on?
- What are the survival strategies? How and why are camel breeders still keeping herds even though breeding is not a cost-effective proposition in the present circumstances?

In the next session, new working groups were formed and each was assigned to discuss a different topic.

- How to overcome the loss of grazing opportunities?

- How to improve access to prophylactic healthcare and medicines?
- How to improve marketing of camel products?

The findings were then presented by each working group in the plenary and a general discussion opened up. At the end, five key recommendations were agreed upon.

What the camel breeders say...

From 17–19 November, Lokhit Pashu-Palak Sansthan organised a national-level workshop for about fifty camel breeders and owners representing various communities, castes, and religions, and coming from almost all parts of Rajasthan. After intensive discussions, the participants unanimously recommended the following actions and changes:

1. Restoration of traditional grazing areas, commons, and identification, restoration and management of new grazing areas with peoples' participation.
2. Inclusion of camel milk in the Rajasthan Dairy Act.
3. Availability of camel healthcare and simple and effective vaccination procedures.
4. Total ban on fertile and healthy female-camel slaughter.
5. The activities of the National Research Centre on Camel should be extended to camel-breeding areas.

We were buoyed by the response and enthusiasm of the camel breeders, all of whom emphasised that this was the first time anybody had ever asked them about their opinion or taken an interest in their situation. One of the leaders, Bhom Singh from Jaisalmer, actually scolded us for having incurred expenditure by booking some of them into local guesthouses. "Why waste money on such niceties; we can just as well sleep on the floor of your training centre," he commented repeatedly.

Only a few days later, from 23–25 November 2004, we organised a "Multi-stakeholder Platform on Saving the Camel and Peoples' Livelihoods," in a big tent in Sadri. Its purpose was to assemble experts from other countries to provide some inspiration to Indian decision-makers about the economic opportunities the country was missing out on. The distinguished international guests included Gaukhar Konuspayeva from Kazakhstan who had done exciting work on camel milk and analysed it for the chemical components that might explain its health-enhancing properties. There was Bernard Faye, a French maverick scientist who had worked with camels all over the world, especially in Niger where small-scale camel dairies were currently being set up. Then there were the drivers behind the cutting-edge camel research in the Gulf countries. One of them was my old friend from Khartoum, Bakri Musa, who now was with the Department of Camel Affairs of the Sultanate of Oman and involved in embryo-transfer for racing camels. Also there was Dr Wernery from Dubai who was heading its Central Veterinary Research Laboratory and had done pathbreaking research not only on camel diseases, but also on camel milk. Not to be forgotten, Dr T. K. Gahlot from Bikaner whose *Journal of Camel Practice and Research* was the vehicle in which new research results were published. The present director of the National Research Centre on Camel, Dr Sahani, also accepted our invitation and presented a paper, in which he echoed our views about the decline of the camel population and the reasons for it. That was progress of a sort as now the trend was officially acknowledged. But despite our many invitations, no representative from either the Indian state or central government departments on animal husbandry made it to the meeting.

So we just compiled all the papers in a report and sent this out to whoever might be interested:

What the scientists say...

Camel experts from research institutions and non-government organisations in India, France, Germany, Kazakhstan, Oman, the United Arab Emirates, and the UK met at the training centre of Lokhit Pashu-Palak Sansthan near Mammaji-ki-dhuni at Sadri, district Pali, Rajasthan, India, on 23–25 November 2004, and issued the following statement:

We draw attention to the dramatic decline in Rajasthan's camel population. This has been caused primarily by the shrinking area of grazing, and the neglect of camels in policies and development programmes.

We believe that the camel is an integral part of Rajasthan's ecology, economy and culture, now and in the future. It is a significant source of employment for the state, enables the local economy to withstand drought, and is vital for Rajasthan's identity and attractiveness as a tourist destination.

We urge the following to conserve the camel in Rajasthan:

- *Urgently investigate how to restore sufficient pastureland for camels in order to halt the decline in camel numbers.*
- *Make camel health services easily accessible to camel owners. This should include prophylactic and curative treatment of trypanosomiasis and mange.*
- *Identify emerging market opportunities for camel products (such as milk and meat), and support changes in the farming system to take advantage of these.*
- *Promote the value-addition and marketing of camel products (milk, wool, leather, dung).*
- *Promote and subsidise the use of camel carts as an eco-friendly source of transport.*
- *Develop an effective, comprehensive Camel Policy, aimed at the long-term conservation of the camel as part of Rajasthan's biodiversity. This should be developed in extensive consultation with the various stakeholders, especially camel-breeding communities.*

Lokhit Pashu-Palak Sansthan

P.O. Box 1, Sadri 306702, District Pali, Rajasthan.
Tel. 02934-285086. E-mail lpps@sify.com

Press Release

Sadri, 25 November 2004

A three-day international conference entitled "Saving the Camel and Peoples' Livelihoods: Building a Multi-Stakeholder Platform for the Conservation of the Camel in Rajasthan" was concluded here today at the training centre of Lokhit Pashu-Palak Sansthan, a non-government organisation based in Sadri, District Pali, Rajasthan. The scientists which represented research institutions and non-government organisations from India, France, Germany, Kazakhstan, Oman, the United Arab Emirates, and the UK, discussed the evidence for the rapid decline of Rajasthan's camel population and the underlying reasons for this trend. Between 1997 and 2003, camel numbers decreased by 25% according to official government figures, but some experts believed that the actual decrease may be much larger. They were especially worried about the sale of large numbers of female camels for slaughter during the Pushkar Fair in the last two years and attributed this to the lack of economic returns from camel breeding which forced the traditional camel breeding communities, such as the Raika, to abandon their hereditary occupation.

During the conference that was supported by the Food and Agriculture Organisation of the United Nations (FAO), as well as Misereor, experiences from other countries were also discussed. According to Dr. Bernard Faye from CIRAD in France, in Morocco and Tunisia an emerging market for camel products has resulted in a revival of camel breeding and resulted in an increase in the population. Prof Babiker Musa from Oman reported that in Gulf countries camel racing was big business and that a single camel could cost as much as $100,000 to $200,000.

The scientists emphasized that in order to save the camel in Rajasthan, the government would have to create an enabling policy framework and they issued a set of recommendations directed at policy makers. In this memorandum they expressed their conviction that the camel must be maintained as an integral part of Rajasthan's ecology, economy and culture, even in the future. It is a significant source of employment for the state, enables the local economy to withstand drought, and is vital for Rajasthan's identity and attractiveness as a tourist destination. They urged the following actions: a thorough investigation in how to restore sufficient pastureland for camels; easy accessibility of camel health services to camel owners, including prophylactic and curative treatment of trypanosomiasis and mange; the identification of emerging market opportunities for camel products and support for changes in the farming system to take advantage of these; promotion of the value-addition and marketing of camel products (milk, wool, leather, dung); subsidies for the use of camel carts as an eco-friendly source of transport; and development of an effective, comprehensive Camel Policy, aimed at the long-term conservation of the camel as part of Rajasthan's biodiversity. This should be developed in extensive consultation with the various stakeholders, especially camel-breeding communities.

Chapter 13

THE YATRA

> *"Camels still occupy a very special niche in the hearts and minds of Rajasthan's rural people.*
>
> *This is obvious from the delighted response and the very warm hospitality the members of the camel yatra (*Unt bachao yatra*) have received during the first week. Their month-long tour will take them from Sadri in Pali District, to Jaisalmer, and then Bikaner.*
>
> *The yatra aims to raise awareness about the rapid decline in Rajasthan's camel population. Thousands of female camels are being sold for slaughter at the state's big livestock fairs."*
>
> – Press Release, LPPS, 22 January 2005

What else could we do to generate interest and concern about the plight of the camel in Rajasthan? How could we spark sustained attention in the media? Did the people of Rajasthan really not mind if the camel became a dinosaur and children would know camels only from pictures rather than flesh and blood? Over the year, an idea had germinated in our minds and firmly established roots: we would undertake a yatra, more specifically a camel yatra, a journey on camelback, through Rajasthan's camel-breeding belt, to really take the issue to the people, to find out their feelings while at the same time raising awareness about the subject.

A yatra essentially means a pilgrimage, typically to a famous Hindu temple, for the purpose of requesting something from god. This could be a wish such as conceiving a child or for a job for your son, or to solve an intractable problem that you can't come to grips with. In return, you make a promise or give something up. Depending on your means, this could be a donation, building a temple, or to stop drinking tea. Very often, a yatra involves some hardship to show god that you are serious – for instance, in the Hindu month of Shravan, tens or hundreds of thousands of people walk hundreds of miles on foot to the temple of Ramdevra in Pokharan.

Yatras are also a tool deployed by Indian activists to generate public interest in social causes. For instance, the Centre for Science and Environment (CSE) regularly organises a *Pani Yatra* (water trip) to learn about and promote traditional rainwater harvesting structures. And the famous Professor Anil Gupta of the Indian Institute of Management (IIM) in Ahmedabad, annually takes interested people on a *Shodh Yatra* (research trip) to investigate and highlight the traditional knowledge and innovations of villagers.

Hanwant and I both agreed that a yatra would serve us well to generate awareness about the dwindling camel numbers. Also, it would be a fantastic way of bringing us into contact with many new camel breeders throughout the state and get the broader picture.

While we were in agreement about the general concept, Hanwant and I disagreed vastly on the finer points – the route to take, the length of the whole exercise, the number of people and camels to take along, the logistics, where to sleep, when to go, and so on. Our ideas were quite different and some of the details were gradually becoming contentious issues. I was rather purist, while Hanwant tended to be more pragmatic, or should I rather say, more practical?

We needed to sort out these questions and decided to do this in a relaxed setting – over a few drinks. So a torrid evening in late June saw us seated on the perfectly manicured lawn of one of the several luxury hotels that had cropped up on the road between Ranakpur and Sadri in recent years. The hotel, although a brand-new edifice, provided a romantic opera-like backdrop, as the façade had been resurrected from the pillars and balconies of a crumbling Rajput haveli. A pair of massive devotional horses made out of clay that are more commonly placed in temples provided additional ethnic décor.

We, and everybody else, had been desperately waiting for the rains to start, but there were no dark clouds that would indicate their arrival any time soon. Instead, the sky was hazy and grey, turning the setting sun into an opalescent ball. There was not an inkling of a breeze and the air was heavy and scented with wafts of frangipani and night jasmine. In the east, the thin sliver of the moon was rising hopefully and peacefully, spreading calmness, albeit not to me. The last few nights I had been unable to sleep, wondering how on earth we would pull off this undertaking. It wasn't just the unknown dimensions of the yatra that were troubling me. I had taken on many responsibilities, including research, writing reports and analyses, as well as preparing meetings and workshops in the context of pursuing the rights of livestock keepers internationally. The foreseeable future just seemed a staccato of deadlines. Much of this was voluntary work which I was doing because I felt it had to be done. As Jon and Aisha were about to start college and would require more financial support over the coming years, any sensible person would have looked for a real job back in Europe and not hung about here in this backwater that was so cut off from the rest of the world that people still practised child marriage and where it was rare for the internet to function. "Grow up," I had been telling myself, "don't plan a dubious adventure which as of now has no itinerary, no departure date, no crew and no supporters. Preparing and going on the yatra will eat up another significant chunk of time during which you will not earn anything."

Right now, Hanwant and I were sitting next to a star-shaped lotus pond, overlooking the Ranakpur road on which Raika sheep and goat herds were walking home from their grazing sojourns in the forest. The bleating of ewes filtered faintly through the heavy air, signalling to the lambs that their moms were coming back and going to feed them. Crouching at our feet was Modaram Raika, the owner of a riding camel, whom we knew vaguely. He had been hovering at the entrance to the hotel, with the intention of offering his camel's services to the hotel for safaris. When we had entered, he had surreptitiously attached himself to us, hoping this would give him the extra bit of courage needed to approach the hotel manager or maybe because he thought we would put in a word for him.

Hanwant ordered a beer for us and tea for our turbaned friend which was served in a dainty leopard-spotted cup, with little sachets of demerara sugar and sugar substitute that Modaram examined puzzledly.

The ensuing conversation about the technicalities of the camel yatra was disillusioning, to put it mildly. It made one point quite clear: after devoting fifteen years of our lives to the camel, there were still enormous gaps in our knowledge of this animal. In fact, we were ignorant about some of its most basic aspects which we needed to know for planning the yatra. For instance, how many kilometres could it walk in one day? Even more germanely – how would we feed it? For me, the latter seemed a minor issue. I recalled what I had read many years earlier in the travelogues of the famous explorers of the Arabian Desert and the Sahara that I so admired: it was just a question of budgeting enough time for the camels to feed on the way - one needed to let them graze whenever good forage was available. Besides, weren't camels supposed to be able to go for days without food? Every schoolkid knew that this was why they had a hump. And hadn't I even written this myself in a summary of scientific facts about the camel?

Hanwant strongly disagreed. As he has caretaking in his genes, the idea that any creature in his possession or sphere of responsibility could be subjected to pangs of hunger was entirely unacceptable. His solution to the problem was to take along a camel cart to carry feed for the camels.

"Taking a cart along is like taking a pram or a wheelchair," I taunted him. "When people trek through the Sahara, they would not dream of taking a cart. They take all their supplies on pack camels."

"But the purpose of our yatra is not adventure - it is for documentation and awareness-raising," Hanwant reminded me.

He had a point there, but I was not ready to admit that.

"Why don't we ask Modaram," I suggested, who was glad to be drawn into our Hindi-English mixed debate.

"You can let them graze in the night, which is the best thing. But if you are tired and the camels are tired because you have walked all day, then it is difficult," Modaram said.

"So what about taking food with us on a camel cart?"

"That is very impractical, because, if you have say eight to ten camels, then you will not be able to put more than a two days' supply on a camel cart."

"But we'll need the cart anyway," said Hanwant. "Nobody can sit for 20 km on a camel for more than one day; the next day one can't walk."

"But that's only a question of getting the muscles used to it. It will pass after a few days," I interjected, feeling like a great explorer surrounded by a couple of pansies.

Hanwant was clearly worried about me (or himself?) not being able to manage the 20 km daily on foot or on camelback. After all, we were not fit at all – Hanwant spending most of his days sitting either in the jeep or in endless Raika meetings, while I was shackled to the desk or in conferences. Hanwant, who had been a sliver of a man when I had first met him, had become pretty stocky and compact. I had also filled out and nurtured the secret hope that the yatra would have a slimming effect on me.

Hanwant was not prepared to let go of the camel cart."When I was a child, my *nana*, my maternal grandfather, always went to buy a whole herd of male camels at the Tilonia Fair. He walked and rode them from there to Jodhpur and then to Barwali, our village. I remember when I was a small child, I rode on the camel cart."

Then he added dreamily, "Such a soothing movement..." It was clear that his fondness for camel carts went back to very dear childhood memories.

We tabled the point for the time being and moved on to another question.

Where and how would we sleep on the way?

I suggested that we take along sleeping bags and sleep in the open. Hanwant thought we needed tents. He was even musing about taking along some charpais, so that I would be more comfortable. I thought that was absolutely ridiculous and said I would much prefer to sleep on the ground, next to the dying embers of the campfire.

At this juncture, the hotel manager appeared, asking if he could be of any help. We introduced Modaram and tried to negotiate a deal for the camel safaris he wanted to offer. But they had vastly different ideas. The manager welcomed the idea of Modaram standing outside the hotel with his nicely decked-up camel and offering rides. But Modaram wanted proper employment with a guaranteed monthly income. This was definitely not on and, with the dejected Modaram in tow, we decided to leave.

We drove home in silence, both in our own worlds. Hanwant reliving his childhood rides on a camel cart, while I wistfully thought about my dreams of becoming a great explorer in my youth. On the winding road leading towards Butibagh, Hanwant abruptly stopped the jeep.

"Look, look! A black cobra!" He pointed through the windshield and, in the shine of the headlines, I could make out the tail-end of a snake slithering into the shrubs.

"That's a very auspicious omen – especially when the cobra crosses the way from right to left," said Hanwant. "You will see, everything will be all right with the yatra. It will be a great success! So just stop worrying!"

"But," he added, "the cobras are why I am afraid of sleeping outside and want a tent. Earlier, cobras never used to climb on to the charpai, but these days they have started doing that."

Over the next few months, we settled on the route to take. As we wanted to cover the major camel-breeding areas, we needed to take in Barmer, Jaisalmer and Bikaner. That amounted to about 800 km. Of course, the details of the route were not discussed, but we now had the cornerpoints. Everything else would have to be improvised.

One of the major challenges was to obtain riding camels. In our area, there were only the breeding herds of the Raika, composed of many females and very few breeding males. Neither would be suitable. Females are not ridden in Rajasthan. Full stop. Hanwant strictly ruled out the option as incompatible with local cultural values: the job of female camels is to give birth and they are not to be subjected to any additional physical exertions. That's what the Raika thought. I tried arguing my case by quoting excerpts from the writings of my heroes, the explorers of the Middle East. They had all used female camels for riding, and eulogised their gentle cooperative nature. But to no avail. Not even the fact that, right here in India, in the neighbouring state of Haryana, farmers preferred to use female camels for ploughing, impressed Hanwant. So training one of our several Miras was out.

That the local male breeding camels were not eligible, even I could see. They have their mind on females and would be impossible to control, especially as the yatra would take place during the rutting season.

So where to get riding camels? I insisted that we needed to assemble them well ahead of the yatra to get to know them and engage in some team-building exercises. Maybe we should also practise riding on camels, since, as noted during our soul-searching exercise at the hotel, we really didn't have any experience in sitting on and steering camels.

But this proposition remained illusive. Although Hanwant sent out word through the Raika grapevine, there were hardly any results. A few times, the existence of a male camel was reported, but they turned out to be old or crippled. Ma'sahib suggested we could find good animals in Barmer district, but to investigate this further would take a few days of travel – time which Hanwant did not have. He was up to his ears with work, as LPPS was helping the Raika in a court case about their grazing rights in the Kumbhalgarh Sanctuary. This had been referred to the Supreme Court in Delhi and now required intense interaction with advocates, as well as compiling solid data to underpin the Raikas' claims.

Our Raika advisors also cautioned against bringing in animals from Barmer, an area that was much drier than ours and where the plant life was different. Such animals were raised on and accustomed to the typical dry desert vegetation and would refuse to ingest the lusher forage around Sadri. I argued that we needed exactly such desert-raised camels for the yatra, since that was the area we were going to cover. Yes, that's true, I learned, but they would lose condition if brought to Sadri much earlier – so we should get them just before the yatra.

As my camel expertise obviously was not called for at this stage, I decided, as usual, to leave all these minor details to Hanwant. I had work in Germany, he kept me updated over the phone, but there was never any substantive development on this crucial matter. While this lack of progress filled me with pangs of anxiety, he was unfazed. Instead, he revelled in the used saddles and camel adornments that he was collecting from the Raika who no longer kept camels. "It is important that we and our camels make a good impression while on the yatra. You will like very much the nice saddle belt that I found – a real antique," he tried to reassure me. Gradually, he assembled the various pieces of proper camel attire which are a specialty of Rajasthan's camel culture. Besides saddles, these included various types and subtypes of saddle-cushions, saddle-girths, saddlecloths, stirrups, saddle-ropes, halters, and reins, as well as ankle-bells, knee-bells, a chest-cover, and a head-covering.

Indian Camel Equipment

Hindi	English
Pilan	Saddle
Thada	Saddle support
Gidiya	Saddle cushion
Tang	Saddle girth
Panchi	Saddlecloth
Pagra	Stirrups
Gudhra	Saddle cushion
Ghassiya	Thin saddle cushion

astonishingly astute and analytical. He knew everything about the history of the area and the genealogies of the leading families. One could pose him any question about local matters, traditional practices, historical personages and information would slowly but endlessly pour out of him, often in a structured way, as if he was a textbook. I could listen to him for ages, enjoying his lilt and distinct pronunciation which was quite different from the language spoken around Sadri.

Although they were feeling the pressure from the loss of prime grazing areas, the camel breeders of Jaisalmer still retained huge herds, often numbering several hundred heads. If we wanted to save the camel, this was where we should be working, as here there were still sufficient numbers to reach some kind of economy of scale to make the marketing of products a viable proposition. And the larger rationale, even urgency, was also there: the depletion of groundwater resources had taken on alarming dimensions, to the extent that the Rajasthan government had now prohibited the drilling of new tubewells. In this scenario, the development of the camel economy offered great opportunities that could benefit many sections of society. In our work in Sadri, the need for poverty alleviation and stopping rural–urban migration had always been the overall justification. But here something else was at stake: the whole ecology of the region and the need for utilising the land in a long-term sustainable manner, without finishing off the groundwater resources for ever.

Out of these ruminations we developed a project proposal that was entitled, "Revitalising Camel Pastoralism for Sustainable Land Use and Improved Livelihoods in the Thar Desert." Its goal was to "economically revitalise camel breeding with the purposes of enabling long-term sustainable land-use, supporting rural livelihoods, and in order to conserve an important component of Rajasthan's biological diversity and cultural heritage." To achieve this, we proposed to secure pasture space and to seek an increase in economic returns from camel breeding. For this purpose, we would explore new marketing options and tap into "emerging consumer demands".

The approach sounded eminently sensible and convincing on paper and we were fortunate that an enlightened and enthusiastic programme coordinator at a grant-making institution liked the idea very much. He was especially keen on catalysing the sale of camel milk and pressed us to make concrete commitments about the amounts of milk that we would turn over. We were a bit reluctant to reach specific targets, as we had no experience in marketing and sales. But finally we agreed – unwisely, as it later turned out – to reach a certain threshold of daily milk sales. This was to be one of the indicators by which the success of the project would be judged.

We were impatient to start the project. I was excited by the raw and romantic atmosphere of Jaisalmer – it somehow reminded me of Jordan and the Middle East in general, with its slow, easy-going pace, the oriental feel of its bazaar, and with its large numbers of Muslim men in flowing robes milling around its main square, the Hanuman Chowk. Even before the project contract had been officially signed, we threw ourselves into the work and the new challenge, by making the project known to important policy-makers, and sent letters to the chief minister of Rajasthan, as well as to the Members of Parliament from the area. LPPS vice-president, Uttra Kothari, and I were granted an appointment with the governor of Rajasthan, Mrs Pratibha Patil who later became President of India. Unfortunately, she was less interested in the issues and the camel than in knowing how I was coping with Indian food and who was cooking my meals.

In Jaisalmer, one of the first tasks was to rent an office and we found it in Achalvansi Colony – a building that was brand new but decorated with the stone-latticed façade that is typical of Jaisalmer's architecture. It was a real beauty of an abode compared to our rustic facilities in Sadri. We interviewed and hired local staff, trying for a balanced representation of the different camel-keeping castes. One member of the team was a woman called Mira Paliwal, a real firebrand and the local leader of the association of unmarried women – widows, divorcees, spinsters.

The next step was to go out and visit the camel breeders in their villages, to find out where they were located, and how they could best be supported. We learnt that all of them gather once every year, on a specific day in the moon calendar, at the shrine of Kaju Fakir, a Rajput who had converted to Islam. For this meeting, they bring their camels along – thousands of them – and get them blessed by passing them under a rope tied to the corners of the shrine. This is believed to protect the herds from disease. Kaju Fakir's place is located in an army firing range and normally off-limits, but Hanwant managed to attend and use the opportunity to inform all of the camel breeders about the objectives and activities of the project.

The interest and feedback was great; the herders were really pleased that somebody was taking an interest in their occupation – repeatedly mentioning that this was the first time anybody from the outside had talked to them about these issues. Encouragingly, they actively got into the fray from the start, formed their own committee and made arrangements for hosting the official opening workshop of the project. For this, they picked a location known as Joshi-ka-talab which was about 15 km from Jaisalmer, near a small lake that had been artificially created for water storage.

On the big day in November, the camel herders turned out in large numbers, some of them on camelback, while a few brought their entire herds along and subsequently plied all of us with fresh milk. They included the Bhatti Rajputs who were the original occupants of the area, as well as Rathore Rajputs and Sodha Rajputs that had migrated here from Pakistan. There was the Bishnoi community that follows twenty-nine rules and worships nature and owns some of the largest herds near Pokharan. Raika that still took care of camels owned by the Jaisalmer royal family were also there, as well as Muslim herders who dominate the camel safari business at the Sam sand dunes. From our side, we had invited government officials from the Animal Husbandry department and local MPs but they did not show up. However, the staff from the National Research Centre on Camel and the Institute of Desert Medicine in Jodhpur participated.

The programme started with a camel competition in three categories – best camel herd, best male camel and best female camel – judged by a committee of camel breeders, rather than veterinary doctors, as is usually the case. The winners received prize money of Rs 1,100, Rs 501 and Rs 201 respectively.

In preparation for the event, I had put together materials and a leaflet that described all the possible products that could be made from camels. By means of a powerpoint presentation, I demonstrated the diversity of goodies made elsewhere, including Camelbert made in Mauritania, flavoured milk from Dubai, camel leather items from Australia, woollen rugs from Turkmenistan, camel bone jewellery from Jordan, camel milk soaps from the US and a camel milk truck from Kenya. Raika leader Bagdiramji, who had recently returned from a pastoralist gathering in Ethiopia, reported how he had met several African entrepreneurs who had established camel dairies in Mauritania, Niger, Kenya, and Puntland; what he had gleaned from them about different production techniques; and that some of them were making cheese from camel milk.

The herders were suitably impressed and gave supportive

applause. As is a well-established practice at LPPS, all of us then divided into three groups to discuss specific topics.

The first group discussed how to market camel products, touching upon points such as: How to build up a milk-production chain? What could be learned from a dairy cooperative? What was the role of entrepreneurs? What was the desired role of women? How to stimulate demand for the products? Was there potential in camel wool, camel leather and bone products? What steps were needed to be taken to access market potential? This group's recommendations included: creation of a cooperative group in which camel breeders would be active members; establishment of camel milk collection centres; processing of milk for different products through an entrepreneur or trained dairy persons; and discouragement of camel slaughter.

The second group tried to solve the grazing problem and how to feed camels so that they could be productive. A key question was investigating the possibility of getting the Forest Department to plant more trees suitable as camel forage. Which ones should these be? How to get the Forest Department on board? Was it possible to have a camel sanctuary, modelled on wildlife sanctuaries? They concluded that forage plants had reduced and provided a list of trees, shrubs and grasses that should be planted, and a selection of dry fodder made available during droughts. The group supported the idea of a camel sanctuary in each pertinent district and emphasised the promotion of low water-consuming fodder, crops and grasses and the replacement of barbed wire with live shrubs.

Finally, a third group delved into policy and organisational aspects, attempting to identify policies that would support camel husbandry and enable camel breeders to make their voices heard. They discussed how to build an effective camel lobby and the need for getting organised as camel rearers. They seconded the establishment of camel sanctuaries, stopping encroachment on village grazing grounds, the establishment of dairying facilities as well as loan and animal-health facilities.

After all this hard work, it was time for the highlight of the workshop: a tasting of camel milk ice cream that our staff had made in two flavours: strawberry and *kesar pista*. We ceremoniously unwrapped a plastic container and the novelty was "inaugurated" by a Raika priest from the Sadri area who was also the chairman of Rajasthan's livestock board. Everybody got to sample the delicacy and raved about its taste. It was this event that caught the attention of the media worldwide. Our press release about the new camel culinary delight was picked up by news agencies not only in India but also around the world, even making it onto the Yahoo news site. Within a day, we received requests for interviews from the New York Public Radio and BBC World Service.

Press Release

Jaisalmer, 9 November 2006

CAMEL BREEDERS OF THE THAR DESERT TO CASH IN ON HEALTH PROPERTIES OF CAMEL MILK

With a camel-milk ice cream tasting, the Rajasthan-based NGO, Lokhit Pashu-Palak Sansthan (LPPS), has launched a two-year project to help traditional camel breeders realise the economic potential of a range of camel products. The organisation sees the revival of camel husbandry as an important tool for supporting livelihoods and sustainable land-use in the drought-afflicted and impoverished far western part of Rajasthan.

Camel milk is different from cow's and buffalo milk, in a very healthy way: it contains enzymes with anti-bacterial and anti-viral properties, which help to fight diseases. This is why it has not only been used traditionally to cure tuberculosis and typhoid, but may also have a positive effect on patients with HIV/AIDS, cancer and Alzheimer's Disease. No allergies against camel milk are known and even lactose-intolerant people can drink it. Moreover, camel milk contains insulin and has been shown to reduce blood sugar levels in diabetes patients.

Camel milk is already marketed as a health food and beauty product in the Gulf and several African countries. The global market potential for camel milk could be billions of dollars, estimates the Food and Agriculture Organisation (FAO) of the United Nations.

From 6-8 November, camel breeders and scientists met in a three-day workshop held near the ancient caravan city of Jaisalmer to discuss potential and strategies for marketing camel milk and other camel products. At the gathering, camel breeders emphasised that their ancestral herds have dwindled by about 50% in the last ten years, because their grazing areas have been eaten up by irrigation agriculture.

"With groundwater levels dropping rapidly, the end of water-intensive land use is in sight and camel husbandry represents a perfect solution to the chronic water woes of the state," states Bagdiram Raika, president of the Rajasthan Pastoralist Development Association.

"We would like to see the camel breeders of Rajasthan make use of their traditional assets to avail themselves of new marketing opportunities. Our role is to support them in this process," explained Hanwant Singh, director of LPPS, an organisation that supports landless livestock keepers.

"This project will not only contribute to poverty alleviation, but also to conserving biodiversity," commented Dr Ilse Köhler-Rollefson, project coordinator of the international NGO, League for Pastoral Peoples and Endogenous Livestock Development. "The camel has been a part and parcel of the Thar Desert ecology for hundreds of years, and there is danger of it becoming extinct unless it generates income. Ultimately, we hope that this project will motivate people to plant trees for camel fodder, which will also help to combat desertification."

The response of the camel breeders to save their animals through value-addition was enthusiastic. "We would like the government to establish camel sanctuaries. The camel is part of Rajasthan's identity and it should be declared as the state animal," said Bhom Singh, owner of a large camel herd.

The ice cream made from camel milk and coming in two flavours – kesar and strawberry vanilla – was a full success. "This is an absolutely delicious desert treat," opined Tommaso Sbriccoli, an Italian researcher, comparing it favourably with the gelato in his home country.

Already the numerous hotels in Jaisalmer are expressing interest in stocking up this new item to attract health- and diet- conscious customers.

We felt positive.

Catalysed by this event, countless camel breeders travelled from their remote villages to our office in Jaisalmer or called us with their problems. Their absolute priority was help with treating sick camels. Many herds were afflicted with mange, a skin disease caused by mites that is highly contagious and causes itchiness. If not treated, the animals lose weight, deteriorate and may even die. Once a herd is infected, it is very difficult to control. There are traditional treatments available, but they are extremely time-consuming, as they involve application of ointments over the whole surface of the camel. In most cases, we were able to treat the outbreaks by means of a single injection per camel and it made quite a dramatic impact. The camel breeders, some of whom had lost significant numbers of animals to this disease, were extremely grateful as a consequence and treated us with even more respect than before.

Gradually, we got a feel of Jaisalmer's unique social and ecological fabric. Very thinly populated, the area had been the entry-point for a series of Muslim invasions into India and thus been at the interface between Hindus and Muslims for well over a 1,000 years. While it gave the impression of being a remote outpost, it had actually been at the crossroads of major trade routes that connected India with China, Iran and the Mediterranean. The Bhatti Rajputs who had ruled the area for more than a 1,000 years had originally had their capital in the town of Lodorva. After this had been ransacked several times by Muslim invaders from Afghanistan, the Bhattis moved the capital to the top of Trikuta Hill and, in 1155 AD, built the golden fort that Jaisalmer is famous for.

The business model of the Bhatti kings had been to levy taxes on the caravan trade in exchange for safe passage. From 1271 onwards, another community had become prominent: the Paliwals – brahmins who had immigrated in large numbers from Pali in central Rajasthan. They knew how to farm and developed a special technique called "*khadin*" that trapped rainwater in shallow depressions and made it possible to cultivate wheat even in the otherwise bone-dry Thar Desert. These people had also engaged in trade and built a large number of substantial settlements, even quite extensive cities, in the desert. In 1818, Jaisalmer came under British rule. It continued to thrive for a while due to extensive trade in opium, silk, indigo, dried fruits and various other goods. But, in 1840, the overland trade – and the associated taxes – came to a halt as a port was built in Bombay. The business people deserted the town, the royal family lost much of its influence and the population of Jaisalmer drastically reduced. Currently, because of army activities and because of mining, as well as energy extraction, the economy was once again up, leading to rapid changes in the landscape. Large numbers of wind-energy projects were cropping up and huge fields were covered with solar panels. Other areas became totally off limits as they were demarcated as army firing ranges or for mining.

From historical facts it was clear that the earlier wealth of Jaisalmer had been entirely dependent on camels. They had been the prerequisite for the establishment of trade routes through the deserts. Furthermore, camels had been required for ploughing the khadin land and for lifting groundwater which was usually at considerable depth from the surface. Not surprisingly, camels had enjoyed an extremely high status. Virtually every household had once owned a male camel for transportation and for household chores. But, ownership of female breeding camels had been the privilege of the local elite, such as the king, noblemen, and leading lineages. The value of the female camel was expressed in an old proverb that was often recited to us: *Mere ko jin gao panaye jisme sandia hain* – "Marry me into a village with many she-camels." In earlier times, girls had pleaded with their parents to marry them into a family or village with female camels, because this meant status, security, and a means of communication.

But now times had changed and the opposite obtained. The older generation was still very fond of camels, but due to the rapid economic development, there were other opportunities around for the younger generation – if they desired them and were not just content with hanging out and whiling away their time, as quite a few seemed to be. Educated youngsters often told their fathers to get rid of the camels. "But it's the camels that paid for the education – how can I now sell them?" one exasperated breeder whose son had become an advocate once told us. Being a camel herder now even made it difficult to get married, and this had to do with the local balance between males and females – there were significantly more boys than girls on the marriage market.

As Mira, who was coordinating the work with women, told us, infanticide of the girl-child – formerly very common among Rajputs because of the expenditure associated with arranging a girl's marriage – continues to be practised in a number of villages in Jaisalmer district. These villages are locally described as "not having seen a *baraat* (marriage procession) for over a decade". What people meant to express with this phrase was that, in these villages, there was a total absence of girls because they were all killed at birth. According to Mira, this was going on clandestinely with the connivance of village nurses who were put under pressure to keep their mouths shut. The deed was performed by means of opium administered right after birth and the burial was quietly taken care of by the *daroga*, a caste of domestic servants for Rajput chiefs and noblemen. Various aid agencies had tried to stop the practice, but without success. It was spine-chilling driving through the villages in question; luckily we did not work in any of them.

The unintended side effect of this archaic behaviour is a local abundance of bachelors for whom no bride can be found. Our kitchen and tea "boy" who was already well in his forties and still unmarried, was a case in point. And, purportedly, young men who were herding camels were regarded as especially unattractive bridegroom material and had low chances of finding a wife. When we talked to the camel breeders about their problems, this point regularly came up. "Instead of a camel project you should have a bachelor project and see that they all get married," became a popular joke in our project.

A few words about the role and position of women in the desert might be in order. Throughout our working area, married women were, and continue to be, in strict purdah and entirely house bound, although, in some cases, they do work in the field during harvest time. In essence, the universe of women is composed of only two places: their pir (parental place) and their *sasural* (in-laws' place). They know about Jaisalmer town because that's where their husbands frequently go by bus to buy supplies or where their sons go for schooling, work or to hang out, but they have never visited it themselves.

After meeting me several times, some of the women spiritedly expressed envy at my ability to roam around and visit different places at will. Although I always invited them to visit us in the Jaisalmer office, no female face ever showed up except a group of widows that Mira had been working with for many years. As it was not part of the normal pattern of behaviour of married women to go to Jaisalmer, Mira and I schemed to organise a women-only trip to Jaisalmer for the wives of some Rajput camel breeders from a particular village with whom I had developed a bantering relationship. In order to avoid any contact with a non-family male, I would drive the jeep myself. This may sound like a simple plan, but it required weeks of persuasion. The women were unsure and one of our field workers who was from the same village and related to some of them, would always distance himself with a worried expression. So I was not sure if and how the female excursion would play itself out. When Mira and I turned up one

Sunday morning ready to provide a ride to Jaisalmer for interested ladies, a large number of women had decked themselves out in shiny new Rajput garments and were raring to go, with babies and small children tucked in their arms. There were so many of them that when they all squeezed in, they did not leave enough space for me behind the steering wheel. We drove off to the wail of some of the school-age children who had never been separated from their mums before, and were determined to hitch a ride on the bumper or by hanging on to the sides of the jeep. It took several attempts to shake them off, but when we had finally tackled the take-off from the village, the mood relaxed and the women broke out into songs and laughter. This gave way to wondrous stares, questions and comments as we reached the outskirts of the town, as traffic increased and we passed shops and hotels and flew by strange-looking, scantily dressed white tourists. After parking the jeep, we wandered in a tightly knit cluster up to the fort, enjoyed the view from the bulwark, sat the children on the ancient cannon, posed for pictures, had snacks and tea, made observations. The colourful wares of the tourist shops only elicited surprise and even slight disdain for being of lower quality and a waste of money. Then the concern to get home and cook food for waiting husbands and family members took over the mood, and we drove home again, still singing, but rather tired from all the excitement. It was a memorable event for all involved and I am still wondering if it awakened any further curiosity and longing to see more of the world outside the villages.

While this may sound controversial, I don't believe that the normally restricted radius of action of desert women makes them unhappy or that they are suffering; in fact, to me, they generally seem much happier and relaxed than the average American or European suburban wife hassled by the double burden of career and motherhood. Lack of knowledge about the big wide world may make them even more content as they are not aware of alternative options. They are always busy with numerous household chores, have children and young animals to take care of and lavish love and affection on. They are never alone, but always embedded into an extended family, with all the give and take that entails. On the other hand, the husbands are out during most of the day, so do not interfere much with domestic affairs and women can call the shots. Importantly, they have numerous outlets for their creativity, embellishing their homes with intricate designs in dried mud and building truly awesome furniture from acacia branches covered with lime. They are usually full of fun and mischief, coupled with enormous dignity and generosity. The older women have an aura of wisdom and spiritual detachment from worldly things (except the welfare of their children), the middle-aged women are warm and active busybodies, astutely leveraging their sons and other male relatives to get certain things done beyond their immediate sphere of influence. The younger set performs roles as obedient daughters-in-law or as playful daughters of the house, usually confident that their father will make the best possible match for them. This was the impression that was generated for me, the total outsider, and one that I also believed to, by and large, be true, for a good mood and a satisfied countenance are not that easy to put on consistently.

The widows of whom there are disproportionately many are a different case. Some of them are Kargil widows whose husbands lost their lives in the recent spat between India and Pakistan. Others were married to old men while still in their teens. The widows are immediately recognisable from their drab maroon clothes and lack of jewellery; they are shunned by society and entirely dependent on their husband's relatives, or sometimes their father, for hand-outs, as they have no opportunity to go out and earn their own livelihoods. While they are entitled to government pensions, filling out the required forms and pushing them through the bureaucracy can be challenging. This was one of the tasks that Mira specialised in, and the reason why she was so popular among the women.

In general, our work seemed to be moving in the right direction, although it took longer than expected to complete the household camel survey that was part of it. This was due to the huge areas that needed to be covered and the fact that large herds of camels tended to be located in extremely remote villages close to the border with Pakistan. These were reachable only by means of kaccha roads that were frequently rendered impassable by moving sand dunes. As a foreigner, I myself could not normally visit these places, except with a special permit. But I observed again and again how the people that were the furthest from "civilisation", that is, resided in far-flung villages, were the happiest and the most hospitable. These villages were not only very clean, but beauteous to behold being composed entirely of mud-brick buildings that were assiduously kept up, repaired and painted by women who exuded self-confidence and hands-on efficiency.

The media attention on the ice cream had raised local awareness about camel milk and its special properties. People frequently came to our office requesting to sample camel milk and then to order daily delivery to their doorsteps. These were mainly elderly people with diabetes, but also one young man who wanted to build his body. There were even phone calls from further afield and Delhi from business people who were interested in starting a market for camel milk there. So the demand was building up. Now we needed to connect the dots and bring the milk from Jaisalmer's thousands of female camels to the waiting consumers. We were excited and tried to infect the camel breeders with our enthusiasm by calculating for them how much money they could make per month by just selling a few litres of milk per day. With the slogan,

"Two litres per day will earn you Rs 6,000 extra per month," we tried to seduce them into production. Yet, while people politely nodded their heads in agreement, echoing our viewpoint that it was certainly a great idea, active participation in starting to sell milk was not really forthcoming. One of our friends told us, "Yes, good idea, you are welcome to milk my camels and take all the milk that you want."

The logistics certainly were not easy, as the camel management system in Jaisalmer was entirely different from Sadri. No friendly kissing camels here. These animals had to fend for themselves for large parts of the year – without a concerned Raika to daily check them for the smallest scratch, to fuss over their wellbeing and have sleepless nights over lack of feed. The Jaisalmer camels were usually not habituated to human handling, and medical interventions such as a jab against tryps or mange that were an easy exercise in Sadri posed a major challenge. It needed a lot of cunning and manpower to catch and restrain camels and every treatment turned into a mad wrestling act, a competition between man and animal over who could outwit the other.

There was quite some variation between herders – and communities – in the amount of attention given to the herds, but the general pattern was like this:

During the breeding season – which is also the birthing season, and lasts roughly from November to March – supervision is required to ensure desired mating of the females with desired males, to prevent fights between competing males and to make sure the babies are taken care of and nursed properly by their mothers. In the rare case that the mother dies or does not accept her young, the orphan is hand-raised by the women.

After the breeding season peters out from March onwards and temperatures begin to soar, the camels are left to range freely. Some herders put the young camels into thorn enclosures during the day, which ensures that their mothers come back in the evening to nurse them. But, gradually, the bond between the mother and offspring loosens and is no longer sufficient to lure the mother back. The female camels disperse in small groups, often composed of related females (grandmother, mother, daughter) or just two or three camels that are friends. The male camels become solitary during this time and roam on their own.

When the first rains fall, the camels need to be gathered to prevent them from causing harm to the crops that are now being sown. Many of the females come back on their own; according to local lore, they return when they see thunder and lightning in the direction of their villages. They seek out places where rain has fallen, apparently being able to detect these over long distances by their sense of smell. According to scientists, they have the ability to sense "geosmin" a substance that is produced by streptomyces bacteria when rain falls.

The camels that don't return voluntarily are brought home in a collective exercise in which all camel breeders join. Irrespective of ownership, everybody gathers each camel he comes across and then brings him or her to a central place. As each animal has a village-specific, or even owner-specific brand, they can then be sorted out easily.

If there are proper rains, then everything is fine and the herds graze in the vicinity of their villages, but if not, then they have to be let loose again, as they become impossible to control in their search for food.

As it dawned on us that the camels of Jaisalmer were kept in a semi-feral state, we began to have second thoughts on the viability of milking them. Was it realistic to collect significant amounts of camel milk under these circumstances - would we even get enough to make a systematic operation viable?

We decided to seek expert advice from the woman who had

done it long before us: Nancy Abeiderrahmane, who had founded the world-famous Tiviski camel dairy in Mauritania a decade earlier and against all odds. Nancy graciously agreed to help us and give us her assessment. She flew in with lots of enthusiasm and her laptop on which she had stored pictures of her state-of-the-art dairy in Nouakchott. In our Jaisalmer office, she gave a presentation to Bhom Singh and other camel breeders who raptly looked at the pictures of the various products as well as of the pick-up trucks which transported the milk from collection points in the desert to the dairy. We drove around the area with her and visited several camel herds. Nancy looked, probed and enquired. Finally, she provided us with her evaluation at a workshop in Jaipur which we had organised and in which many important people participated: Dr Agrawal from Bikaner Medical College who presented his data on the impact of camel milk on diabetes and insulin metabolism; representatives of the Rajasthan dairy federation; Dr Wernery from Dubai; and notably, the president of the Raika Education Charitable Trust (RECT) who was a banker. Everybody was excited about camel milk marketing and Nancy's verdict was that it was definitely feasible. In her opinion, the infrastructure in Rajasthan was actually better developed than Mauritania, so, in some ways, it should be easier. However, she also cautioned that in order to get everything going it would require quite a substantial investment in cooling tanks and in a processing unit. The figure she mentioned for her own unit was around USD 800,000. Not to be daunted, the Raika banker and the people from the state milk cooperative put forward plans for how this kind of funding could be leveraged.

The workshop in Jaipur felt like a breakthrough. And we had another uplifting experience. One day we were driving to Jodhpur when Hanwant received a phone call from a Raika leader urging us to participate in a meeting that the community had organised with Vasundhara Raje, the chief minister of Rajasthan. The Raika had always been a votebank for her party and she had been very close to our dear Bhopalaram, the most respected and sincere pastoralist leader who had sadly passed away recently. Hanwant immediately redirected the jeep towards the venue where tens of thousands of Raika, both men and women were assembled. We were ushered to the dais and seated next to the local dignitaries, the district collector and other bureaucrats, and within minutes her aides introduced us to Vasundhara just before she was to give her speech. While I was thinking she must be busy with other things at this particular moment, she knew how to handle the situation perfectly and greeted us with regal charm, "Oh you are the famous camel people! Where have you been all this time? I have been desperately trying to contact you! The camel is so important for Rajasthan." She then went on to say that she had directed the Rajasthan Cooperative Dairy Federation to start producing camel milk and to put it on sale in Jaipur. Perplexed, I handed her some of our camel promotional material and one of our newsletters, but she was already urged on by the local organisers to start her speech. With panache and warmth she began to address the huge and adulating crowd. I could not understand every word she said but I got the drift and, suddenly, to the cheers of the masses, she started waving the camel brochure in her hand and holding forth about the importance of the camel and the need to save it. The speech went on for some time and, afterwards, Vasundharaji was engulfed by the crowd as she was led to her waiting helicopter, but the remarks by this gifted politician made us feel good.

Meanwhile, back in the Thar Desert, things were moving a bit slower. Our staff had worked hard to set up a collection and distribution chain. They collected the "white gold of the desert" in the early morning by motorbike from the producers, then pasteurised it in the office kitchen, filled it into plastic bags, and finally delivered it to about a dozen camel milk aficionados in the town. It was working in a way, but there were lots of hiccups – both on the supply and demand side. Sometimes milk was not available or had gone off; the customers complained that it came in too late in the morning to be used for their morning chai and that they wanted it earlier. There was constant fluctuation among clients, with some dropping out and new ones joining. We never sold much more than 30 kg per day.

We thought that not much more could be expected at this stage, considering all the hurdles involved – the wildness of the camels, the novelty of the concept, the problems with transportation, the sometimes unbearable heat and electricity outages, but our donor was not impressed. He cited figures from another project with buffalo milk producers in Gujarat where a minimum of 1,000 litres, and a maximum of 3,000 litres per day had to be turned over in order to make a profit. We argued that it needed time to build up to such volumes and that camel milk was not a mass market proposition like cow and buffalo milk, but a premium product with medicinal and health benefits. Therefore, it could generate a higher price and could be made profitable with smaller quantities.

Be that as it may, there was another unanticipated hurdle of which we got an inkling one chilly morning when we left before dawn to get to one of our main milk suppliers in time for the morning milking. He, his five brothers and their families lived in a small hamlet on top of a hillock somewhere in the middle of nowhere. When we reached there it was not yet light, except for a shimmer in the east, and everybody was still sleeping. One of the brothers called us into a community meeting room where he had slept and which was used for storing sacks of grain. We insisted that we only wanted to pick up the milk. It had not yet been collected, but there was no hurry. Sometime later, three blanket-clad figures ambled down the slope to where a number of camels were assembled, while their youngsters were caged in a small enclosure made from dried trunks of the aak tree.

We were directed not to follow because the milking camels might be scared of us and then not let go of their milk. Unlike the camels in Sadri, these ones didn't just stand there and let themselves be milked. They had to be held and soothed by one person, while another one milked and a third one managed the calf whose presence was necessary to stimulate the milk flow. It took about thirty minutes to milk the six camels which together provided about 20 kg of milk.

It was an achievement for this extended family to have habituated their previously semi-feral camels to milking. Their efforts had been financially rewarding and they had earned around Rs 20,000 over the last two months – a sizeable income by local standards. The extra income had enabled them to pay back an outstanding loan, as one of the brothers told us when we had given in to his pleading to have another cup of tea – traditional hospitality outweighing the theoretical imperative of getting the milk to town as speedily as possible to be pasteurised and delivered to the waiting customers. Although I was impatient to move on, the ensuing conversation gave us a taste of local sentiments and attitudes with respect to making money from selling camel milk. To the donor and to us, it sounded great that poor people had made significant income through the project and we were expecting the "beneficiaries" to be jubilant about this and wanting to expand their activities and rake in more cash. But they were strangely unexcited and noncommittal. When the men expanded about their household income it became clear why. Each of the five brothers generated income from different sources – one from crop cultivation, one from sheep and goats, one from a small herd of cows whose milk was picked up by a private dairy, and one had an army pension. So these people were not poor at all and certainly did not consider themselves as such. They had various types of resources to fall back on and their cost of living was very low. For instance, they had very little expenditure on food, cultivating their own millet and obtaining plenty of buttermilk and ghee from their cows. Various desert trees, such as kair, kumbat and khejri, yielded fruits and pods from which nutritious and delicious "vegetables" could be made. If cash was needed, this could always be generated by selling some sheep – demand for whom as a source of meat was extremely high. There was such a run on mutton that traders were continuously roaming around, seeking to get their hands on any lamb over four to six weeks of age. It was clear that these herders felt they had everything they required to satisfy their needs, so why overexert themselves with the bother of getting up early to milk reluctant camels?

Moments such as this made me think that poverty in the desert was either a myth or a foreign invention.

Some time later, we had another eye-opening discussion with Bhom Singh who had now become the elected president of the Jaisalmer Camel Breeders' Association – a kind of apex organisation of the seven or eight camel breeders' saving groups that had been established as part of the project. Commanding huge respect among the camel breeders, Bhom Singh liked to spend his days in a teashop in Pokharan, discussing local affairs with friends and contacts and taking care of far-ranging businesses over his mobile phone. He invited us to his house in a village near Pokharan which was reachable only over a sandy track, and ushered us into a small square guest reception room, separate from the domestic complex to which only family members had access. The guestroom was a dark place constructed out of roughly hewn stone. It doubled up as storage place for broken charpais and agricultural implements which were piled up in one corner.

We were handed some coarse and heavy blankets to roll up as back rests and to protect us from the cold. After we had seated ourselves in the dark interior, Bhom Singh barked orders to a bevy of thin young men scurrying around to serve tea. After the routine morsels of opium had been parcelled out, Bhom Singh leaned back and was ready to talk. We wanted to know from him how life had changed in the last half century.

"When I was a child, my family made its living as *dakoos* (dacoits). We stole camels in Sindh which we then sold here in the Pokharan area or in Barmer, in exchange for *bajra* (millet). In those days, we lived off only the products of our animals – ghee, milk, and buttermilk. Water was very difficult to get in those days – much rarer than milk! Sometimes, we hardly had any bread and lived for weeks off camel milk. We obtained millet in exchange for ghee and wool. We started growing our own millet only in 1974 and one sack of millet had to last for the whole year, so we never had roti more than once a day. Sometimes, we had to mix the millet flour with the seeds of *matira* (melon) and *tumba* (a wild creeper) to make it last longer. In drought years, we tried to make flour from the bark of trees such as khejri and kair. When it became really bad, the whole village migrated to Sindh where we found work. Sangria, the pods of the khejri tree and pilu, the fruit of the jal tree, were very important for us." He paused, and I asked him, "And what about tea? When was that introduced?"

"Oh, tea – that only started about fifty years ago. And I can still remember very well when that happened. My mother did not know what these dried black bits were, and she thought it was a dried vegetable, so she fried the tea leaves and made a *terka* (garnish) from them."

"So what kind of things did you need to buy?"

"We had to purchase red chilli, salt, sesame oil, sugar and matches."

"And what about opium and alcohol – how important were they?"

"Oh, opium is very old, we have used it for many generations. But drinking of alcohol was restricted to the thakurs, the large landowners; ordinary people did not use it."

After an hour or so, the young men brought in trays of food – *bajra ki roti* (millet bread) with chutney from green chillies, and with generous amounts of homemade ghee from Bhom Singh's cows. It tasted delicious and felt healthy – easily one of the best and most satisfying meals I could imagine. It was served under the light of a flickering oil lamp by solicitous and respectful attendants hovering over us to be at immediate service. Listening to Bhom Singh's stories, with the cows that had provided the ghee ruminating away on the other side of the wall, I wondered what more could one want from life – it couldn't get any better, I was sure.

The next morning, we were again served wonderful food, then Bhom Singh showed us a stone mine that had been set up on his land. Granite had been found beneath it, worth many crores of rupees, he had been told. But, just like the camel breeders in the dhani we had visited to collect milk, he was not particularly excited about this development – if anything he was somewhat puzzled about how to handle this new situation. For him, it was more important to sit, have a good talk, relish opium, dispense nuggets of wisdom and enjoy the respect of his fellow camel breeders and others, rather than accumulate money.

For me, these interactions were eye-openers. The camel breeders were tough, resilient people used to hardship; they were not materialistic and rather indifferent to personal luxuries. They were quite happy with their situation (except for the involuntary bachelors who were yearning for a wife and a nuclear family of their own) and could obtain most of their immediate survival needs from their animals or from nature. How could we get a milk market going to provide income if people were not really inclined to exert themselves for the opportunity of some extra cash in their pockets, but preferred to take it easy and enjoy life? Apart from that, where would the substantial investment for cooling tanks and qualified dairy experts to get the camel milk "industry" going, come from? We had looked into creating a producer society and the camel breeders had already organised into clusters of self-help groups and were making regular savings. An Indian dairy consultant had developed a very detailed and intricate plan projecting a daily milk turnover, the number of families benefited, margins, specialty products for the Jaisalmer market, needs for investment and so on. But in the absence of a groundswell of support, it all felt risky and I baulked at taking it further around Jaisalmer. The Rajasthan dairy cooperative had never come forward with the support they had promised at the Jaipur conference. Vasundhara Raje had not been re-elected and the present chief minister had no interest at all in doing anything for camels.

It was also the plain truth that the camel breeders were much less interested in milk marketing than in other types of support they received from LPPS. One of them was, of course, camel healthcare. Another issue important to them was the prevention of thefts and accidents. Losses were high from both factors, as thieves were stealthily roaming about and regularly rounding up camels to truck them out of the state – probably to the meat markets in neighbouring Uttar Pradesh. The presence of LPPS and the creation of the Jaisalmer Camel Breeders' Association had already curbed these activities, as they felt these were strong institutions that would take up the fight. There were also accidents both on the road and the railway tracks, as well as when camels strayed into the army shooting range. Our staff had set up a task force to pursue the drivers who had been involved in accidents with camels and managed to extract substantial compensation money which pleased the camel breeders. We had also put up signboards warning drivers about camels crossing the road. Alas, they were also stolen eventually – prices for scrap metal being pretty high.

At the end of our project, a repeat survey of 10 per cent of the households investigated at the outset of the project in 2006 showed that herd sizes had increased by 26.5 per cent over the last four to four and a half years. This was supported by the government livestock survey which showed that Jaisalmer was the only district in Rajasthan in which camel numbers had not diminished further but had actually increased. The members of the Jaisalmer Camel Breeders' Association had no doubts why this had happened. For one, it was the availability of genuine medicines for treating trypanosomiasis and mange. The mange outbreaks had been controlled to a large degree. Another factor was the prosecution of camel thefts and accidents. The third element was more psychological: their changed perception of the camel. Previously, camel keeping had been seen as a backward, dying profession. But, because of all the hullabaloo we had made around camel milk, they felt that they were engaged in an activity with economic potential for the future. So it was better to hang on and take care of camels, just in case.

While we conceded that our milk marketing venture in Jaisalmer had been a failure and that we had disappointed our keen and supportive donor, we still felt we were on the right track and closer to a solution. If camel milk marketing was too difficult to tackle because of the product's perishability and the amount of infrastructure required, then other products might work: camel wool and camel dung. But this work could also be pursued from Sadri where time had not stood still either.

Chapter 15

RECOGNITION AND RIGHTS

"We recognize that the genetic resources of animal species most critical to food security, sustainable livelihoods and human wellbeing are the result of both natural selection, and directed selection by smallholders, farmers, pastoralists and breeders, throughout the world, over generations."

– Interlaken Declaration on Animal Genetic Resources, 7 September 2007

"Each contracting party shall, as far as possible and as appropriate: Subject to national legislation, respect, preserve and maintain knowledge, innovations and practices of indigenous and local communities embodying ***traditional lifestyles relevant for the conservation and sustainable use of biological diversity*** *and promote their wider application with the approval and involvement of the holders of such knowledge, innovations and practices and encourage the equitable sharing of the benefits arising from the utilization of such knowledge innovations and practices."*

– Paragraph 8j, United Nations Convention on Biological Diversity (CBD), 2007–the present

While we had been absorbed with the Jaisalmer camel milk puzzle, work had piled up in Sadri. The grazing conundrum in the Kumbhalgarh Wildlife Sanctuary had taken on new twists and turns, involving legal action by a Raika struggle committee that LPPS had supported, and eventually ended up in a limbo at the Supreme Court. At the global level, some of the larger development trends, which we had been grappling with for so many years, were coming into the limelight: the neglect of traditional types of livestock (such as the camel) in favour of western high-yielding animals, the lack of respect for the traditional ecological knowledge of communities (such as the Raika), the unravelling of the customary ways of life, the mindless modernisation. These are trends that are recognised as undermining the sustainability of life on earth. Two UN bodies were zeroing in on the complex set of issues around the loss of "genetic resources", of biodiversity and of traditional knowledge.

One of these was the Food and Agriculture Organisation (FAO) in Rome which is concerned with domestic animal diversity: thousands of farm animal breeds that were developed by farmers and pastoralists over centuries or even millennia are currently becoming extinct or have already disappeared. They are being replaced throughout the world by uniform masses of high-yielding chickens, hybrid pigs and black and white Friesian cows bred in western countries. While the local breeds certainly can't provide the same amount of eggs, meat and milk as their high-tuned and scientifically selected cousins, they have many advantages over them, especially if their owners are poor: they can sustain themselves on local plants and crop by-products, they can cope with the local climate, they rarely get sick. The western breeds, on the other hand, require expensive feed, regular doses of medicines and can perform really effectively only under controlled climatic conditions.

While their global takeover has precipitated a glut of cheap livestock products, for which many are certainly grateful, this is also a risky and dangerous drift. Total reliance on genetically narrow, high-performance animals means the loss of human ability to adapt to climate change and even to utilise the extensive deserts, steppes and mountainous zones of the world for food production. Therefore, it endangers long-term food security for humanity at large.

The second UN body was the Convention on Biological Diversity (CBD), a binding international legal framework whose goal is to conserve and ensure the sustainable use of biodiversity, as well as to make sure that the people and countries that steward biodiversity receive benefits if the biodiversity is commercialised. The CBD goes back to the Rio Convention in 1992 and has been signed and ratified by practically all nations, with the notable exception of the USA. The signatory countries meet regularly every two years to discuss progress, or the lack thereof, in biodiversity conservation.

The FAO and the CBD not only provide a forum for official debate at the government level, but also develop strategies and issue recommendations to counter the loss of biodiversity; they do this based on research as well as their consultations with governments, non-government organisations, industries and communities. Arriving at a consensus with so many stakeholders involved can be quite time-consuming, taking several years or even decades; sometimes the processes become stalled because opinions and interests are just too divergent. But they do have the advantage that once guidelines are developed, they provide an official standard that is followed by governments around the world.

The League for Pastoral Peoples (LPP), the German-based non-government organisation that I had initiated in 1992 with the original intent of providing emergency relief to the Raika, engages in these formal discussions. Based on the long interaction with the Raika, LPP is emphasising that pastoralists are "guardians of biological diversity", on two levels. For one, they produce food without directly impacting wild biodiversity. Instead of tilling the soil and growing crops, they use their herds of domesticated animals to convert wild vegetation into highly nutritious and valuable products. Secondly, pastoralists are the ones that conserve the vast majority of domestic livestock breeds as only these can survive and perform in the rough and remote expanses that pastoralists occupy – no western, modern breed has a chance here.

The overall argument of LPP is that local livestock breeds, the eco-systems to which they have adapted, and the livestock keepers can only be conserved as a package ("in-situ") and not separately and out of context. While I had learned this from the example provided by the Raika, there are countless other cases throughout the world of pastoralists stewarding important genetic resources by means of their traditional knowledge – the Samburu and Rendille in Kenya, the Maasai in Tanzania, the Afar in Ethiopia, the Tuareg in Niger, the Bedouin in Jordan, the Pashtoon in Pakistan, the Mongolian herders, to name just a few. Over more than the last decade, LPP has put in a lot of effort in identifying leaders from these pastoral communities, making them aware of the global discussions and in enabling and facilitating them to participate in these UN and other high-level meetings. Between 2003 and 2007, LPP organised discussions and interactions in Kenya, Italy, Ethiopia and, of course, in Sadri that were attended by hundreds of livestock keepers representing more than twenty countries. Through this grassroots consultation process, the concept of "Livestock Keepers' Rights" crystallised. Its basic premise is that in order to conserve domestic animal breeds - and rangelands - the communities that steward them need to be provided the rights already accorded to them under various international laws and legal agreements - including the CBD and the UN Declaration on the Rights of Indigenous People. In addition, they require proper services to ensure animal health and market linkages.

The first international conference on animal genetic resources was to be held in Interlaken in Switzerland in the autumn of 2007. Organised by the FAO and the government of Switzerland, its purpose was to agree on an official joint plan for saving the multitude of locally adapted farm animals for posterity, the "Global Plan of Action for Animal Genetic Resources". The governments from more than hundred countries, as well as representatives of research bodies, the animal industries and civil society, were to attend. This conference was what we had been waiting for to draw the attention of the global community to the role of the Raika and other pastoralists as guardians of local breeds and of diversity. In preparation for it, we had churned out research papers, pamphlets, and even a book and a film called *Keepers of Genes* with FAO support.

We were determined that the Raika with their immense traditional knowledge and as caretakers not only of the camel, but also of various other breeds, would be part of this crucial event - as key witnesses, so to speak. But who would represent them, how should the delegation be composed? Hanwant consulted extensively with the Raika. There was a clear split in the community - on the one hand are the traditionalists who love their animals and will get really upset if somebody tells them to stop livestock keeping. On the other hand, there is the educated section that regularly exhorts the traditionalists that they should "stop running after the tails of their animals". Hearing about the planned trip, many of the latter were highly interested in attending and begged Hanwant and me to provide them with this unique opportunity of travelling "foreign". But we did not want fake pastoralists who had an authentic background but otherwise could not care less about their heritage. We wanted genuine herders who were proud of what they were doing and provided good examples of pastoralist virtues and knowledge. These people were wary about going abroad, besides having the logistical problem of finding a replacement to take care of their herds during their absence. Finally, Dailibai, my favourite animal healer and long-time friend, was the first to agree when I told her she would stay in my village in Germany and get to meet my mother and other family. With this choice clear, we now needed a man closely related to her as chaperone, as otherwise her reputation among the community would be endangered. The candidate for this was her cousin Mangilal, a sedentary Raika who kept buffaloes and impressed people with his friendly demeanour and huge turban. His wife and daughters would look after the buffaloes, so there was no problem there. The third person in the group was Ramaram Raika, a highly respected and deeply knowledgeable sheep breeder who had six brothers, one of whom could herd his flock temporarily.

For good measure and moral support, we decided to complement the group with Tolaram Bhopa, the musician who had been so important to the success of our yatra. We were hoping that he would repeat the remarkable feat he had achieved then of keeping spirits high and of sustaining the esprit de corps in uncharted territory. Because this it certainly was. None of the group had ever travelled anywhere outside the vicinity of Sadri and when Hanwant explained to them they would have to sit in an airplane for ten hours to reach their first destination, there was worried silence.

But first there were the formalities to be taken care of and passports and visas to be obtained. This turned out to be a long-drawn-out battle stretching over several months. The various officials that needed to sign and pass files did not see the need for such "illiterate" and "backward" people to go abroad, laughed at them and treated them condescendingly. Dailibai got stalled early on, as for some reason or another she could not get the required police certificate necessary for applying for a passport. It was a battle of nerves and we were unsure, until practically the last minute, whether she would be able to travel.

Finally, I received the group – the men in their red turbans and Dailibai weighed down by kilos of silver jewellery – at the Frankfurt airport, all happy smiles and totally jetlag-free despite the overnight flight. The plan was for them to stay in my native village for a few days to acclimatise and get over the first culture shock. All wired up, they talked non-stop about the difficulties of getting through the security check in Mumbai (apparently, Dailibai's heavy adornments had the X-ray machines going haywire), and mimicking the flight-attendants' query of "veg or non-veg?" They found the phrase hilarious and repeated it non-stop, cracking up with laughter. As soon as they reached my home, there was no question of wanting to rest – they wanted to work and help with running the household, although the electrical appliances and the absence of a wood chulha and proper brooms stopped them temporarily.

During the next few days, my house turned into a remote outpost of Rajasthan, with whiffs of masala chai floating through the air, the kitchen resounding with the pounding of garlic and green peppers (German garlic did not pass the test), chapatis burning on the electric stove, jokes, banter and laughter, astute observations about Germany and my village. In between, Hanwant coached them how to deal with the challenges expected at the

Interlaken conference. The only temporary problem was how to negotiate western bathrooms, as all of them much preferred to use the open, but could not find an appropriate place when they nipped out the first morning before dawn.

On the second day, a visit by public bus to Darmstadt, the next bigger town, was on the agenda. No sooner had they all seated themselves, than Tolaram, cutting a resplendent figure in his ankle-length crimson gown, with a rather cunning and watchful expression on his face, playfully put the bow to his ravanhatta and experimentally extracted some haunting tones that drifted through the entire – by Indian standards rather empty – bus. Amazingly, no harsh admonishment by the bus driver or outrage about the disturbance by the passengers came forth – instead there were curious stares, giving way to surprised smiles and finally, rhythmic clapping. Even the driver visibly enjoyed this break from routine.

The Raika delegation spread good cheer wherever they went and after a successful press conference in our garden that resulted in colourful spreads in several daily newspapers, Switzerland was next. Tolaram, by now bare of any inhibitions he might have previously had, used the airport to test his crowd appeal. By performing a few gigs from the epic of Pabuji – who must have been applauding this pluck from heaven – he quickly assembled a rapidly increasing audience. With great difficulty, Hanwant had to pry Tolaram away from the captive spectators and herd him onto the plane – only stopping him at the last minute from selling off his instrument to one of his newly acquired fans.

In Interlaken, we put up in a youth hostel built in traditional Alpine style. It was already filled with pastoralists and activists from twenty-six countries invited by LPP, and a couple of like-minded organisations to hold a parallel civil society meeting to the government conference and to discuss their take on the situation of genetic resources and livestock keepers.

The next day, the participants, all dressed in their ethnic attire, took the whole morning to introduce themselves and provide some background on their relationship with livestock. Plenty of common interests and problems were discovered between pastoralists from Ethiopia and Kyrgyzstan and livestock keepers from West Africa, Pakistan and even Canada. Dailibai, Ramaram and Mangilal listened agog through their headphones to the plight of Ethiopian camel pastoralists who could not access medicines for their camels – a problem to which they could relate so well. When it was their turn to speak, they talked about how they had been herding camels, sheep and other livestock for many generations in the Aravalli Hills and that their traditional grazing area had now been turned into the Kumbhalgarh Wildlife Sanctuary for which they had lost the grazing rights. This meant that livestock keeping had become a hassle and younger people were no longer interested in this profession. If there was neither pasture nor herders, how could livestock survive? What good would it be to deep-freeze animals or keep them on government farms? If the camel and other breeds of livestock were to be conserved for the future, then this required secure access to grazing and to animal healthcare, as well as some respect from the outside world. If given this kind of support, they would be able to continue raising livestock, and both their livelihoods and the survival of their herds would be secured. Plus the rest of the world would benefit.

All the conversations at this meeting revolved around vital and existential issues that went to the core issues concerning the extinction of livestock biodiversity. The contrast of this colourful multi-ethnic, multilingual gathering to the official government conference that took place in Interlaken's venerable Kurhaus could not have been greater. Here the participants wore suits and ties or business costumes and were poring over a text that had already been drafted by a preparatory group and was projected onto a huge screen. Passages that were deemed as controversial were put in brackets. It was the task of the government representatives to come to an agreement on this bracketed text. To an outsider it often seemed that the debate was more about form than content, as there were heated and extended discussions about the positioning of commas or insertion of colons. Notably, the negotiations between the countries were organised in various regional blocks - such as Africa, Latin America, Norh America, European Union, and G77, and were, of course, held in English with simultaneous translations into all official UN languages.

Our single-minded and ambitious goal for the conference was the inclusion of a reference to Livestock Keepers' Rights in the Global Plan of Action for Animal Genetic Resources, as this document would provide a reference point for government interventions and actions in the years to come. As negotiating language and its finer nuances is a science on its own and requires specialised legal training to do a proper job, the Raika could not actively participate in the debate. Nevertheless, their mere presence made a huge impact. Wherever they went, they drew crowds. There was no way of overlooking the red turbans among the grey suits and ties of the bureaucrats - many of whom probably understood for the first time what we meant by "livestock keepers". The press also loved the ethnic attire and Hanwant, as the only English speaker, was busy attending press conferences. Ramaram was interviewed by a radio reporter and when asked to give a message to his loved ones, he sent his greetings to his wife and his children, but then burst out, "Most of all I miss my sheep." As soon as the group sat down anywhere on the promenade in Interlaken, they were surrounded by fans - mostly middle-aged ladies who wanted to have their photos taken with the turbaned men. In an exhibition showcasing Swiss agricultural products, Tolaram engaged in a spontaneous jamming session with Swiss Alphorn musicians. During the conference dinner on a boat cruising the Swiss lakes, our Bhopa, for the first time in his life, had a sip of red wine which put him in a good mood but somehow led him to play the same tune over and over. Although generally well received, one high-level UN bureaucrat was overheard saying, "I just wish he would do a Jimi Hendrix act and smash up his instrument."

While our Raika delegation was basking in the admiration and adulation of the general public, other NGO representatives were doing their best at the negotiating table to get "Livestock Keepers' Rights" into the text of the official document. One of them, a lawyer named Justice Nchunu from Cameroon, advised the governments of the African countries and managed to convince them that livestock keepers' rights were important. The African group made LKR part of their agenda but, unfortunately, North America and Europe were entirely against it. In the end, the "Global Plan of Action on Animal Genetic Resources" that all the countries agreed upon contained a number of references to the rights of livestock keepers.

This was significant as the GPA was an official UN document and, therefore, provides guidance and a reference point for all future action. It would give us a foot in the door in the years to come.

But the tour of the Raika was not yet over, although by now it was not just Ramaram who was missing his sheep. Dailibai was also beginning to feel homesick, wondering about her two cows, the calf and other animals, and even whether her children were protecting her stack of manure that was piled up next to the road.

Immediately after the Interlaken conference concluded, all of us were on a plane to Madrid to participate in the "World Gathering of Nomads and Transhuman Herders" that was held near Segovia. More than a hundred pastoralists from thirty-eight countries representing fifty different ethnic groups had already assembled; amongst them was Bagdiram Raika, as one of the counsellors of WAMIP, who had come directly from India.

The most exciting and eye-opening part of the programme was the annual march by 200 Spanish pastoralists and thousands of sheep through downtown Madrid, as part of their regular migratory route between summer and winter pastures. Spanish shepherds have ancient, 800-year-old grazing routes, including 120,000 km of livestock trails which have been protected by an Act of Parliament passed in 1995. All participants joined this special spectacle and Ramaram felt right at home among the many sheep, Dailibai joined a Kenyan colleague in riding on a bullock-drawn cart, Bagdiramji, Hanwant and Mangilal carried a banner and Tolaram sang, danced and fiddled to his heart's content. In between the rally, a resolution about pastoralism was read out on Madrid's central square and, in the evening, UN officials explained the rights of indigenous people and how pastoralists could make use of them.

It was a notable demonstration of pastoralist strength, but our small Raika delegation was tired out and wanted nothing but to get home to their loved ones, especially their animals.

Special Correspondent *(The Hindu)*

The Rajasthan camel breeders sought recognition for their role in bio-diversity conservation.

109 countries, including India, agree upon Global Plan of Action for preventing the further extinction of local breeds.

Trip's high point was rally through heart of Madrid together with Spanish shepherds and others from Africa, Asia and the Americas.

JAIPUR: A delegation of "Raikas" (camel breeders) from Rajasthan who visited Europe recently to meet fellow pastoralists and share traditional wisdom on livestock keeping, have returned after successfully convincing the decision-makers at global forums of the need to preserve livestock bio-diversity and indigenous production systems.

Attending a series of high-level meetings in Europe, they advocated the rights of herding communities and sought recognition for their role in bio-diversity conservation.

In Interlaken, Switzerland, the group attended the first international conference on animal genetic resources, organised by the Food and Agricultural Organisation (FAO). The conference addressed the worldwide loss of livestock bio-diversity, a trend that is happening because of the replacement of local breeds – for instance, Tharparkar and Rathi cattle – with a small number of international high-performance breeds such as Holstein-Friesian or Jersey cattle. "It is regarded as dangerous because exotic breeds are more susceptible to diseases and require higher inputs. In the long term, disappearance of locally adapted breeds may impact human ability to utilise dry lands and cope with climate change," said Ilse Köhler-Rollefson of the Germany-based NGO, League for Pastoral Peoples, which arranged the tour on behalf of the Rajasthan NGO, Lokhit Pashu-Palak Sansthan (LPPS).

In Interlaken, the governments of 109 countries, including India, elaborated and agreed upon a Global Plan of Action (GPA) for preventing further extinction of local breeds. The action plan recognises the role of herding communities as custodians of local breeds.

"There seems to be light at the end of the tunnel for the pastoralists of India after a quarter-century-long struggle. With the GPA it would be easier for these communities to get their rights established," said Uttra Kothari, an academic from Jaipur, who accompanied the camel breeders as interpreter. "Unlike in Europe, India has no organised form of pastoralism. Here the traditional livestock keepers get shunted everywhere and their flocks often looked down upon as a menace while in Europe they get subsidies for preserving the indigenous breeds."

The GPA is to support indigenous and local production and associated knowledge systems with the help of veterinary and extension services, delivery of micro-credit for women in rural areas, appropriate access to natural resources and to the market, resolving land tenure issues, the recognition of cultural practices and values, and adding value to their specialist products.

Hanwant Singh, Director of Lokhit Pashu-Palak Sansthan who was part of the group, said, "It was very encouraging to see that the traditional knowledge of pastoralist groups in upholding genetic diversity is finally getting due recognition. By agreeing to GPA, India has committed itself to supporting them in their role as custodians of valuable breeds. "

In Spain, Raikas attended a global gathering, which brought together hundreds of pastoralists. Organised by Spanish shepherds, the purpose of this meeting was to draw attention to the role of herders in eco-system management. At this event, Bagdiram Raika, a community leader from Chittorgarh, was elected to serve as councillor for India to the World Association of Mobile Indigenous People (WAMIP).

For the visiting camel breeders the high point of the trip was a rally through the heart of Madrid together with Spanish shepherds and their colleagues from Africa, Asia and the Americas. This is an annual event which marks the passing of Spanish migratory sheep herds from their summer to their winter pastures, and has been revived by Spanish conservationists who see pastoralism as an important tool for bio-diversity conservation.

"The event proved very refreshing for us. In India we are

always blamed for our role in damaging the environment wildlife," commented Ramaram Raika.

* * *

The Interlaken and Spain trip was an important, but small step forward in a very long journey. For the time being, this particular international process around animal genetic resources had come to an interim conclusion with the "Global Plan of Action", and there was no longer a forum in which to push the issue of Livestock Keepers' Rights further. The situation remained in limbo until 2009 when a legal NGO named Natural Justice based in South Africa stepped into the gap and opened up a new avenue for advocacy. We were contacted by Kabir Bavikatte, the young Indian lawyer and co-founder of the NGO, who wanted to test a new approach he had conceived for communities to invoke their rights. He suggested that the Raika develop a "Biocultural community protocol" to obtain their credentials as being *relevant for the conservation and sustainable use of biological diversity* under one of the provisions of the CBD. The idea was that the Raika would make their own statement about the genetic resources they are stewarding, about the traditional knowledge used to manage these resources and their role in biodiversity conservation. This statement would then be complemented with references to the CBD as well as other national and international legal frameworks that supported conservation by communities, thereby creating a document with considerable legal gravitas.

Hanwant and I enthusiastically agreed to this proposal, optimistic about the concept, but also curious how the Raika would respond and collaborate. So, within a short time, Kabir and a colleague, Harry Jonas, travelled to Sadri where the LPPS staff introduced them to the Raika. The idea was discussed with

Raika elders, including Dailibai, Ramaram and Mangilal who through their excursion to Interlaken had had enough exposure to understand the significance of the proposed Biocultural Community protocol. They compiled a text that put on record the Raika, the types of livestock they owned and their customary practices. It also detailed their complicated relationship with the Kumbhalgarh Wildlife Sanctuary. Harry assembled and organised all the information and material on paper, then with Hanwant's help, the manuscript was discussed in detail with Raika elders who gave it their final seal of approval. Pictures were added to underline the points made as well as a legal appendix which listed both the national and international laws and official agreements that supported the claims of the Raika. This, of course, included the Interlaken declaration as well as the Convention on Biological Diversity, but also the Forest Rights Act, the UN Voluntary Guidelines on the Right to Food, and so on. It turned into a powerful document. For the first time, the Raika were not written about, but actually spoke themselves. It started out with, "We are the Raika, an indigenous pastoral community who live in Rajasthan, northwest India. We number about one million people..." and explained how the Raika had developed and preserved unique breeds of livestock and traditional knowledge associated with them, and how their pastoral lifestyle had shaped the eco-system of Rajasthan's forests which they had traditionally conserved and sustainably used.

When the Biocultural Protocol was finally available as a printed brochure, in both English and Hindi, we felt we had a milestone in our hand. Whatever would happen in the future, at least the Raika heritage could no longer be ignored or talked away. This was an official document that was submitted to the National Biodiversity Authority of India and acknowledged by this autonomous body.

The printed brochure certainly put across who the Raika were and compiled systematically all the legal arguments that favoured their way of life. For the Raika, this was, first of all, a handy tool that they could hand over to forest officials and bureaucrats as a sort of introduction to who they were. The list of laws and legal frameworks that supported their herding way of life made it all the more powerful. Yet, for the Raika themselves – still basically an oral society – to completely grasp the full implications of the Biocultural Protocol would take years.

In the international circles that deal with indigenous people and with biodiversity, the protocol was taken note of and it immediately became a point of reference that several UN agencies put up on their websites. It also set into motion a round of international travel for Dailibai who unwittingly had taken on a role as brand ambassador for her community. Within a couple of months, she was invited to a meeting of African indigenous peoples in Nairobi, where there was a major push going on for indigenous peoples to get more recognition for their role in biodiversity conservation and for building their capacity to participate in and influence the on-going negotiations about the CBD. At the same time, another group of pastoralists in Kenya, the Samburu, had expressed interest in following suit and developing a Biocultural Community Protocol (BCP). Natural Justice was keen to support them, and also to enlist Dailibai's help in the process – sharing the BCP context from one pastoralist community to the next.

So, in September 2009, Dailibai, with me in tow as her interpreter, journeyed to Nairobi where we met the Natural Justice team and then jointly set off to Maralal, our base in Samburu. The Samburu, who are closely related to the better-known Maasai, are traditional cattle keepers but, over the years, had also started keeping camels as a way of coping with the worsening drought situation. They also kept the Red

Maasai sheep, a small but very drought-resistant breed that had long been the object of scientific curiosity for its genetic resistance to stomach worms. Most sheep around the world have to be routinely dewormed several times a year, causing considerable expenditure. So the genetic resistance to worms of this indigenous breed developed by the Maasai and the Samburu was of great interest to sheep producers all over the world, with possibly enormous commercial value. Scientists believed it would one day be possible to transplant the genes into other breeds, saving enormous sums in dewormers. It was this long-standing commercial interest in the Red Maasai sheep that made the case very interesting for Natural Justice.

The meetings with the Samburu took place in a small schoolhouse and both men and women attended. They were fascinated by Dailibai and immediately classified her as belonging to the Rendille community – a camel-breeding tribe in northern Kenya with whom the Samburu have close linkages. In the discussions, we learnt that the area was experiencing an unprecedented drought and that many of the "more productive" livestock promoted by the government, such as crossbred cattle and Dorper sheep had perished. By contrast, the Red Maasai sheep breed and the camel, as well the local zebu cattle still looked in good condition.

The drought was not the only challenge the Samburu and other Kenyan pastoralists faced. Another big threat was posed by bandits that were out to raid livestock and were armed with AK 47 machine guns. While cattle-raiding has always been part of Kenyan pastoralist culture (and successful participation is necessary for obtaining enough cattle to be able to marry), the introduction of guns had turned this into a deadly enterprise. Our Kenyan counterparts were deeply concerned about our safety. And with good reason: Just two days after our team left the area, thirty-two people – mostly women and children – were killed in a fight over cattle.

Back in Nairobi, Dailibai had to make her presentation to the African indigenous peoples representatives about the Raika BCP. I felt this was a major challenge, as she did not understand a word of English and, although a good orator, was not used to giving a structured talk. So, together, we prepared a series of slides that illustrated the way of life of the Raika and were intended to be self-explanatory. While I was nervous, Dailibai was full of self-confidence and made a brilliant presentation for which she received much applause. In the end, the participants of the meeting made a resolution recommending the promotion of Biocultural Community Protocols in their inputs to the Draft International Regime on Access and Benefit-sharing that would be discussed at another meeting on the CBD scheduled to take place in Japan in 2010.

Dailibai had thus become an international ambassador for her community. Despite being illiterate – barely able to write her name – she was somehow able to cope with and adjust to any situation she was thrown into. She charmed people with her open smile and made friends wherever she went. This fame and international acclaim had not necessarily made life easier for her back home. Many of her fellow-Raika were not ready to accept a woman as their spokesperson and, at local meetings, they would tell her to sit down and keep quiet. Within her family too, the response was mixed. Her husband, a very quiet and introverted man working in the Ranakpur temple, fortunately, was supportive. But one of her sons, who was otherwise quite modern and enjoyed hanging out with foreigners, did not approve and complained that she was not taking sufficient steps for getting him married. There were also problems with her elder son's marriage which she urgently had to sort out, and even being temporarily excommunicated was looming over her. So, she was not really inclined to undertake any more travel that year. When an official invitation arrived to introduce the Raika BCP at a meeting to be held at the UN Convention's Secretariat in Montreal, Canada, it took some convincing to get her to agree to go but, finally, she consented and we – Dailibai, Hanwant and I – arrived in Montreal on a freezing November morning. While Rajasthan was basking in warm and balmy weather, Daili made her first experience with cold weather, refusing to wear the heavy parka that we had brought along for her, instead preferring to wrap herself in her traditional shawl. Fortunately, the city has extensive subterranean passageways and we found a way of walking to the meeting place without actually having to surface into the icy outside. The highrises were another shock, as was the bland fast food. But, as usual, Daili did not let on her culture shock and graciously received the congratulations of a high-level UN official for the Raika Biocultural Protocol.

The fact that the Raika, their traditional knowledge, their special relationship to animals, and also their problems were presented and discussed in the hallowed and air-conditioned halls of the UN was encouraging. But it was also clear that it would take years, or maybe decades, before this appreciation would trickle down and bring tangible benefits, or contribute to the revival of Rajasthan's camel culture and economy. For the time being, LPPS sometimes resembled a resource organisation and travel agency for pastoralists, with frequent requests by conference and workshop organisers to "send a pastoralist". It had become proper procedure to include a few people with turbans or in traditional dress among one's participants to demonstrate grassroots inclusiveness.

On the national level too, there were promising developments. In 2006, the Indian Parliament had enacted the Forests Rights Act (FRA) that had been promoted by the Ministry of Tribal Affairs to correct the "historic injustice done to forest-dwelling communities" by handing over forest management to a government department and thereby depriving them of their rights and often livelihoods. The purpose of the FRA is to provide use and access rights to people who have traditionally lived in forests. Because of intensive lobbying by a group of NGOs, the FRA also made specific mention of mobile pastoralists that use the forest only seasonally and declared them to be eligible for claiming and receiving forest rights. This was a momentous breakthrough that LPPS wanted to share with the Raika around Kumbhalgarh, as well as of course the Adivasis in the area. It provided hope that the long-standing conflict with the Forest Deparment could finally be resolved and the customary rights that the Raika had been deprived of, reinstalled.

So together with Raika elders, LPPS called for a meeting at Sonar-ki-Bagiche, the only place in Sadri big enough to hold several thousand Raika. Also invited to the meeting were the Adivasi, as well as the assistant conservator of forests, a local member of the Legislative Assembly of Rajasthan and a Bhopa from the Raika community who was highly respected, but had recently been co-opted by one of the political parties – to ensure the Raika vote.

Close to a 1,000 Raika streamed in, as well as a smaller group of Adivasis and sat down on the floor under a colourful canopy to listen to the day's speeches. Hanwant gave a brief welcome, then Babu Lal, a Raika elder addressed the crowd. Hanwant explained about the rights that were provided by the Forest Rights Act. Then the assistant conservator of forests elaborated that while the rights had indeed been accorded, there was no experience yet on how to implement them. However, he and his staff were standing by on a twenty-four-hour basis to help everybody, and grievances could be addressed to the sub-divisional officer at the district level. Next was the MLA who cautioned that the new rights were in conflict with a Supreme Court order that prohibited grazing in forests. He heaped praise on the priest and listed all that he had achieved for his community, including construction of hostels, establishment of livestock insurance schemes, even reservations for government jobs. The priest, almost bare-chested and sporting a huge red turban and bushy beard then addressed his Raika brothers. As he was speaking in Marwari, I could understand him only partially. But I could understand enough to comprehend what he was saying: that the FRA existed, but that it was not applicable to the Raika. That he, in fact, had looked at it in the internet, but nowhere did he see the word "Raika" mentioned.

I could not believe my ears. Here was a very popular, even venerated, personage who denied that a legal provision which had profound significance for the future of his community actually existed. I was aghast, although Hanwant seemed unperturbed. But a few Raika from the audience stood up and queried the Bhopa on the matter. The Bhopa vigorously continued to refute the validity of the Forest Rights Act and had the last word. The meeting wound down and people drifted away to eat the food – dal-baati-churma, my favourite – that LPPS had sponsored.

Fuming, I pushed through the crowds to catch hold of the priest to confront him but he just kept insisting that he was right.

Nobody else seemed to share my anger. In the end, I sought consolation from the usually outspoken and forthright Dailibai who put me straight. Shaking her head, she reminded me that this was how politics worked.

Over the coming months and years, it became clear that many politicians and interested parties, including the Forest Department itself, were opposed to the FRA and systematically denied its existence. Even now, years later, the implementation of the Act is in limbo, although NGOs, including LPPS, have made diligent and sustained efforts to help communities file their claims under this Act. To my knowledge, so far, no forest rights have been granted to any pastoralist community in India. But we are working on it, together with many other civil society groups in India, and we are optimistic that, eventually, the effort and struggle will pay off.

On the positive side, the Raika have become more aware of their rights and are no longer willing to pay huge bribes to obtain their customary access to the forest during the rainy season. The last couple of years have seen huge demonstrations of Raika men, women and children in Sadri providing a show of strength at the beginning of the rainy season, when the foresters usually issue their demands and determine fees.

The Hindu, 26 July 2010

RAIKAS DEMAND GRAZING RIGHTS IN FOREST LAND

By Sunny Sebastian

JAIPUR: Raikas, the community of herders, have sought the application of Forest Rights Act and the UN Convention on Biological Diversity (CBD) in ensuring grazing rights to their animals in the forest land. The monsoon season is a testing time for these livestock keepers who graze large herds of sheep and goats – as well as a diminishing number of camels – as crops are sown in the farm lands and the animals can find food only in the forest.

Raikas refer to the Article 8j of the UN Convention on Biological Diversity, to which India is a partner, to support their demand. It commits countries to "...subject to national legislation, respect, preserve and maintain knowledge innovations and practices of indigenous and local communities embodying traditional lifestyles relevant for the conservation and sustainable use of biological diversity."

Hundreds of Raikas – men in their trademark multicoloured turbans and the women folk in their traditional attires – took to the streets of Sadri, a small town in Rajasthan's Pali district the other day to press for the demand. The immediate cause for their anguish was the Forest Department's decision to impose a levy of Rs 11 per day for each sheep. The amount is unaffordable by the Raikas and even if they pay up, the authorities do not issue a proper receipt.

"It is not the payment for grazing that matters," points out Dr Ilse Köhler-Rollefson of the LIFE Network, which promotes community-based conservation and development of indigenous breeds. "They want their grazing rights under the Forest Rights Act and CBD re-instated," she observes.

Last year, with the help of the NGOs, Raikas developed a Biocultural Protocol in which they establish themselves as a local community whose lifestyle protects biological diversity. In the protocol, they document how they do it: by preventing forest fires, guarding wildlife, and by keeping locally evolved livestock breeds. This document, and the underlying approach, generated much attention nationally and internationally.

Within the country, several other communities – such as the Maldhari in Kutch and a group of Lingayats living in the Bargur forest in Tamil Nadu – followed suit. Internationally the Raika have shared their protocol with the leaders of African indigenous communities during a meeting in Nairobi and with a working group of the Convention on Biological Diversity held in Montreal last year.

The Raika struggle for grazing rights has a long history. In the year 2003 they took their case to the Supreme Court though the matter remained unsettled. With the passage of the Forest Rights Bill in 2007 – which provides rights not only to forest dwellers, but also to seasonal forest users – the situation changed. But the initial jubilation turned to dismay as the herders found that there was no clear procedure for claiming the rights.

"Raikas are known to be peace-loving people whose main concern is to make sure that their livestock has enough to eat. In fact, they are the keepers of the genes and they take upon themselves the duty of taking care of camels," notes Dr Köhler-Rollefson who helped the community to get organised under an NGO Lokhit Pashu-Palak Sansthan (LPPS). Both LIFE Network and LPPS helped Raikas to find their voice and link themselves with herders in the rest of the world.

Dailibai Raika, a traditional animal healer, explains that in Germany the local shepherds are paid by the government for conserving the environment. She and Hanwant Singh Rathore, the director of LPPS, visited Germany earlier this year and interacted with parliamentarians.

Both are scheduled to attend the next meeting of the CBD in Japan. A preparatory meeting of Indian and international herders will be held in Kuttupalayam near Coimbatore from August 13 this year.

At a rally in July 2012, Dailibai Raika stepped onto the podium and gave a flaming speech to a sea of red turbans. Before the meeting, both she and Hanwant, inspired by the model of Anna Hazare and Arvind Kejriwal, had emphatically stated that they would rather go to jail than give up their rights.

In 2013, the usual announcement of grazing fines by the Forest Department did not come forward. There was silence. Maybe it was because of fear of the Raika reaction. Or perhaps it is because the Kumbhalgarh Wildlife Sanctuary has been slotted to be turned into a National Park and any untoward incidents are to be avoided.

Chapter 16

AVATAR

CAMEL MILK AS APHRODISIAC!

"Is camel milk the Viagra of the desert? It appears so in the arid state of Rajasthan, where thousands of men have been clamouring to get their hands on camel milk after an 88-year-old man who fathered a child several weeks ago attributed his virility to the drink. Since the man, Virmaram Jat, a local farmer, revealed what he believes to be the secret of his sexual prowess, sales of camel milk have shot up and dealers have doubled their prices in the western state, a paper reported.

One vendor, Samran Singh, told he now charged 40 rupees (US$ 0.8; euro 0.66) a liter, up from 20 rupees (US$ 0.4; euro 0.33) a few weeks ago.

However, doctors and scientists in Rajasthan said it was unlikely the milk was responsible for his achievement.

The director of the National Research Centre on Camel, M. S. Sahani, said there was no scientific basis for the claim."

– *Associated Press*

New Delhi, 29 August 2006

It is many years since that chilly morning in Bikaner on which I first stepped into the captivating, seductive, endlessly absorbing world of rural Rajasthan, the Raika, and their camels. At that time, the only vehicle to transport me to the single hotel in town, the Dhola-Maru Tourist Bungalow, was a horse-drawn tonga. Since then, time has flown by - almost imperceptibly, as it does when a journey has its own momentum.

In between, the world has changed.

Back then, trunk calls had to be booked days ahead in the telephone office and a telegram was the only means of urgent communication. Now, practically everybody has a mobile - except for the nomads because they lack a place to recharge it - and not long ago, telegrams were officially phased out in India.

The Ambassador car, inextricably associated with my early field work has become almost extinct and replaced by sleeker foreign models.

Traditional social institutions are losing their sway and giving way to social media, even in rural areas.

We ourselves have also changed. From a chivalrous taxi driver, Hanwant has turned into a passionate advocate for the camel and for pastoralists. Dailibai has grown from a stigmatised and silent rural woman to a bold, charismatic and globally recognised pastoralist leader. I am no longer a disoriented academic but on a mission - for humane and responsible livestock keeping. There has also been institutional development - pastoralists have become more prominent on the national and world stage as several organisations apart from LPP and LPPS have evolved to support their cause.

Considering the almost ubiquitous technological progress, however, is there still a place in this universe for the camel and for the Raika and other nomads, or have they run their course and should be phased out, like the telegram and the Ambassador?

I often wonder and ponder about this myself, when I see how towns are bulging at their seams and gobbling up pasture and agricultural land, how the once open fields along the road from Sadri to Butibagh have almost all been walled in, how - often unnecessary - asphalt roads are built into the remotest nooks of the interior, how values have changed, how young educated Raika drift into the cities and can quickly forget their heritage - sometimes within a single generation.

Despite all our efforts, the camel in India has not fared all that well - its numbers continue to dwindle, as demand for working camels has become almost negligible. No, not 50,000 camels, as some irresponsible media and tourism operators say, but less than 5,000 camels, came to the Pushkar Fair in 2013. Even worse, the vast majority could not find a good buyer - either they went for meat or their breeders took them back home. So it does seem as if we are flogging a dead horse, or rather, dead camels here, doesn't it?

But stop! Like always in India, there is more to it than meets the eye. Despite the rapid development, I see a future, and even an urgent need, for both the camel and for the Raika and other nomadic livestock keepers. I'm optimistic for several reasons (and besides that, everything in India is cyclical). Let's not forget that the camel is a versatile and multipurpose animal that can fulfil many basic needs of humans. Its role as a transport and farm animal is certainly on the retreat, at least temporarily, as long as oil is available and affordable.

Yet, its potential as a dairy animal remains huge - although it needs to be developed with substantial investment and commitment from both the public and the private sectors.

Apart from that, there is a range of other eco-friendly products that can be made from happy living camels and that may just satisfy that budding urge of urbanites - in India and abroad - to re-connect with nature. We are now on a new journey seeking to connect the camel with this new clientele.

A few years ago, a friend forwarded me a news item about elephant poo paper – yes, paper, made from elephant poo – that was being manufactured in Jaipur by a firm called Haathi Chaap and processed into a range of stationary. Hanwant and I had already come across elephant poo paper in Thailand, so what would be more natural than trying out the same method with camel poo? When we contacted the people behind this venture, Mahima Mehra and Vijendra Shekhawat, they quickly agreed to undertake the experiment. We shipped off a big burlap sack of dried camel dung to the factory in Jaipur and soon held the first sample of camel poo paper in our hands. It was a bit grainy and bumpy from the seeds of the acacia and other trees that camels browse on. But it had a distinct and unique character – it was brown and natural and felt very substantial to the touch. Subsequently, Haathi Chaap was kind enough to develop a small range of products, including notepads, notebooks and greeting cards; with great enthusiasm and generosity, Virendra helped us set up our own handpaper-making unit on our Butibagh campus in Sadri and now we are producing this "desert paper" locally.

By some serendipitous coincidence, Kamal Kishore from Kullu in the Himalayas, stepped into our lives. Kamal is an animal scientist with extensive experience in wool processing. Besides owning an Angora rabbit farm and his own eco-textile company making hand-spun, hand-woven vegetable-dyed garments, he is also on the board of the Kullu shawl weavers' cooperative. He opened our eyes about the potential of camel wool. I had always believed that the short and rather coarse wool of our dromedary camels did not provide scope for producing anything worthwhile – their hair definitely not being in the same league as the luxuriant and lustrous pile of the Bactrian camels that we had seen in

Mongolia. But Kamal taught us differently. He did some tests on the fibre length and fibre diameter of camel wool from both the Jaisalmer and Sadri areas and found out that it actually contained a significant proportion of fine wool with long and thin fibres that were almost equivalent to Cashmere quality. Kamal suggested that it was a matter of separating the wool into different types – according to both fineness and colour. The fine wool could be used for making stoles and shawls, the rougher section could be turned into rugs or dhurries. Separation by fibre colour would allow us to make designs with naturally coloured wool eliminating the need for dyeing the wool. He also noted that the quality of wool from Jaisalmer was even higher than the one from Sadri – possibly because of the much lower winter temperatures there.

We spread the news that we wanted to purchase wool amongst our Jaisalmer breeders. Many of them had been shearing their camels to keep mange mites under control but had discarded the wool because they no longer had a use for it. Our staff collected the wool, then Kamal and a pair of designers from Delhi who we had enlisted for the cause came to Jaisalmer and separated the wool into two piles – one of long and fine fibres and another one composed of coarse and rough hair. With temperatures in Jaisalmer soaring to about forty-five degrees Celsius, sitting in a small room packed with dusty and dirty wool, was an almost superhuman task. But, in the end, it proved really worthwhile. The designers, Anurag and Shalini, developed exquisite rugs, while Kamal's team of spinners and weavers up in the Himalayas created a range of beautiful and soft stoles. The pieces were so pretty that we spontaneously decided to exhibit samples at the international eco-fashion fair in Paris. Several international designers immediately expressed interest in using dromedary wool – later renamed "desert wool" to distuinguish it from the conventional camel wool of Mongolian Bactrian camels.

Together with the desert paper, the desert wool items from "free-ranging and happy camels in the Thar Desert" have been doing well at the Pushkar Fair and at the Nature Bazaar, an annual crafts sale in Delhi.

It was at the Nature Bazaar that Harshita, an elegant lady from Delhi's elevated social circles, walked up to us one morning and told us about her autistic son and how well he was responding to camel milk. She was sourcing it from a camel herder who lived on the outskirts of Delhi. Unfortunately, he was preparing to migrate elsewhere because there was no longer enough feed for his camel. Harshita was desperate to find an alternative source as she feared her son's condition would once again deteriorate without his daily intake of camel milk. She also told us about a Facebook page called "Healing with camel milk" on which mothers of autistic children from around the world exchange their experiences with camel milk therapy. Here, they also share where to source camel milk – no small matter, if you are living in, say, Singapore.

How on earth could camel milk have a benign effect on autistic children? Of course, as elaborated at length in earlier chapters, there are many claims about the therapeutic effects of camel milk. Often these can be explained with the immune-enhancing qualities of its proteins. But how could camel milk influence autism, which is not an infectious disease, but apparently a neurological disorder? It was a mystery, and a quick scan of the scientific literature confirmed that these assertions were made, but without any explanation given. Sceptically, I was wondering if the whole tale was cooked up by the rumour mill, the result of desperate parents, clinging to straws. As Harshita and her son suddenly moved to the US, we did not have a chance to follow up with her, but, in the meantime, we developed a better understanding of how and why camel milk can have real therapeutic properties.

It all has to do with the fact that the camel – at least here in

Rajasthan – is feeding on a very wide range of plants, especially trees. These contain known phytochemicals that can cure or relieve a range of diseases. We only became really aware of this ourselves when we were preparing for the inauguration of our camel-dung paper unit. At that time we were looking for a catchphrase or slogan that could popularise camel poo paper with environment-conscious customers and hit upon the idea of calling it the "most biodiverse paper on earth." This was not just an advertising gimmick, but the absolute truth. Normal paper is made from trees that are grown on plantations and belong to the same species. And even elephant poo paper is composed of only a limited range of plants, as captive elephants have a fairly restricted diet. But our free-ranging camels feed on thirty-six different types of plants according to local knowledge. Actually, they feed on more than that, but thirty-six is some kind of magic number and is mentioned by camel breeders around Sadri, in Jaisalmer, and even in Kutch in Gujarat.

In order to illustrate the biodiversity that is contained in the camel-dung, pardon, desert paper, Aisha who was interning with LPPS identified, photographed and researched the thirty-six camel forage plants. It quickly became evident that practically all thirty-six plants are also used in folk medicine and have been described in ancient Ayurvedic texts as treatment for different types of diseases.

For instance, for *desi babul*, scientifically known as *acacia nilotica*, one of the trees most favoured by camels, Aisha compiled the following information:

> **Medicinal use:** *Acacia nilotica* is a popular medicinal plant in many countries. The bark treats coughs while also acting as an astringent. Besides, the bark can also be used to treat diarrhoea, dysentery and leprosy. The bark can also be

used to treat asthma, excessive external bleeding, problems related to urination or menstruation, vaginal discharge, diabetes, infections, allergy, skin ailments, hair related problems, sore eyes, impotency, and so forth.

The Maasai of Kenya drink a decoction made from the bark of the tree as part of an intoxication ritual meant to impart courage. The drink is also thought to be an aphrodisiac while the root is said to cure impotence. In West Africa, the gum is useful to treat cancerous tumours, indurations of liver and spleen, condylomas, and excess flesh. In Lebanon, the resin is mixed with orange-flower and works as an infusion for typhoid convalescence. In Tonga, people use the root as treatment against tuberculosis. Egyptian Nubians even believe that diabetics can eat unlimited carbohydrates as long as they also consume the plant's powdered pods. (Source: *Camels of Kumbhalgarh. A Biodiversity Treasure*, LPPS, 2013).

If the camel is eating all these wild plants of medicinal value, then it is no wonder that its milk is such potent stuff, since it represents a distillation of these healing plants! Compare that with the milk of a buffalo that is mainly fed with a genetically modified cottonseed expeller or of a cow stuffed with a diet of concentrate feed! Camel milk would be so much healthier and contain so many more important micronutrients.

This scenario should also mean that the value of camel milk very much depends on what the camel eats and that the milk of camels fed a "western diet" of hay and alfalfa may be far less wholesome than that of our free-ranging camels. Hanwant has often remarked that after drinking a glass of camel milk he feels really relaxed, almost as if he had taken opium. While only pharmaceutical research could pinpoint what this could be attributed to, I would find it plausible that some of the phytochemicals in the trees that camels forage could be causing this effect. And this could be why autistic children respond positively. Modern urban diets with their emphasis on highly fertilised crops (wheat, rice, corn) may just miss out some important ingredients necessary for complete nutrition and it is possible that camel milk from free-ranging camels can provide it!

Because we currently do not have the resources to build up the value chain for fresh camel milk, we are processing it. The highly popular camel-milk ice cream requires a functioning cool chain so, at the moment, we are only able to produce it for special occasions. The other product – soap made from camel milk is proving extremely popular, both in India and abroad.

People, of course, have not only material needs, such as nutritious food, paper to write on, and fabric to wear and to decorate their home with. Maybe even more importantly in these times where many people are oversatiated with *things*, they have emotional needs. And camels can satisfy these too. The kissing camels herded by the Raika around Sadri provide unforgettable encounters for visitors and tourists that can't be found anywhere else in the world. The dependable and stout companionship of camels that we experienced during the yatra is priceless. A couple of months ago, Bhom Singh gifted us two calves whose mothers had died, so we could provide them with special care here in Butibagh. Baptised Moomal and Mahendra, these orphans now brighten up our campus. Moomal, the girl, is a cuddler and a kisser, while Mahendra is more reserved. After the Pushkar Fair, they were joined by three other young camels – grandsons and great grandsons of Mira, who I bought in 1991 – who failed to find a buyer at the fair. They are still getting acclimatised, but we are determined to find work for them as cart and riding animals, maybe to ferry tourists between Ranakpur, where Dailibai has opened a small shop that sells camel products, and Butibagh.

Apart from being the operational centre of our NGO, Butibagh also houses the processing facilities for camel raw materials to turn them into paper, ice cream and woollen goodies.

All these activities are from the perspective of not only the urban consumer and national or international tourist, but more importantly for the rural people, many of whom are forced to move into the cities for lack of income opportunities in their villages. Although many of the Raika youths drift to the metro areas, quite a few of them would much prefer to find jobs locally. Aisha, while doing research for her geography degree on the situation of young people from pastoralist families, interviewed youths who were working in cities. She heard terrible stories about their working conditions: eighteen-hour workdays, no place to sleep and unhygienic water that often causes debilitating diseases.

By developing camel products, a good number of jobs can be created in rural areas to provide alternative options to a debased urban existence. Already widows in Jaisalmer spin camel wool into yarn with the traditional spinning wheel, a weaver couple in Jalore is making rugs, some ladies around Sadri knit toys and caps from camel wool, while others process camel dung into the most bio-diverse paper on earth. This fledgeling enterprise will take time to grow, but grow it will and eventually generate extra income for camel breeders and thereby not only encourage them to hang onto their wonderful animals, but also restore pride in their profession.

In November 2013, we celebrated the launch of a small booklet entitled *Camels of Kumbhalghar: A Biodiversity Treasure* that makes the case for integrating wildlife conservation with support for the Raika and that documents the camel forage plants and their medicinal value according to traditional knowledge. It was released by the director of the National Research Centre on Camel, Dr N.V. Patil, who is ever so supportive of the work done by NGOs, and with a message by His Highness, the Maharajah of Jodhpur, brought by Colonel Umaid Singh, the secretary of the Marwari Horse Society.

To be sure, there were many unknowns. The talk of the conversion of the Kumbhalgarh Sanctuary into a national park gave us many sleepless nights. It is a move that will bring with it greater, if not total, restrictions on grazing. It will be the death knell for our Raika herders from Latada, Anji-ki-dhani and other villages. We're doing our best to prevent this and to show that wildlife and camels, as well as other livestock, can be compatible, and that, in fact, this coexistence may very well be beneficial for the predators that are to be protected – the leopard and wolf.

But then, under the new government of Vasundhara Raje that came to power in 2013, the Rajasthan Assembly declared, on 30 June 2014, the camel as "state animal" and accorded it a variety of protective measures. So the story of the camel in Rajasthan did not end – rather we found ourselves at the beginning of a new cycle and the rebirth of this magnificent animal in a new avatar!

AFTERWORD

IT'S NOT JUST ABOUT CAMELS

"You can judge the morality of a nation by the way the society treats its animals."

– Mahatma Gandhi

What is at stake in Rajasthan goes far beyond the camel. It also goes beyond the future of the Raika and beyond finding a place for camels, people and wildlife in the Kumbhalgarh National Park, as important as that is to us. It's about whether we, as humans and as a society, value a humane relationship with livestock and are prepared to support it.

The Raika relationship with their animals strikes the delicate balance between care on the one hand and use on the other. It's a relationship between people and herds that goes back countless generations and that is embedded in innumerable shared experiences. When a baby camel is born, lifts its head, starts tottering around, and then forms friendships with its peers, its behaviour will trigger reminiscences about its ancestors who had the same peculiarities and oddities. "Look, already it is obvious it will have hairy ears just like its grandmother..." "It has the same curious black patch on the right flank as its aunt..."

When an old camel dies, the family will remember the circumstances of its birth and the events that occured in their own lives at that time. The thoughts of the woman of the house will wander back and she will remember how the mother of this animal was part of her *dhamini* and her familiar presence provided solace while she was still getting used to the ways of her in-laws. The life histories of the Raika and their animals are deeply interwoven and this endows the relationship with responsibility and humanity.

But the world is currently moving towards industrial livestock production – systems in which farm animals are no longer given respect as sentient beings; systems in which they are reduced to mere cogs in the wheel, to machines that are being stoked to churn out produce.

While I was writing in the isolation of Butibagh, I received regular email messages from the Veterinary Forum for Responsible Agriculture, a quickly expanding group of German colleagues that is expressing its abhorrence with the system in which they are caught – the inhumane industrial mode of livestock production that has become the norm. In this group, both practising and government veterinarians share with each other the shocking experiences and observations they make in their daily practices: the excruciating pain that many farm animals experience throughout their short lives, because treatment is not worthwhile; the massive and routine use of officially banned antibiotics; the pressure that farmers face to go into ever bigger debt and to cram more and more animals into small spaces, in order to stay in business; the reluctance of the mainstream to openly discuss these issues.

The future of livestock production is now on the agenda of the Food and Agriculture Organisation. This is the same body where we have advocated for "Livestock Keepers' Rights" to be given to responsible livestock keepers and cultures so that they have a chance of competing with the industries. While we will continue the pressure, it will be a long struggle, as there are huge vested interests in the further industrialisation of livestock keeping.

My hope for change rests on India. It is the country with the largest number of livestock-dependent people worldwide and it has an amazing and unique heritage of livestock cultures of which the Raika are only one. My fervent hope is that India will recognise the value of its pastoralist legacy and make it the starting point for carving out its own more humane and more ecological path of livestock development that the rest of the world will eventually follow.

POST SCRIPTUM

Tough times came after 2014, when this book was first published – for the Raika, the camels and for us personally. We have experienced a daunting roller-coaster ride – shuttling us back and forth between the depths of despair where we thought all was lost and the exhilarating heights from which we fleetingly espied camel nirvana: a scenario where camels, people, and the environment live together in harmony and mutually support each other.

We were hoping that state animal status would mean public investment in the camel economy and in support for the Raika and other herders as keepers of the state animal. Instead, in 2015, a new law was put in place, the Rajasthan Camel (Prohibition of Slaughter and Regulation of Temporary Migration or Export) Act, 2015. It was based on the (erroneous) assumption that the slaughter of camels in some states in South India was the reason for the dramatic population decline of 35% within the five years from 2007 to 2012.

This law, which the Raika community tried to prevent, had exactly the opposite effect than was intended. What happened next was a horrible calamity of camels being smuggled across the state border and then driven on foot towards slaughter houses somewhere in South India, regularly intercepted en route by animal welfare groups who then raised funds to truck them back to Rajasthan "where they belonged", but where they often arrived more dead than alive with broken limbs. And where there were no adequate arrangements to take care of them so that they sometimes were resold to start another trek southwards. This scenario still prevails, with 111 camels recently "rescued" near Nasik in Maharashtra with much fanfare in the media, and then walked back to Rajasthan. At least 10 of them died.

But, slowly, there is realisation that "rescuing" camels is not a solution and causes terrible cruelty to the long-suffering camels. Instead, we need a long-term plan, and there is imminent hope that this might be designed and implemented. The United Nations General Assembly has declared 2024 as the International Year of Camelids. In combination with the Indian government's recent discovery and appreciation of the country's pastoralist cultures, this may be just the constellation that successfully revives India's camel sector.

As I write this, I can hear the guttural noises of a camel herd that has spent the night just below my house at the edge of the Kumbhalgarh Sanctuary where it has found a seasonal sanctuary during the monsoon. More than 100 head strong, the herd is composed, among others, of the offspring of Mira and Moomal, as well as some that were saved from slaughter. All of them are in good condition, and there are many youngsters cajoling around on their stilt-like legs. The morning milk has just been transported by motorbike to the micro-dairy that we have set up on our campus where it will be processed and then shipped to customers throughout India. Some of it will be made into cheese that is on offer in Rajasthan's top hotels.

So there is hope in the air!

Indeed, much has happened between 2014 and now. I hope to bring out a sequel to *Camel Karma*, which I'm tentatively calling "Camel Dharma". A fitting title, I feel, for a book about finding the right way of living with camels!

APPENDIX

Camel population in India

Year	Total number
1945	380000
1956	436000
1966	653000
1977	752000
1982	756000
1987	719000
1992	746000
1997	670000
2003	498000
2007	422000

ABBREVIATIONS

BDR: Bangladesh Rifles

BSF: Border Security Force

CEC: Central Empowered Committee

FAO: Food and Agriculture Organisation of the United Nations

FRA: Forest Rights Act

LPP: League for Pastoral Peoples and Endogenous Livestock Development

LPPS: Lokhit Pashu-Palak Sansthan

NGO: Non-Government Organisation

GLOSSARY

Aakra: A central place in a Rajasthani village where all the cows assemble in the morning before being led to grazing by the *gual*.

Aiye, aiye: Please come in.

Anafi: A racing camel breed from Sudan.

Angrezi babul: A thorny shrub or tree that is not eaten by livestock (*Prosopis juliflora*).

Awlia: A yellow flowering shrub (*Cassia auriculata*).

Babul: A thorny tree (*Acacia nilotica*).

Baniya: Trader/merchant caste.

Bhakal: Rug made from camel hair.

Bhabhi: Husband's sister.

Bhoot: Ghost.

Chappa: Village cowherd.

Charpai: A local type of bed, made from wood and string.

Chithi: Letter, mail.

Chowdhury: Farming caste (in the context of Rajasthan).

Dahi: Curd.

Daroga: A caste that serves Rajput rulers and originated from their liaisons with inofficial wives.

Dhaba:	A roadside restaurant.
Dera:	An encampment where nomads spend the night.
Dharamshala:	A hostel for pilgrims.
Dharma:	God-given duty.
Dhani:	A hamlet or outlying part of a village.
Dhoti:	A loincloth, traditional garment of Hindu men.
Dulaa:	The soft palate of the male camel which is ejected during the rutting season.
Ghagra:	A wide skirt worn by Raika ladies.
Ganja:	Marijuana.
Gauchar:	Village grazing ground.
Ghee:	Clarified butter.
Gual:	A herder – somebody who takes care of a cow or camel herd.
Gudara:	Forested areas reserved for grazing by livestock during the rule of the maharajahs.
Holi:	A Hindu holiday marking the beginning of the hot season.
Jagir:	Estate.
Jai Mataji:	A traditional greeting among Rajputs (literally meaning: long live the Mother Goddess).
Jarri roti:	A very big and thick flat bread.
Jauhar/Johar:	Mass suicide committed by Rajput women when their men were defeated in battle
Jal:	*Salvadora persica*, a shrub.

Jhoopa:	Round hut.
Kaccha:	Literally raw or unripe; for instance, refers to a dirt road or uncemented house.
Kair:	An important fodder shrub of the Thar Desert (*Capparis decidua*).
Kartik:	A Hindu month (falls in October/November).
Khejri:	Important fodder tree whose pods are locally used as a vegetable (*Prosopis cineraria*).
Kotli:	A platform in the centre of villages where men hang out.
Kuffieh:	Arab headgear.
Lakh:	One hundred thousand.
Lapsi:	A sweet dish made with wheat, ghee and gur, that is served at weddings and special functions.
Marwar:	The kingdom of the Maharajah of Jodhpur.
Mela:	A fair, often with religious background.
Mewar:	The kingdom of the Maharajah of Udaipur.
Odhni:	A veil worn by women in Rajasthan (literally meaning: cover).
Oran:	Land that is sacred and therefore protected from use.
Parantha:	Fried flat bread.
Patwari:	A land registration office.
Pilu:	Fruits of *Salvadora persica* (jal) shrub.
Pir:	Parental village.
Pukka:	Cemented, permanent.

Purdah:	State of seclusion of Hindu women.
Rajput:	The ruling and land-owning caste.
Rakhi:	A band tied around the wrist - usually by a sister to her brother.
Ram Ram:	Raika greeting (referring to God Ram).
Roti:	Traditional flat, unleavened bread.
Sangria:	Pods of the khejri tree, which are made into a traditional and delicious dish.
Sasural:	Home of the in-laws.
Sati:	Self-immolation by Hindu women when their husband or close relative died (prohibited now).
Seth:	A trader/merchant.
Shwarma:	Meat cooked on a spit (*Arabic*).
Sorio:	A ritual among Gabbra people in Kenya that involves killing and consumption of camels.
Tell:	A hill formed by successive layers of human occupation (archaeological term).
Tibursa:	A camel disease caused by biting flies.
Teeka:	Injection.
Tola:	A camel herd.
Tumba:	A melon-like creeper whose fruits are used in traditional medicine (*Citrullus colocynthis*).
Trypanosomiasis:	Scientific name for tibursa.
Wadi:	Seasonally dry riverbed (*Arabic*).
Zenana:	Women's quarter in palaces.

NOTES

Chapter 1: Camels

A. **Musil**, 'The Manners and Customs of the Rwala Bedouins', in *American Geographical Society, New York, 1928.*

D. **Stiles**, 'Stopping Desert Spread with a Camel' in *The Ecologist* 1984.14/1: 38-43.

W. **Thesiger**. *Arabian Sands*, Viking Penguin, a division of Penguin Group (USA) LLC, 1959, 1983, renewed (c) 1987.

Chapter 2: Bikaner

N. **Patnaik**, A *Desert Kingdom: The Rajputs of Bikaner*, Weidenfeld and Nicolson, London, 1990.

R. Kumari **Bikaner**, *The Maharajas of Bikaner*, Amaryllis, Delhi, 2012.

Chapter 3: Sadri

R. **Bharucha**, *Rajasthan: An Oral History. Conversations with Komal Kothari*, Penguin, India, 2004.

A. S. **Leese**, A *Treatise on the One-Humped Camel in Health and Disease*. Haynes and Sons, Stamford, 1927.

M. H. **Singh**, *The Castes of Marwar*, Book Treasure, Jodhpur, 1990, reprint from 1894.

V. K. **Srivastava**, *Religious Renunciation of a Pastoral People*, Oxford University Press, Delhi, 1997.

Chapter 4: Anji-ki-dhani

J. D. Smith. *The Epic of Pabuji: A Study, Transcription and Transliteration*, Cambridge University Press, 1999.

Chapter 5: Pushkar

V. S. **Srivastava**, *Cultural Contours of India*, p. 178-187, Abhinav Publications, New Delhi, 1981.

Chapter 6: The Camels of Nachna

R. V. **Somani**, *History of Jaisalmer*, Panchsheel Prakashan, Jaipur, 1990.

Chapter 7: The Ear-tag Project

I. **Köhler-Rollefson**, 'Rajasthan's Camel Pastoralists and NGOs: The View From the Bottom', p 115-128 in D. **Stiles** (ed.), *Social Aspects of Sustainable Dryland Management*, John Wiley & Sons, Chichester, 1995.

Chapter 8: The Milk Miracle

Z. **Farah** and A. **Fischer** (eds.), *Milk and Meat from the Camel: Handbook on Products and Processing*, vdf Hochschulverlag AG, Zürich (Switzerland), 2004.

Chapter 9: Ethnoveterinary Medicine

I. **Köhler-Rollefson**, P. **Mundy** and E. **Mathias**, *A Field Manual of Camel Diseases: Traditional and Modern Health Care for the Dromedary*, ITDG-Publications, London, 2001.

C. **McCorkle**, E. **Mathias**, and T.W. **Schillhorn van Veen** (eds.), *Ethnoveterinary Research & Development*, Intermediate Technology Publications, London, UK, 1996.

Chapter 11: The Forest

H. **Gauthier-Pilter** and A. **Dagg**, *The Camel: Its Evolution, Ecology, Behavior and Relationship to Man*, University of Chicago Press, Chicago, 1981.

N. S. Jodha, *Life on the Edge: Sustaining Agriculture and Community Resources in Fragile Environments*, Oxford University Press, New Delhi, 2001.

LPPS, *The Camels of Kumbhalgarh: A Biodiversity Treasure*, LPPS, Sadri, 2013.

P. **Robbins**, *Political Ecology: A Critical Introduction*, John Wiley and Sons, 2012.

P. **Robbins** and A. **Chhangani**, 'Protecting the Wolves from the Sheep?' Paper presented at the Rajasthan Studies Group Conference, Jaipur, 29-31 December 2005.

P. **Robbins**, A. **Chhangani**, J. **Rice**, E. **Trigosa**, S. M. **Mohnot**, 'Enforcement Authority and Vegetation Change at Kumbhalgarh Wildlife Sanctuary, Rajasthan, India' in *Environmental Management 4(3): 365-378*, 2007.

Chapter 13: The Yatra

I. **Köhler-Rollefson** and H. S. **Rathore**, 'Camel Yatra', in *Down to Earth*, 15-31 May 2005, New Delhi.

Chapter 15: Recognition and Rights

I. **Köhler-Rollefson**, *Keepers of Genes: India's Pastoralists and their Breeds*, LIFE-Network/LPPS, Sadri, 2007.

LPPS, *Raika Biocultural Protocol*, Sadri, 2009.

websites: www.pastoralpeoples.org, www.lpps.org

ACKNOWLEDGEMENTS

As this book covers such a long period of my life – almost a quarter of a century – the debts I have accrued are endless.

My initial research was supported by the American Institute of Indian Studies, later stints by the National Geographic Society, the Alexander von Humboldt Foundation, and the German Research Council. The projects with the Raika have been made possible by Misereor, our most steadfast donor, by the Ford Foundation, by the German Technical Cooperation, now GIZ, as well as many others. The recognition by the Rolex Awards for Enterprise in 2002 was crucial and continues to be a source of great encouragement, as was the Trophée de Femmes of the Yves Rocher Foundation in 2010. Most recently the Marwar Ratna Award by H. H. Maharajah Gaj Singhji II of Jodhpur for "Exceptional and Outstanding Contribution in the Field of Conservation, Preservation and Promotion of Regional Culture and Heritage" bestowed upon us in May 2014 has uplifted our spirits and hope for saving Rajasthan's camels.

Dr Dewaram Dewasi, Professor Vinay Kumar Srivastava, Dr S. M. Mohnot, Dr N. D. Khanna, Dr T. K. Gahlot, Dr Arun Srivastava, and Dr Shravan Singh all helped at various stages of the work.

I am very grateful to my friends in Delhi – Premaliya and Purnima Singh, Sanjay Barnela and Anjali Khosla, as well as Kamal Kishore and Kanika Chandel, for providing me temporary homes and hospitality when travelling through. Tragically, my friend Namitha passed away, but I am grateful that the friendship with her husband, Dipak, and son, Anant, continues.

Gunnar and Birgit Denecke were exceptionally supportive during their two tenures at the German Embassy in New Delhi.

In Rajasthan, Uttra Kothari and the whole Kothari clan, starting with her eminent father Komal Kothari and now continuing with Kuldeep Kothari, has been a pillar of support. The directors of the National Research Centre on Camel, including Dr Sahani, Dr Pathak, and Dr Patil, as well as principal scientists, Dr Sumant Vyas and the members of the Quinquennial Review Team looked at our work benevolently.

I am extremely grateful to Dr Colonel Umaid Singh, Secretary of the Marwari Horse Society, for his interest and generosity and drawing the interest of H. H. Maharajah Gaj Singhji of Jodhpur to the plight of the camel. High Highness has gone out of his way to provide the Foreword not only for this book, but also for the earlier publication, *The Camels of Kumbhalgarh*.

The Raika are too numerous to mention, but still I would like to single out Dailibai, Adoji, Gautamji, Ghisulal, Ruparam, Ramaram and Mangilal Raika. Both the Godwar Raika and Maru Raika communities have adopted me almost as one of their own.

The LPPS staff in Sadri, currently encompassing Ramesh, Jagdeesh Paliwal, Khetaram Raika, Shanta, Gulabji, Kastu and Ramji, plays an essential and important role.

In Jaisalmer, the LPPS staff, Mira Paliwal, Narpath Singh, Khetaram, Gyan Singh and Ramswarup did great work, and camel-breeders, Bhom Singh, Padam Singh, Sode Khan, Mool Singh and many others were sources of information and inspiration.

Chanda Nimbkar, the late W. M. K. Warsi, Samreen Farooqi, Mahima Mehra, Dr Balaram Sahu and all the members of the LIFE Network generously helped me at critical junctions. Thanks also to the international students and interns who researched different facets of the Raika animal husbandry system.

Annabelle Descamps helped with the map at the beginning of the book.

Back in Germany, my close friends, Tita and Alex, Juliane Bräunig, Sabine Poth, Evelyn Mathias and Paul Mundy, Astrid and Reiner Stürz, and Bettina Bock provided major moral support. Heather Meurer, Yvonne Mabille, and Peter Laufmann commented on earlier versions of the manuscript, while in the final stages the detailed inputs by Kate Hardy of Indian Moments were invaluable. I am grateful for the diligent editing by Aradhana Bisht of Westland Publishers.

The gratitude to my long-suffering family cannot be expressed. First of all, there is my mother, Brigitte Köhler, who was burdened with extensive grandmothering duties due to my long absences, Gary Rollefson, who put me on the right track for research and always supported me, my wonderful children, Jon and Aisha, as well as their equally wonderful partners, Konzy and Frederik. Hope you all forgive me for my absorption with camels, Raika, pastoralists....

The last and biggest thanks to my soulmate who made it all possible and without whom the world of the Raika and their camels would forever have remained a closed book: Hanwant Singh.

ALSO FROM SPEAKING TIGER

RUNNING AWAY FROM ELEPHANTS

Adventures of a Wildlife Biologist

Rauf Ali

'The memoirs of a self-confessed maverick wildlife biologist, full of fascinating information, and stories told with humour. A must for wildlife lovers and all who enjoy a unique read.'—Mark Tully

Beginning with his interactions with Dr Salim Ali, the legendary ornithologist—who was also his grand-uncle—wildlife biologist Rauf Ali takes the reader on a journey through India's natural history and the beginning of ecological studies in India.

Rauf was one of the first Indians to complete a PhD in wildlife biology—he researched the social behaviour of bonnet macaques in the forests of Mundanthurai region in Tamil Nadu. In the late 1980s, he was instrumental in setting up one of India's first Masters programmes in ecology, and later, as an ecologist, Rauf undertook the task of delineating Protected Areas in the Palani Hills of the Western Ghats. He was also among the first to conduct environmental research in the Andaman and Nicobar Islands, and in this book, he provides eye-opening information on the environmental damage caused by the introduction of chital and other species alien to the region.

Enlivening the narrative are anecdotes drawn from a career spanning over three decades: of encountering wild elephants; dealing with red tape; and whiskey-laced brainstorming sessions with students and Nobel laureates alike.

Through these personal accounts, Rauf reveals the state of environmental conservation in India, and the complex relationship between locals, wildlife researchers and forest officials. Quirky, candid and informative, *Running Away from Elephants* is an invaluable addition to writings on natural history in India.

ALSO FROM SPEAKING TIGER

WHERE THE INDUS IS YOUNG

A Winter in Baltistan

Dervla Murphy

'Such is the author's love of travelling and of this untouched wilderness, that the lasting impression left by this book is one of sheer joy.'—Colin Thubron, *Sunday Telegraph*

One winter in the mid-1970s, Dervla Murphy, her six-year-old daughter Rachel, and Hallam, a hardy mule, walked into Baltistan close to Pakistan-held Kashmir—the frozen heart of the Western Himalayas. For three months they travelled along the perilous Indus Gorge and into nearby valleys, making a mockery of fear, trekking through the forbidding Karakoram mountains and lodging with the Balts, who farm one of the remotest regions on earth. Despite the hardship, Dervla never forgot the point of travel, retaining enthusiasm for her magnificent surroundings and using her sense of humour to bring out the best in her hosts, who were often locked into the melancholic mood of mid-winter. This hair-raising, quirky and vivid account of their adventure is a classic of travel writing.